*Women Pioneers of the Louisiana Environmental Movement*

# WOMEN PIONEERS
of the Louisiana Environmental Movement

PEGGY FRANKLAND

with Susan Tucker

UNIVERSITY PRESS OF MISSISSIPPI • JACKSON

www.upress.state.ms.us

Designed by Peter D. Halverson

The University Press of Mississippi is a member of the Association of American University Presses.

Photographs © Gabriella Mills

Copyright © 2013 by University Press of Mississippi
All rights reserved
Manufactured in the United States of America

First printing 2013
∞
Library of Congress Cataloging-in-Publication Data

Frankland, Peggy.
 Women pioneers of the Louisiana environmental movement / Peggy Frankland, with Susan Tucker.
    p. cm.
 Includes bibliographical references and index.
 ISBN 978-1-61703-772-6 (cloth : alk. paper) — ISBN 978-1-61703-773-3 (ebook) 1. Women environmentalists—Louisiana—Biography. 2. Environmental protection—Louisiana. 3. Environmental justice—Louisiana. 4. Louisiana—Environmental conditions. I. Tucker, Susan, 1950– II. Title.
 GE55.F73 2013
 304.2092'5209763—dc23                                        2012038297

British Library Cataloging-in-Publication Data available

*To my grandchildren, Nicholas, Logan, Alexis, Cade, and Addie, and my great-grandchildren, Robert and Madeline, and those who may follow*

# CONTENTS

Preface and Acknowledgments    IX
Introduction    XIII

Chapter One. "HOW COULD I STAND BY?": PROTECTING ONE PLACE, PROTECTING MANY    3
    Sally Herman    5
    Fernell Cryar    9
    Barbara LeLeux    12
    Catherine Holcomb    15
    Monica Laughlin Mancuso    18
    Helen Solar    21
    Miriam Price    25

Chapter Two. "WE ARE BLACK AND WHITE, RICH AND POOR": CROSSING BOUNDARIES, REMAKING LOUISIANA    30
    Ann Williams    31
    Rose Jackson    35
    Marietta Herr    40
    Ruth Shepherd    44
    Theresa Robert    49
    Kay Gaudet    53

Chapter Three. "I KNOW THAT IT WAS A REVELATION FROM GOD": RELIGION AND ENVIRONMENTAL ACTION    59
    Lorena Pospisil    60
    Shirley Goldsmith    65
    Gerry Ardoin    70
    Janice Crador    74
    Debra Ramirez    80

Chapter Four. "WHAT A FEW PEOPLE CAN DO": LEARNING TO ADVOCATE FOR OTHERS    85
    Jessie Price    86
    Gay Hanks    90
    Mary Brasseaux    94
    Florence Robinson    97
    Mary Ellender    101
    Carol Savoy    105

Chapter Five. "YOU ARE NOT SOMEBODY PRETENDING TO BE A MAN": SUCCESS, POLITICS, AND GENDER     110
    Mildred Fossier        112
    Mary McCastle         118
    Florence Gossen       123
    Clara Baudoin         127
    Liz Avants            132
    Les Ann Kirkland      136
    Mary Tutwiler         140

Chapter Six. "WHEN SOMETHING IS NOT RIGHT, YOU HAVE TO DO SOMETHING ABOUT IT": CAREER ACTIVISTS BUILD BRIDGES     145
    Sister Helen Vinton   146
    Lorna Bourg           151
    Marylee Orr           157
    Linda King            162
    Wilma Subra           166

Chapter Seven. "WE AS A PEOPLE ARE BETTER THAN OUR POLITICS": ALLIES, EXPERTS, AND ADVERSARIES     174
    Charles Elson "Buddy" Roemer     175
    Carroll Wascom        179
    Maureen O'Neill       185
    Kai David Midboe      191
    Dan Borne             197
    Robert Kuehn          203
    Audrey Evans          207
    Paul Templet          211
    Will Collette         217
    William "Willie" A. Fontenot     221

Chapter Eight. "THERE WAS NEVER A QUESTION OF DATA": PERSPECTIVES FROM TEN YEARS OUT     228
    Wilma Subra           231

Supplemental List of Women Environmental Activists     242
Notes     245
Index     251

# PREFACE AND ACKNOWLEDGMENTS

Louisiana is to the environmental movement what Selma, Alabama, is to the civil rights movement.
—BILL MOYERS

This book presents a history that touches countless Louisiana citizens today in the early twenty-first century, as well as the memory of their ancestors and the future of their descendants throughout the nation. Yes, these stories reflect a commitment to make safe the land, air, and water of a certain place in time. But they also tell of how caring and active leaders are made, how families lived in the past, and how we might best teach children that they may teach their children how to live in the centuries ahead.

Like protecting the treasures of our environment, writing a book is an act of faith that requires daily work, constancy, and, most of all, community. This project was a huge undertaking that could not have been accomplished without the support of many people. I thank first the Louisiana Endowment for the Humanities, a state affiliate of the National Endowment for the Humanities, whose grant made parts of the work possible. The opinions expressed in this book, of course, do not necessarily represent the views of the Louisiana Endowment for the Humanities (LEH) or the National Endowment for the Humanities (NEH).

Next, and most critically, I thank key editors and writers for this project, Amy Clipp and Susan Tucker. This project would not have happened without their involvement and steady guidance.

I am also grateful to the thirty-eight women and eight men who graciously shared their expertise, insights, and experiences; allowed Jennifer Abraham Cramer, Sharon Barrow, and me to interview them for this project; and gave permission to publish the results in this book.

Words cannot convey adequately and in such a short space how deeply appreciative and indebted I am also to nine gifted individuals who volunteered their expertise and invaluable time to serve on an advisory committee. Their involvement and generosity were essential to the success of the project, and although the process has taken many years, they have remained staunch supporters. Their encouragement and involvement helped me maintain my own interest in the project. First in this list is, again, Amy Clipp of New Orleans, who brought her skills as writer and editor to the project. In the late 1990s one night at a party, we discussed an idea I had about writing a book about women environmental activists. Amy surprised me the next week when she called and volunteered to work with me on a yet undeveloped plan. That telephone conversation was the seed planted that motivated me to move forward with this project. She also taught me about using my time wisely, but most of all she taught me about tenacity. I deeply appreciate her patience, skill, and good advice.

At that same party, I also talked to Barbara Ewell, professor of English at Loyola University in New Orleans. My initial thought about a book was to focus on different women activists around the nation. It was Barbara who suggested that there were so many wonderful women in Louisiana that I should write the book about them. Barbara also suggested I contact historian Mary Hébert Price, director of the T. Harry Williams Oral History Center at Louisiana State University (LSU). It was Mary who suggested that the book be an oral history of the women so that their stories would be preserved for future generations. Mary trained me to interview the subjects, loaned LSU equipment for interviewing and transcribing, and furnished various supplies. Her staff also transcribed many of the interviews. Mary brought national attention to the project, then still in its infancy, by making it possible for us to speak at the National Oral History Association's 2001 Annual Meeting, "Bearing Public Witness: Documenting Memories of Struggles and Resistance." Under Mary's direction at the Williams Center, she also allowed the talented Jennifer Abraham Cramer to interview many of the subjects. Jennifer approached the developing project with enthusiasm, boundless energy, and total dedication. In 2004, after Mary retired and Jennifer became director of the Williams Center, she continued to promote the project by conducting workshops and presentations at LSU. In 2011, she was responsible for my participation in the Listening to Louisiana Women Symposium, which featured many of the state's women activists and their oral history projects. Jennifer also interviewed Wilma Subra for the book's conclusion and assisted in editing the interview. Jennifer is an amazing young woman.

Susanne Dietzel, former director of the Women's Resource Center, Loyola University, New Orleans, Louisiana, and now a professor at Ohio University, is an accomplished author and researcher. Susanne always allowed the advisory committee the use of the Women's Center conference room for meetings. Along with Barbara Ewell, Susanne was responsible for arranging a presentation featuring three of the women activists at the National Women's Studies Association (NWSA) conference in New Orleans in 2003. At this stage Barbara Ewell once again offered both professional and personal advice. She knew firsthand about environmental issues since her father's farm, adjacent to Devil's Swamp, north of Baton Rouge, Louisiana, was contaminated with toxic waste. Gabriella Mills, photographer and exhibit designer from Lafayette, Louisiana, donated her remarkable talents, capturing the beauty of the women, their inner strength, and true grit in her photographs. Thanks Gabe. You did the women proud. Marylee Orr, executive director of the Louisiana Environmental Action Network, is not only featured in the book but also contributed immensely to the project. She held a fund-raiser in 2002 that celebrated the women's work and provided key funds for the project.

Jerry Speir, former director of the Tulane Environmental Policy Institute, New Orleans, Louisiana, brought his many years of personal experience as an environmental advocate to the book project. As an attorney, his legal expertise was very important. He also provided thoughtful edits and support throughout the process. Susan Tucker, archivist at the Newcomb College Institute of Tulane University, brought her experience as an author. Her book, *Telling Memories among Southern Women*, was made up of oral history narratives that allowed me insight into the genre. It is difficult to find the words to describe how grateful I am to Susan. Since 1999, she has been consistent in her belief and support of the manuscript. After Hurricanes Katrina and Rita and the devastation that occurred to me and many of the women featured in the book, I found it hard to focus on the manuscript. After many delays and often despair, Susan took the lead and prodded me back into action. She took the manuscript on her European sabbatical in 2011 and volunteered to edit the manuscript and to bring it up to date. This project could have never been completed without Susan encouraging me to continue and then giving me a deadline. I am truly indebted to her.

Special appreciation goes to Janet Allured, associate professor of History at McNeese State University, Lake Charles, Louisiana. She served as the scholar and evaluator. She also supported the project by inviting me and five of the activists to speak at the 2002 Women's Studies Lecture series.

Grateful thanks are also extended to Candis LaPrade and Gloria Hendrickson. Gloria especially helped by putting the book in draft form—and working two months beyond her initial agreement. Her talent and dedication to this project are deeply appreciated. Michele Bulet is a light designer and videographer. Her project role was to videotape interviews, which are now housed at the T. Harry Williams Oral History Center.

My thanks also go to relatives and friends who made my work always more rewarding; to my children, Vicki, Charles, and Jennifer, who supported me regardless of the hours I spent away from home; and to my sister, Sharon Barrow, who conducted several of the interviews for me. Thanks also go to Elaine Smythe, Alecia P. Long, Laura Cox, Patsy Dean, Ginger Horton, Kay Kiker, Reverend Tracy MacKenzie, Esperanzia Grijalva Maya, Doug McNeill, Mike Tritico, and, especially, Elizabeth Vincent, who graciously allowed me to interview her for practice, which brought a lot of much-needed laughter to the project. I also thank Henry Sirgo.

# INTRODUCTION

Not long ago, Louisiana was renowned for the uniqueness and beauty of its landscape. This magnificence was the backdrop of my early life when I came to Lake Charles as a young woman of eighteen in 1959. Today, so many years later, I still think of the brilliance of the gifts of air, land, and water that we have. You will hear of those gifts in the essays of most of the women and men in this book, and, more, you will hear of the resilience of both the state and its residents. Touted as "the Sportsman's Paradise" for decades, the state's vast wetlands, bayous, and upland forests are remembered for nurturing the communities of families who hunted, maintained gardens, and created distinctive cultures, in parts, Creole and Cajun, in other parts, more mainstream southern.

This natural bounty formed the backbone of Louisiana's economy. Fisheries, timber, agriculture, and oil and gas—all of these industries and many others took root in Louisiana over the centuries and greeted me as a young woman who married into a family whose members have lived in Sulphur for six generations. This community is located in Calcasieu Parish (called *counties* elsewhere in the United States), along the coast of the southwestern part of the state.

Early on, I saw how the petrochemical industry, in particular, had come to dominate the state's economy after World War II. The Mississippi River and the Calcasieu Estuary were close enough to southern Louisiana's oil and gas fields to provide both fresh water for production processes and major navigation channels for shipping products. By the 1970s, over two hundred petrochemical facilities were operating along the river and the estuary, making a range of products used worldwide. These industries brought new wealth to Louisiana and created tens of thousands of very welcomed jobs.

Yet after years of what I can only describe as both a lovely and sheltered life of being a mother and a wife, I came to see that industry had other, less beneficial consequences as well. To a large extent, the state's petrochemical facilities operated with a free hand. The state's Department of Environmental Quality (DEQ) was not established until 1984, and even then its power to enforce laws and levy fines was restricted. The combination of intensive production and decades of lax regulatory oversight devastated Louisiana's environment. By 1990, Louisiana ranked first in the nation for discharging toxic pollution into the air, ground, and water.[1]

My first venture into promoting a different sort of response came earlier. On September 28, 1982, the national (NBC) evening news showed a huge, billowing, and uncontrollable fire that was releasing chemicals into the atmosphere. The fire had erupted when forty-one Illinois Central Gulf (ICG) railroad cars carrying toxic waste derailed in Livingston, Louisiana. Many of them burned and exploded, sometimes hurling flames and toxic ash more than 110 feet into the sky. It was reported as the worst train derailment accident in Louisiana's history, and twenty-seven hundred people had to be evacuated. I registered this as a problem that I could do nothing about.

On October 23, 1982, a month after the accident, the headline on the front page of our local newspaper read, "BFI, ICG Pass Dumping Buck." The article stated that contaminated soil from the Livingston train derailment was being shipped in overloaded eighteen wheelers from Livingston, Louisiana, and being dumped in Willow Springs in an eighty-five-acre landfill owned and operated since 1972 by Brown & Ferris Industries Chemical Services, Inc., a subsidiary of Brown & Ferris Industries (BFI).[2] No one wanted to take responsibility for transporting the toxic waste to Calcasieu Parish. When the news media found out about the waste entering our area, forty truckloads had already been dumped in the landfill.

This angered me, but what spurred me into activism was the fact that the Department of Transportation and Development (DOTD) had dismissed speeding and other violation tickets to the truckers hauling the waste. Questioned by the media, DOTD secretary Paul Hardy said, "I will ask the Violation Review Committee to review all tickets pertaining to this emergency situation on a case by case basis, and request that the committee consider voiding these citations in view of the extenuating circumstances."[3] What he failed to mention was that by voiding the fines, it would cost the State of Louisiana thousands of dollars. I was astounded that the contaminated soil had been left on the ground in Livingston for nearly a month and suddenly state officials were deeming the removal of the waste as an emergency.

I also learned that allowing the trucks to overload meant substantial savings for BFI. The weight limit on tractor-trailer rigs using the interstate highway is eighty thousand pounds. State officials admitted that the trucks carrying the waste had overloads ranging from five thousand to seventeen thousand pounds.[4]

Again, I felt outraged. The truck drivers and those to whom they reported clearly did not think of the residents living along their path. I did not want these trucks potentially spilling waste on our streets.

My schooling in Louisiana politics commenced. It was soon revealed that the trucks hauling the waste belonged to BFI, which also owned the landfill, and a subcontractor, Strainco, Inc., which was owned at the time by State Representative Bill Strain of Abita Springs, Louisiana.[5]

Interviewed by the local newspaper, the BFI manager was quoted as saying that the ICG made the decision to dump the waste in Calcasieu Parish, though reports indicated that BFI/Willow Springs was the highest bidder on the disposal project. Supposedly, the BFI facility in Livingston (located near the explosion site) also bid on the project and lost to BFI/Willow Springs. It seemed odd to me that BFI owned the two sites, yet they were bidding against each other.

I began to see that many environmental problems are linked to one another. With the news media on their trail, everyone involved was blaming the other person. Jim Glasch of ICG's corporate headquarters said the railroad had virtually no option in selecting a dump site. A day later he said that the decision to use the Calcasieu facility was made after the mayor and commissioners of Livingston passed an ordinance making it illegal for the railroad company to have the waste dumped in Livingston. The secretary of the Livingston Parish Police Jury said she thought the decision had been made because the people in Livingston had suffered enough.[6] (In Louisiana parishes, the police jury is the equivalent to a county board of commissioners or other governing body. The police juries of several parishes are mentioned throughout this book.)

Every day the local newspaper ran a story related to the waste, and it became clear this was a big story with a lot of important players. Concerned, I decided I was going to go to the top and find out what was going on.

The first agency I contacted was the Environmental Control Commission (ECC), which then regulated all industries in the state. It was the first time I had ever contacted a public official. When the secretary at the ECC answered the phone, I asked to speak to the person who held the highest position in the agency. To my surprise, she directed my call to the director, Frank Simoneaux. As it turned out he had no reassuring words for me. Rather, his response was, "Hazardous waste has to go somewhere and you have to accept the fact that it is going to be in your backyard." It was a frightening conversation for me, and I asked him why he was being so rude. Immediately I had the feeling that I had done wrong. I had done what we call here "talked back" to an official. I even worried that he could sue me for the way I spoke.

Still I persisted, and next I contacted my state representative, who also worked for a local chemical plant. He told me that I was worrying too much and assured me that it was a common practice to send waste to other areas.

As a matter of fact, he said, "Just yesterday we shipped a load of really bad stuff to Texas from a local petrochemical plant in Westlake."

Understand that I had never known a reason to worry. I believed in the word of the government and in the best intentions of elected officials. I believed in the best intentions of business people who ran such waste sites. My husband was a farmer and the owner of a service station, a place where the community came for coffee. There was a group of businessmen who went there every day. And my place was in being a mother and, at most, a member of the Parent-Teacher Association. The youngest of my three children was ten that year.

I became something else, someone else, rather quickly. Hoping to go straight to the heart of the problem, and after the negative responses from the two officials, it was apparent that if I was going to get involved, I needed to educate myself. I got in my car and drove around for hours looking for the site. Close by but secluded in the piney woods, I found a narrow road that led to the BFI facility and the Willow Springs community. This discovery was not what I expected; I expected something more remote, not one road that would serve both a residential community and the landfill. This road was the only way into or out of the Willow Springs neighborhood, a small African American neighborhood established by slaves in the 1800s, five miles northwest of Westlake, Louisiana.

I immediately smelled a foul odor. I also noticed that many of the small wooden-frame houses had open windows and no air-conditioning units. A few didn't have screens on the windows or doors. Finally, I observed that their animals were grazing on the levee surrounding the unfenced landfill. Once a self-sufficient community and still one filled with residents who supplemented their food supply by tending gardens and raising chickens, pigs, and cattle, the Willow Springs community looked very vulnerable to me.

This initial ride was a pivotal turning point for me. It was my environmental awakening. Going home, I contacted Mary Ellender, whose narrative appears in this book, and asked her if she would assist me in distributing petitions to ask the ECC to close the Willow Springs facility. We collected 4,389 signatures and delivered them to both the ECC and then Governor David Treen.

Mary and I also began gathering information about the health of the families in the Willow Springs community. In a sense, this was my neighborhood. I lived only four miles away. In a sense, it was another world. Many of their homes were less than one hundred yards from the landfill. I do not mean this to sound as if I was "lady bountiful"; I thought rather that if I did not begin I would be less than the citizen I was taught to be. I would be letting down my neighbors.

We knocked on all doors within a one-mile radius of the landfill. In the first house, I found an amazing man and his wife. I also found living conditions that made me worry even more about their proximity to the BFI facility. They had such large cracks in their walls that the winter wind whipped through the house. The wife was very sick. She sat silently in front of a wood-burning stove holding a bloody handkerchief the whole time we spoke. I noticed her stomach seemed abnormally large; her husband told me she had an inoperable tumor.[7] He told of the death of all his pigs after a heavy rain and the resulting overflow of the levee. The toxic waste running over the levee and his yard had flooded his small pond where the pigs drank. He said, "When they died, they were foaming from the mouth."

In the next household we visited, the man told us, as he had also told a reporter earlier, that one evening his chickens had been roosting in the pine trees and when he awoke the next morning they were lying on the ground dead.[8]

These were stories we heard over and over again. But more significantly, every household had some kind of illness. Equally worrying to me was that people reported that BFI told them that they were building fishing ponds for the community's recreational use.

I learned that BFI had opened seven lagoons or pits, with no specific guidelines for construction and with no liners. Trichloroethylene (TCE), polychlorinated biphenyls (PCBs), vinyl chloroform, mercury, lead, and formaldehyde are some of the many chemicals that were dumped into the unlined pits/lagoons. They also constructed a four-thousand-foot injection well in an old, abandoned natural gas well, which they used to inject liquid chemicals.

Even though significant groundwater contamination was found in fifty-foot-deep sands in 1982, citizens living near the site were told that they could use water drawn from their own fifty- to sixty-foot shallow water wells. Their wells were also linked to the Chicot Aquifer.[9] This connection is significant. By 1987 the US EPA released a study that revealed that toxins at the facility had spread into the two-hundred-foot-deep sands that are at the top of the Chicot Aquifer, the sole source for drinking water for fifteen parishes, or eleven thousand square miles.

Finally, just as the man in one of the houses had told me, I learned the result of locating the facility adjacent to Little River. When there was a heavy rain, the pits often overflowed toxic waste water, which overtopped the levee and went directly into the river, where the people swam and fished. It also went into their yards, where children played and their animals grazed on the grass.

The lives of these people meant nothing to BFI officials, who gave a few families turkeys at Christmas and promised them safe drinking water. One family that lived near the facility accepted their offer, and BFI ran a long, above-ground, exposed pipe with a single outdoor faucet from their facility to the resident's home. They had to go outside to get their water. The turkey and the pipe silenced that family. It seemed criminal to me.

These problems and responses had been happening long before I heard about them. For the citizens of the area, it took six years and many hearings, but the landfill was capped and closed in 1984.[10] In the same year, state officials passed a law to outlaw contamination of groundwater with hazardous waste. The law was written because of the Willow Springs site. It should have always been illegal to leak poisonous chemicals into our groundwater.

I learned so much from this experience at Willow Springs. One lesson was that taking on such a challenging issue requires community involvement and support. In the beginning there were just a few small voices like Mike Tritico, Leonard Knapp, and the High Hope Road Committee calling for justice. However, things changed after six hundred people showed up for an Office of Conservation permit hearing (January 23, 1985) regarding the injection well at the BFI facility. Then all the mayors, city councilmen, and police jurors in Calcasieu Parish supported the closure of the facility.

The other thing I learned occurred both in Willow Springs and elsewhere, and it concerns a much wider world. I now understand that it is a mistake to think only "I live in a democracy." I think now we are always being tested to ask, "What does it require to live as part of a democracy?" It is the community that matters, and the environmental movement taught me that.

I remember that once for a congressional hearing on groundwater contamination being held in Washington, D.C., Herbert Rigmaiden, a farmer from Willow Springs, was invited to speak. His fifty-foot water well was believed to be contaminated. He was probably my age, and his family, like my husband's family, had lived there for six generations. He would not let me call him Mr. Rigmaiden, and I would not let him call me Ms. Frankland.

We were on the same side, but we had to learn how to be together. Still, unlike me and many of my in-laws who had ventured outside Louisiana and Texas, Herbert had never traveled more than twenty miles from his home in his lifetime. He wanted to be sure that it was me who arranged his travel to Houston to catch the plane to Washington. He would not sit in the front seat with me since that was the way the code of the South was shaped. African

Americans rode in the back seat when whites were in the front seat. Before we got out of the car to enter the airport terminal, he told me where to find his valuables if he did not return.

Herbert raised cattle on his farm and sold them at the local cattle auction, and from there they were shipped all over the country. In D.C., he told the committee how his cattle roamed the area.[11] He told about finding six of his cattle dead near the landfill. Their bodies were swollen. Herbert decided to cut open the stomachs of several and was shocked to see a thick green liquid. They clearly had been eating grass and drinking water from storm water runoff.

To many in Congress, he appeared as a character, but he did so according to old rules and with a truly noble and persuasive power. "You gentlemen have got to remember that every time you throw a beefsteak or hamburger up to your face, you are eating that meat which comes of that contaminated water underneath because I have no other way to water my cattle."[12] He said it in a beautiful way, with an African American, Louisiana accent, in a voice that was strong, humorous, eloquent, and evocative of a way of life we knew.

I found my voice, too. I learned to speak of facts. At first when we testified, it was always the emotion of the crisis that we wanted to convey, but later we knew that if we did not have documentation, nothing we said would be taken seriously. Even then it was not always taken seriously. I have had legislators say they support us and turn around and vote the other way. I have been in hearings where not one person listened, where even sometimes a legislator would be asleep.

This was politics, but it was also the dark side of Louisiana's economic dependence on petrochemicals. My neighbors and others like them in other parts of the state began to notice increased incidences of cancer, birth defects, miscarriages, nervous system disorders, and other health problems. By the late 1970s, the health impacts were too numerous and severe to be ignored. Like the people of Willow Springs, others had begun to link the pollution surrounding their communities to the health problems plaguing their families and friends. They could smell the stench that engulfed their homes and neighborhoods. They could see the skies filled with billowing black smoke. The women particularly emerged as leaders even as they tended husbands and children who were suffering from unexplained illnesses. About them, they also saw fish and animals killed by contact with contaminated land and water. Their observations led them to challenge the status quo in fundamental ways. They demanded that dangerous sites be cleaned up and closed. They also stopped poorly conceived proposals for new sites from being passed through the system.

What has stayed with me is that women in so many communities did the work of making safer their communities and those of others in the state. They fought and won many battles with oil refineries and petrochemical industrial facilities that release millions of pounds of chemicals into the air and waterways.[13] They created policies and activities that yielded at least some newly renewed estuarine systems where once lived contaminated fish, shellfish, birds, and mammals. These women, like me, came to know meanings and often the chemical makeup of bio-accumulating toxic compounds, mercury, hexachlorobenzene, hexachlorobutadiene, and polychlorinated biphenyls (PCBs). We have spoken together in such a way that the public was made aware that waste associated with these industries went into 744 solid waste landfills, one thousand hazardous waste dumps, fifty hazardous waste landfills, and four thousand injection wells.[14] We have also made sure that legislators know that approximately thirteen hundred orphan wells and ten thousand waste pits were created by oil and gas production facilities, and over one thousand groundwater contamination plumes were documented in the decades that ended the twentieth century.[15]

Our women's campaigns occurred between 1976 and 1996, an era when the nation learned the power of grassroots environmental organizing. One early pioneer of this era was Lois Gibbs, a wife and a mother from Love Canal in Niagara Falls, New York. In the late 1970s, she organized her small blue-collar community of nine hundred families to protest the pollution found near their homes, and she did so in a way that captured the interest of the national news media. She and her neighbors were extremely effective; not only were the families of Love Canal eventually relocated, but also their action helped spur the creation of the federal Superfund Program.[16] Gibbs would later say, "[Louisiana's first women environmental activists] are some of the most courageous, brave, smart, and skilled people that I have met throughout the country. And I think on average they have had to overcome more barriers—social, political, and economic—than people in most any other geographic area that we work with. That is the stamina of the people in the South. They are fighters."[17]

In the period of which Gibbs spoke, societal trends were arrayed against such fighters. The concept of environmental stewardship had barely entered the lexicon, Louisiana was experiencing an oil boom, and many citizens allied with industry were reaping the profits. The civil rights movement was no longer as active, and for many people, tensions between whites and blacks seemed worse than ever.

Edwin Edwards was governor, and he would dominate Louisiana politics from 1972 to the mid-1990s. A charismatic Cajun, Edwards was known for his quick wit, extravagant lifestyle, and fondness for gambling.[18] His freewheeling style embodied another aspect of Louisiana's political tradition—one that discouraged substantive interaction between the powers-that-be and citizens. One of the interviews in this book tells how he changed the whole goal of a meeting to a discussion of his jewelry. All of this type of disregard for the lives of the people and the work of those who live here was new to me but also motivated me to work for change.

What I discovered was that the governor and legislators were accustomed to acting as they saw fit without considering the viewpoints of those outside the inner circle. Like other twentieth-century Louisiana governors before him, Edwards waved the banner of populism. In his speeches and campaigns, he embraced the poor and African Americans as allies, claiming to fight for the "little guy" in the tradition of Huey Long.[19] Many citizens believed Edwards's rhetoric and trusted he would not compromise their health in exchange for jobs.

In reality, Edwards was offering tax breaks to encourage new industries to build facilities in Louisiana. He could do so more easily than other governors in other states not only because of natural resources but also because of the particular social and political structure of the state. Various constitutional conventions have given the Louisiana state governor the position as one of the strongest governors in the nation. In addition, historic patterns of land ownership have meant direct ties between a few wealthy elites and large outside corporations. In contrast, neighbors in Texas with similar natural resources live in a state where the governor is one of the weakest among political players, and profits from industry, at least historically, stayed in the local communities.[20]

This type of Louisiana politics played out in the placement of most industries in poor, often African American communities like Willow Springs, where resistance to the plant sites was expected to be low. Ironically, many of the citizens living near these facilities were poorly educated and so were not considered for work in the plants. Louisiana's fence-line communities came to embody the classic scenario of environmental injustice: select groups of low-income people bearing a disproportionate part of society's overall environmental burden.

Given this social and political climate, Louisiana's first environmental activists faced an enormous task. It is hard for me to say I was a part of that fight, to claim even a small victory, because so much is yet to be done and because, too, I did such a small part. But the reader should know that the women and men who appear in the pages that follow not only corrected flagrant abuses but also valiantly and often successfully worked within a power structure that paid lip service to environmental protection and ignored opposing viewpoints. One of the most critical achievements of the women was the 1984 IT decision. Formally called *Save Ourselves v. Louisiana Environmental Control Commission*, the IT decision is mentioned often in this book. It established that the government of Louisiana has a constitutional obligation to protect the natural resources of the state in making decisions for permits.[21] This ruling was one of the most important of its kind for the whole of the United States.

Not surprisingly, given women's caretaking roles in our communities and the flexibility of time allowed to housewives and others in occasional jobs, women were the first and the most numerous among those promoting change. Yet, again, not unexpectedly, when the women first brought their concerns to public officials, most were ignored. When questions went unanswered, just as in my conversation with the Environmental Control Commission in 1982, these women realized that many officials had financed their campaigns with donations from industry and were not likely to embrace change. As a result, much early activism in Louisiana focused on creating new tools and protecting communities. Grant funds were rarely available, so the women used personal resources, including grocery money, to finance work.

Direct involvement in politics became one avenue for reform. Some women ran for office themselves or supported candidates who would protect their environmental interests. All over the state, working in our separate communities, women like me discovered that there were few laws prohibiting polluting activities. Many of us, then, began working to establish rules and regulations to address specific issues. In other cases, regulations were on the books, but state agencies were not enforcing them. Our testimonies at hearings helped establish better enforcement at the state and national levels.

Who exactly are these women I came to know? They are black and white, working class and wealthy, school teachers, secretaries, pharmacists, housewives, small business owners, civil servants, nuns, and housewives. Some were mothers, some single, some widowed. All discovered a calling to step outside their established routines and demand changes in their communities.

In some ways I came to know them out of my own attempts both to take a break from the intense and often depleting work of activism and to fulfill a dream from the 1950s, one I left behind in East Texas. In 1989 I went back to school, attending first a women's history class at McNeese State University, where I was astounded to learn that books describing women's involvement in social issues were hardly written until the mid-1960s. After hearing this, it occurred to me that a book needed to be written about the first women environmental activists. As I mentioned in the preface, my thought was to write the book about the different women I had met around the United States. Writing on my home state, however, proved much richer to me. I chose the oral history format because, although many of the women have been interviewed countless times, they had never had an opportunity to tell their stories in their own words. By recording the women and transcribing their words, I could make sure that their stories were told just the way the women wanted them to be.

To be interviewed for this project, each woman had to meet three criteria: First, she had to have been active between 1976 and 1996, the era when the national grassroots environmental movement was just beginning. Second, each woman had to have improved Louisiana's environment by changing a law, policy, or major land-use project or by founding an environmental organization. Third, each woman's work had to take place without institutional support. There are thirty-six women in this book who met those three criteria.

I also felt it was important to interview a few others, who made the work of these activists become laws enacted and obeyed. The reader thus will find here interviews with two women and eight men who made up a part of the communities of the women's day-to-day work: a former state governor, two former secretaries of the Louisiana Department of Environmental Quality, the head of the Louisiana Chemical Association, and the former director of the Tulane Environmental Law Clinic, among others.

Between 1999 and 2012, forty women (thirty-eight featured in book) and eight men were interviewed. Most of the interviews date from 1999 to 2002. All the interviews were tape-recorded, videotaped, and transcribed using standard oral history practices as prescribed by the T. Harry Williams Oral History Center at Louisiana State University. Completed interviews and videotapes will be archived at the Williams Center and other institutions as requested.

In many cases, the transcribed interviews ran over fifty pages. To present the stories in condensed book form, the project editors left out material and rearranged the order of sentences to present the stories as a single monologue. Successive edits were performed to create a clear text that faithfully represented the person's experiences. Although sentences were moved to maintain a narrative thread, the interviewee's actual word choices were not altered.

The voices do not tell easy stories to read. Although these women enjoyed remarkable success, their work was often discounted. Some were told to go home and bake cookies. They were labeled kooks and hysterical housewives, even country goats. In many instances they were accused of harming the economy and being anti-business. One large corporation sued a retired schoolteacher for $1 million because she spoke out against them. Other women were physically threatened and harassed.

Given all that they were up against, the individual victories described in each of the stories in this collection are impressive enough. Collectively they are inspirational. The women featured in these pages changed the way business was conducted in Louisiana. By insisting on being heard, they forced government to be more accountable to its citizens. By conducting thorough research and clearly demonstrating how pollution was harming people and the natural world, the women illuminated the need for change in the state's regulatory system. They were among the first to challenge the timeworn precept that the state had to choose between good jobs and a clean environment. In all of these ways, the women created a template for progressive change that Louisiana is still struggling to fulfill.

The work goes on. Not all victories are clear victories. For example, in 1985 the citizens living in Willow Springs, with assistance from local environmental groups, one concerned legislator, and then Governor Treen, were given a $150,000 grant for a community water district. The citizens no longer have to drink from their shallow wells, but the downside has been that most of the people live on a limited income, and the monthly water bill is an added burden. They, innocent citizens, are paying for a problem they did not create.

Consider too that the victories are always tempered victories because we want jobs, and we are constantly told that regulations will work against jobs. Even if we do not believe the two conditions—jobs and regulations—are antithetical, this argument is pervasive and, in a poor state, very much on the minds of many people. One of our tasks, then, is to convince others that better policies and industrial expansion are attainable together.

Most of all, though, the work behind us forms stories of communities working together. No more powerful message than that of community can be told. More than any national environmental organization currently does, these early grassroots efforts were those of people, especially women, forging new alliances. In Louisiana, this meant that white, African American, and Native American people worked together. This was a revolutionary step that we should both applaud and continue.

Finally, and again, I did not begin this work for myself but for others. Yet I have gained much: insight into the place I call home, insight into the people who live around me and those who make communities farther away, insight into the work ahead, and finally a feeling that seems at once known and unknown. This final feeling concerns the type of survey I did once at Willow Springs. It made me realize that though I am lucky enough to own my own house, to have a deed to my land, I have now learned that I cannot ever, nor can anyone else alone, own the air we breathe or the water we drink. We must own them in common.

The narratives that follow tell personal battles, often formulated at a kitchen table and considered as carefully as the food placed there to nourish friends and family. I offer the words told to me in the hope that they will inspire others who seek to change their own communities.

*Women Pioneers of the Louisiana Environmental Movement*

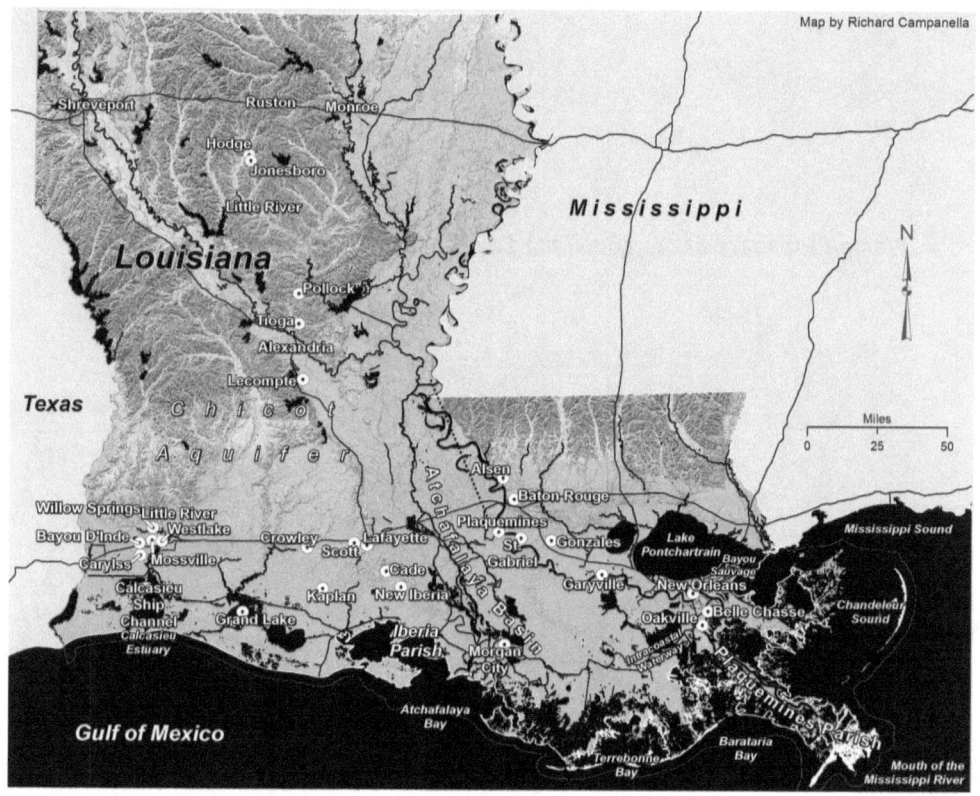

Sites of the women's homes and their activism. Map by Richard Campanella.

Chapter One

# "HOW COULD I STAND BY?"

## Protecting One Place, Protecting Many

*In 1997, Marine Shale agreed to pay more than $10 million to settle federal and state allegations that it incinerated hazardous waste without a permit and planned to sell the contaminated ash as fill material to the public. Sally Herman, Fernell Cryar, Catherine Holcomb, Barbara LeLeux, and Monica Mancuso were the 1995 recipients of an Environmental Protection Agency (EPA) award for their role in ensuring the safety of their community in the closing of Marine Shale's waste operations in Morgan City.*

We begin with a group of seven women, united in one place, Morgan City in Saint Mary Parish, Louisiana. Their stories may seem familiar: like so many others, these women made a leap from the household and schoolroom to public arenas, passing petitions, writing press releases, and testifying at permit hearings. Their work united caretaking for children with caretaking for the environment. We start with them since they tell not only of horrors but also of appreciation, a garnering of strength that rested primarily on education and values located in their families, churches, and, indeed, Louisiana itself. Their stories are those of great sorrows redeemed through action. Their stories are an awakening to the tragedies within their own families and beyond, to others of excluded groups, to even finding themselves among these excluded groups, and, of course, too, to deadly serious issues in the industrial pollution of their hometown.

Morgan City is not a large place. With only some twelve thousand residents, their parish ("county" elsewhere) is also small, with only some fifty-four thousand people. The city sits on the banks of the Atchafalaya River, and its people's livelihoods have always been tied to this river, as well as to the land itself, the trees, and the nearby Gulf of Mexico.

In some ways, it is a typical Louisiana community, known for its annual blessing of the fleet that comes within the festive Shrimp and Petroleum Festival. The combination of these two products in an annual celebration, complete with a ritualistic ceremony of thanksgiving and prayer for safety,

Morgan City women: Front row, from left, Helen Solar, Barbara LeLeux, Monica Laughlin Mancuso, and Miriam Price; and, second row, from left, Fernell Cryar, Sally Herman, and Catherine Holcomb

calls forth the richness of natural resources. Salt, water, oil, and natural gas are celebrated in good food, booths of handicrafts, decorated boats, music, and dancing. The women in this chapter, as elsewhere in the book, value this honoring and its foundation upon jobs based on seafood and oil. Many in the community shape their lives around such products.

Residents are generally proud of the state's natural resources and grateful for industrial growth. A government website lists seventeen industries for the state, and first on this list is the fact that "Louisiana has the greatest concentration of crude oil refineries, natural gas processing plants and petrochemical production facilities in the Western Hemisphere." Second, Louisiana is "America's third largest producer of petroleum and the third leading state in petroleum refining ... [pioneering] offshore oil and gas exploration and drilling." Third, the state also holds the distinction of hosting "the first [oil] well ever drilled out of sight of land." These are the categories the residents associate with prosperity. Tenth out of seventeen industries contributing to this feeling of plenty is shrimping.[1] Enriched earlier with the timber business, Morgan City has at times, then, been among the centerpieces of the state's industrial growth.

In other ways, Morgan City has been somewhat different, somewhat unique. Even in the late eighteenth and early nineteenth centuries, its population was more in flux than most other communities in the state. English-speaking migrants from the Carolinas were the first fishermen here; later came the Acadians, Creoles, and others who followed the dredging of the Atchafalaya to allow for ocean-going vessels. Still later, in the 1930s through the 1970s, came those from within Louisiana and from across the United States who participated in the drilling of the first successful offshore oil well. In the early 1980s a downturn in this work occurred. Then the city looked to another employer, Marine Shale Processors, which had established an incinerator to process non-hazardous oilfield wastes coming from other places.

Waste—the very word, unknown at first except domestically to these women—began literally to destroy lives. Was this waste truly without hazard? That was the question these women grew to ask as the many by-products of "modern life" entered their community and, especially, their families' homes. What was later learned was that Marine Shale started out burning non-hazardous oilfield waste but could not make enough money. Thus, it started taking creosote and other waste from Southern Wood Piedmont Company (1923–1985), which had manufactured railroad ties and telephone poles. The women eventually learned that the combination of materials was very different than the original permit had allowed.[2]

## SALLY HERMAN

In the 1980s, Sally Herman and her husband had an oilfield equipment rental business, where her children often came after school. Their place of work was located across the street from Marine Shale's industrial incinerator. On days the company was burning creosote, employees and children alike would be made sick. Sally became, then, one of the first women to connect illness to waste being burned. She became one of the first to challenge Marine Shale. Her story is a telling one of courage, but also of the context of Louisiana: Like Sally, many of the women had family members who worked in businesses connected to the petrochemical industries. Seven of the thirty-eight women mention direct ties via husbands, fathers, and brothers, and four of these are in the Morgan City area. Many more mention neighbors and friends who worked for petrochemical concerns. Though Marine Shale had a different focus, it was part of the web of conducting business without much oversight.

Sally's narrative also sets the tone in other ways for those women's voices that follow. Notice that she does not begin, or even end, thinking of herself as an activist, but rather, she draws from lessons of religion and citizenry and considers her actions as "right" and logical.

### Narrative from Sally Herman (b. Morgan City, Louisiana, 1947)

My mother worked for the *Morgan City Daily Review*, which was called *King Hanford's* then.[3] My dad worked for Texaco. I have two sisters and one brother. Growing up, my mother tried to shelter me, and I remember her saying, "Don't try. You might fail, and then you will be upset. It was meant to protect me, but I was a rebellious child, so it didn't work. I learned as I got older that if you didn't try—you didn't win either.

I grew up in Morgan City and went to Morgan City High School. I was editor of the school newspaper, and I was in the foreign language club. My first job was at L&H Printing Company in Morgan City, where I did a little bit of bookkeeping and waited on customers.

I got married in 1972, and our first child was born in 1975 and our second child was born in 1977. My husband is a business owner. We rent oilfield equipment, so wherever the oilfield is doing well we just move where the rentals are. We moved to Lafayette, Metairie, Luling, Morgan City, and now we are back in Lafayette.

After our two children were born we really got strongly back into the church. We were living in Luling, and with the help of a friend we started a babysitting co-op and a mother's group. I was president of the Methodist women in Luling, and I also taught several bible studies. We became more and more involved in the church, and my husband eventually went into the ministry, but not full time.

Not only were we active in the church, but when we moved to Morgan City, my husband started the first soccer league because they didn't have one in the area. Our children were involved in both soccer and baseball.

I am not an environmental activist. I do care about the environment, but I would not go out of my way to be involved in a cause [such as joining a group organized around one cause]. That is not my reason for doing what I did. I am a person with strong convictions, and I guess I have something in me that likes to make what is wrong right, and Marine Shale was such a horrendous situation that I felt I could not keep quiet about it.

Our oilfield rental business in Morgan City was directly across the street from Marine Shale. When they would burn creosote for fuel we would have to close down and send our employees home because tears were running out of their eyes. Our children would have rashes and we would have sore throats. I had strangers calling me at night that were deathly ill, that were working there [Marine Shale] and they were begging us to help. We decided not to take it lying down. In 1985, we started looking into what we could do to stop it. Linda King [also featured in this book] helped to find an environmental doctor because the company employees were only allowed to see the company doctor.

We also learned that Marine Shale was taking waste they weren't supposed to take and had sworn they didn't take. We would follow them [trucks] to the gates of Marine Shale as they went in. We would scrape things off barrels and there would be skull and crossbones. We did this because we wanted to know as much as we could firsthand about what was going on. We had people calling us saying they were taking in fetuses from abortion clinics. We had three or four eyewitnesses. I don't know if that is illegal or not, but to me that was horrendous. Babies being incinerated with hazardous waste was just more than I could bear to think about.

When we started fighting Marine Shale, it was a fairly small group: Melanie O'Neill, Kim Folse, and me. We were the main thorn in their flesh for probably five years. Then in 1987, right after the floating garbage barge incident, where they were trying to find a place to bring the [New York] garbage, we learned that the owners of Marine Shale thought they had the perfect solution and that was to bring it [garbage] to their facility for incineration. It was like the last resort. We said, "No, this is enough." The Citizens' Clearinghouse for Hazardous Wastes (CCHW) gave us an award for stopping the barge.

We were attending a parish council meeting [in reference to the barge], and we were trying to think of a name to call our group because they just kept calling us those "crazy people." One of the ladies said, "Let's be South Louisiana against pollution—SLAP." We said, "Yes, that is it—SLAP." The name was so distasteful to Marine Shale that we just loved it. I was the president of SLAP when it was founded.

SLAP was the sole group for probably five years. We had no funding so we joined with the Hazardous Waste Council [HWC] out of Washington, D.C. A lot of people felt we were joining the enemy because they were basically a consortium of hazardous waste treatment plants that wanted to knock out one of the competitors. I didn't care what their motives were. They were going to help us get rid of Marine Shale. They used us and we used them, but it worked. Industry had an unlimited amount of money, lawyers, and politicians. We had nothing except our voices. We basically had no clout and they had it all. This is one of the reasons we joined [HWC] in order to level the playing field.

From [Governor] Edwin Edwards on down, every time we turned, there was a politician involved in some kind of way with Marine Shale. There were many things that we couldn't prove, but in my opinion, Edwards had a financial interest in Marine Shale. We were told he was also a friend of Jack Kent, the owner of the company. Edwards made it impossible for us to do anything about closing the company down or getting any laws enforced, or even letting the LADEQ [the Louisiana Department of Environmental Quality, most often called DEQ] do their job.

We have contacted public officials on several occasions to ask what they could do to help us. When Mike Foster was a senator, I had numerous phone calls and conversations with him. Unfortunately, he never kept his word. He would tell us what he thought we wanted to hear and then would do what he wanted to do.

Senator John Breaux and Congressman Billy Tauzin were almost as bad.

We fought mostly at the parish level, and they, too, pretty much ignored the issue. We begged them not to give Marine Shale a permit, but they kept saying their hands were tied, which was not true because we had lawyers that said so. They just didn't want to take a stand or hurt the economy in the community. Of course, this was 1985, and the economy was already bad in the oilfield business.

I remember Linda King telling me that when they couldn't refute my facts they would attack me, so it was very difficult in the first five years because so many people would say, "You are going to run Marine Shale out of town and there aren't going to be any jobs." A lot of people thought we were doing it for the glory. If they only knew, there was no glory involved. It was hard work and a lot of tears. In the long run it cost me a lot more than I got out of it. I would never let them see me cry in public, but I would go home and cry a lot of times.

I spent a lot of time away from home [fighting Marine Shale], so years later I wrote a letter to my children and I said, "I'm so sorry for all the times you had to order pizza, or I couldn't be at a baseball game, or I couldn't be here or there." Both of them were so sweet and said they felt like I gave them a lot and they realized they could speak out for what they believed in. I think it has made little crusaders out of them.

If I had not been at the point in my spiritual life that I was, I could not have done it. It was only after a lot of prayer with my husband that we decided that I should go ahead because it was the right thing to do. Most of the people being hurt were poor or less-educated people, and a lot of them were Vietnamese, and if somebody didn't speak for them what was going to happen? It's important to realize that what we are doing is for the good of everybody, not just one social group or one racial group. The environment is an area where the rich and poor will all suffer the same consequences—if we lose.

### *Afterword*

There were times when I felt we had lost, and probably a year or two went by with them [Marine Shale] operating business as usual. But the bottom line is that in federal court they lost and they were closed down and they paid all these fines.

# FERNELL CRYAR

As Sally Herman points out, battling an industry as powerful as Marine Shale could be overwhelming. Fernell Cryar, who now lives in Mandeville, Louisiana, expresses similar sentiments. Marine Shale had the support of the town's mayor, its city council, then-Governor Edwards, as well as many residents worried about keeping their jobs.

### Narrative from Fernell Cryar (b. Ville Platte, Louisiana, 1948)

I grew up in Bunkie, Louisiana.[4] I have two sisters and one brother. My parents were good, hardworking people. My father was a farmer and my mother was a homemaker. Mom always helped at school as room mother and things like that. And I don't think I have met anybody more honest than my father. He was always helping somebody. He taught us to do the right thing. Until the day dad died he had a garden. It was huge and he was always bringing stuff to people. We ate all kinds of fish. We would eat venison. Whatever they hunted we always ate, ducks and things like that. At times we had chickens and lambs and pigs.

Even though my dad did not graduate from high school, it was important to him that his kids went to college. I went to Bunkie High School and then to college at Louisiana Tech in Ruston. I have a bachelor's degree in business. I did research papers and that taught me how to do research. Even though Tech was a small school, it had a lot of foreign students because of the engineering program, so I met a lot of different people. It expanded my horizons.

My husband and I got married in 1968, our last year of college. We lived in Ruston for the first year until my husband was drafted, and then we ended up living in Texas the whole time he was in the military. We also lived in New Orleans for seven years. Then we moved here to Morgan City. We have three children.

My first job was right here at Morgan City High School. I was an assistant to the librarian for three years. When I moved here, most of my volunteer work was in the schools. I would substitute teach. I would help in the office and that kind of thing. I also worked in my church, the Holy Cross Catholic Church, and I was on the school board. I have always been a good government type of person, so I belong and am the secretary of the Alliance for Good Government of the Saint Tammany chapter. I am in the League of Women Voters and I belong to the Sierra Club.

I was very aware of social issues. I am a product of the 1960s, when they were protesting the Vietnam War. I am an avid newspaper reader. So in 1987, when I really got started, I had been reading about Marine Shale and what was going on when Barbara LeLeux [also featured in this chapter] called and asked if I would speak at a hearing. I think it was a water hearing, but we have been to so many of them that they kind of run together sometimes. And so I said yes. It was like I was ready to do something and she was the catalyst. Well, I think she dropped the phone when I said yes because, later on, I found that it is very difficult to get people to speak at hearings for various and sundry reasons.

And that was my start. The more I got involved, the more I learned. I would go to the library and look through documents and read and write stuff down and send it to Wilma Subra [also featured in this book] about all the tests they were supposed to be doing. I didn't know much about chemistry. Wilma taught me a lot. She was my professor. I learned by on-the-job training.

Wilma taught me how to speak to the newspapers and how to get out there because the bad guys always had their public relations people there. One time, after I had been on television for an interview, some lady at the bank went on and on about what a great job we were doing, but to my knowledge she had never been to a hearing. Usually you did not get negative responses. Most people would just avoid you. I didn't have any direct pressure, however, because my husband was fully supportive of what I did [he is a financial advisor], although there were people that backed off because they owned businesses.

At times, I would get really down because some days everything looked so bleak because we were not making any progress, or we didn't feel there was any progress. You would go to a hearing and another hearing, and another. And you begin to feel like a bad guy. One time I told my husband, "I think I am going to join the garden club. You just plant plants and everybody likes you and they like your flowers."

This issue was very divisive because Marine Shale came in at a time when there was a high unemployment rate. The oil industry was just about gone, but Marine Shale was hiring. Some of my daughter's friends worked there. They were not bad people. They were just trying to earn a living and stay in this community. These companies have lots of money and manpower, and we usually have very little money and sometimes very little womanpower. They used to fuss about us having Wilma. They had all of these experts from this university and that university. We had one expert. Wilma is better than six of theirs and she never charged us a dime.

When we started working on this issue, the mayor, the city council, and Governor Edwin Edwards were all pro Marine Shale. Edwin Edwards, I believe, was instrumental in helping this company not only get started but stay in business. It gave us a big hill to cross. Politics was very important to them to keep that company operating. Buddy Roemer, I think, really cared about the environment and the state.

Everything I did, including telephone calls, stamps, and gas, I paid for myself. I didn't even take it off on my taxes. Everybody involved in opposing MSP donated their time. It was a grassroots effort. We did have a few people donate money, who did not want to get actively involved. To get the word out about a hearing, we would make homemade posters for the meetings. My son, who is a good artist, drew something and we would run it off and make fliers.

In working with other women, I found that nobody cared about being number one or about getting the glory because we were not in it for ourselves or for any gratifications or any awards. We were all in it for the sole purpose of shutting the company down and making Morgan City a better and safer community. I don't mean this to be male bashing, but sometimes men want a leadership role. The women rotated and we built on each other's strength. If somebody was a strong speaker, this was great. If somebody was better at research, that was also good. I like writing letters, so I wrote a lot of letters to public officials. We worked as a team. Women seem to do that.

We have been called "hysterical housewives," and I think that was just a way of trying to dismiss us or to make people think: do not listen to them, they are just kind of crazy, and they haven't taken their hormones. Most of us are mothers and we care about our kids and other people's kids. We just want a better place for children to live and grow up in. I think it scares people because they know we are going to just keep coming.

I admire Lois Gibbs because she would not let her issue go. I loved it when she locked her house and would not let public officials out. I don't know if I could ever be that strong, but she influenced me because she accomplished so much. She went from being a housewife and a stay-at-home mom to getting all of Love Canal cleaned up, when the EPA was saying there was not a problem.

Part of it [involvement] for me was about giving kids a good environment to grow up in. They do not have a choice about being born, so we need to take care of them. And part of it was when Helen Solar and Miriam Price [also featured in this chapter] learned that their granddaughter Nicole was sick. I knew what she went through during her illness. But there were far too many children in the area sick. But even if it was one [child], how could I stand by? I know the scientists and the Louisiana Health Department and all of those people say we cannot prove anything, but I will believe until the day that I die that those children got neuroblastoma because of that company.[5] Before they located here, we did not have any clusters like that. We had the clusters when the company was burning bad stuff, pulling the filters out, and letting the stuff go into the atmosphere.

I think women in Louisiana have made a tremendous difference. They have made people aware. They have done their homework and they have a lot of credibility today: Marylee Orr [also featured in this book] in Baton Rouge and Wilma Subra, of course, and women all over the state. Now there is an awareness of how our state has been raped over the years by oil companies and other companies who cared only about making a buck and not about what was good for our state. Monsanto in California operates with no emissions, and if they can do that in California, they can do it in Louisiana.

## Afterword

In 1995, when we decided to move from Morgan City, I told my husband, when we were driving around looking at places in Mandeville, that we were going to live where all the lawyers live because they are not going to put a Marine Shale there. The lawyers would fight them. They have the resources and they know congressmen and senators. They know the people to call and those people will listen to them. They are not going to listen to some person who is poor or dropped out of school in the eighth grade. They are not going to listen because they do not feel like this person can impact them. These people don't generally have the resources or the education to fight them.

I think everybody should be a steward of the environment even if it is just recycling. You don't have to do great things. There is always something each of us can do as stewards.

# BARBARA LELEUX

When Barbara LeLeux joined the campaign to close Marine Shale Processors, she knew it would be an uphill fight. As she puts it, "There were about seven of us and the odds were not in our favor, but I don't think we ever felt we would win or lose. We never saw it in terms of that." Barbara got involved because she thought the company was taking advantage of naive, uneducated people.

### Narrative from Barbara LeLeux (b. Jeanerette, Louisiana, 1947)

My paternal grandfather was a mechanic.[6] My maternal grandfather was a sugarcane farmer. In Jeanerette my grandmother lived in a one-hundred-year-old cypress house with a tin roof. It was a wedding gift. When she got married, one of the wealthy members of the family gave her and her sister adjoining houses. My grandfather caught crawfish from ditches and in the water barriers and sold it for five cents a pound during the Depression. They were not raised in artificial ponds. My grandmother kept her coffee grinds and eggshells and stuff like that to put in her garden. They made jams and jellies sealed with paraffin. They reused jars. They fished and hunted. That was all part of their food—especially during the Depression. They did not waste anything.

I grew up in Jeanerette, the second of four children. My father worked in the oilfield. I graduated from Jeanerette High. I wanted to be a nun, but my father would not allow me to go to a convent. Then I wanted to join the Peace Corps, and he wouldn't hear of that either. In those days, you listened to your parents.

I went to college at U.S.L., Lafayette, Louisiana [University of Southwestern Louisiana]. I was an English major with a minor in library science, but then I quit college to get married. When I went back to school, I got a degree in elementary education. Then I got an administrative degree. We have two children.

My husband was in the Air Force during the Vietnam War, very active in the space program as a project engineer. He worked at Cape Kennedy, so we lived in Cocoa Beach, Florida. My husband now builds boats here in Morgan City. Boats are his first love.

I did not want to move here. It was a rough place to live. There were a lot of transients and tough people. I was from a small town where everybody knew everybody. When you were born, you bought your plot. It took me years before I considered it [Morgan City] home.

I first started teaching in New Iberia in 1968. I taught in a Catholic school for seven years, thinking that was the only place that I could serve God. I realize now that the real service is in the public school with the truly poor. I did not realize that there was so much poverty. I always wanted to be a missionary, but I didn't know I could go across the street and become one. Poverty, neglect, and abuse, it's all right here.

When I was in a classroom, and I am not anymore, one thing I made the kids do several times a day was to tidy their desk. I thought if they learned to have a tidy space, they would go home and tidy their room, and then when they grow up, they are going to tidy their home. They would ask, "Is it tidy the desk time yet?" People would come into my room and say, "Your kids are so neat." And that is catching. You know those little things we do are contagious, and that is how you change the world.

I have grown to be very close to people like Monica Mancuso and Catherine Holcomb [also featured in this book] because we are teachers to begin with. When you share a vocation with someone, you have a lot of the same interests and values. We are very family oriented. Monica had talked to me about Marine Shale because we were good friends. So I became involved. She had a science background with a degree in horticulture and she was very concerned about what was going on.

We met many times—especially around the hearings. And, of course, Wilma Subra was instrumental in guiding us because we didn't have the technical experience. She gave us the artillery to fight with and helped us to know what was really going on. It [data] has to be recorded, so you get the stuff written down, and that's the part we played. We had to get up [at public hearings] and say the things that needed to be recorded. It seemed like there were a lot of failures, but Wilma's point was that you just had to get the data read into the record, and that is what we did. I think that being tenacious and believing that if you are right—eventually right will win because the system works. It's slow, but it works. This is the story of the game. One thing Wilma kept telling us was, "They are going to run out of appeals." And they did. We lost a lot of the time, but we won the war, and that was the whole point.

I found a lot of people were complacent, thinking it was easier to look the other way. They would prefer someone else do the job. It wasn't that they didn't have their suspicions, but they didn't want to get involved because it could hurt them financially, or it could hurt them socially, or it could hurt them in some other way. My husband got a lot of questioning and criticism because some of the backers of the plant were my neighbors. So it could be very intimidating.

My children were older when I started. They always thought they were going to find me floating in the river. I think they had a lot of pride though and especially towards the end when Marine Shale started trying to move the aggregate [by-products of incineration]. They wanted to put some of it at the country club. Here were all of these people and this was their country club, but they would not fight it. Instead they would ask, "What is Barbara going to do about this?"

It takes a tremendous amount of effort to fight something like Marine Shale. At the time Marine Shale was going, we had this tyrant for a superintendent of education. He had written a letter and they gave it out parish wide. It said that when we spoke at hearings we were not to say that we were teachers. We could speak—but not say we were teachers because they were intimidated by that role.

We were so calm when we spoke at public hearings that I think it was disarming. Imagine having women, who are teachers, in a sea of people, and no one is on your side. You go into this hall and there might be seven of us, and maybe five hundred others, all wearing caps with Marine Shale Processors written on them. It was a wild experience. They had so much money. No one would have placed a bet on us in this community.

Monica was an inspiration to me, also, because she has the wisdom of Solomon and is still fighting. At this time in my life I don't think I would. Those hearings take something out of you. They are horrible. They harass and yell at you while you are talking. Seven years is a long battle. I don't know how we did it.

Once, when Monica and I were going to LSU [Louisiana State University] to get some information for a hearing, an eighteen-wheeler almost drove us off the road. So I said to my husband when I got home, "The superintendent shred me publicly because I got up at a school board meeting and said that he had lied, then we almost got run off the bridge by an eighteen-wheeler." That was at a time when a guy had gone in and shot fourteen engineering students in Ontario, Canada, and my husband said, "Barbara, you and Monica are the kind of women men kill."

Most women will have a different motivation in everything they do because of who they are and because they are life givers. And as life givers, they want to be life preservers, and consequently, they will do things that might seem unsafe or risky to be sure that life is preserved. But I think that things are better and are continuing to improve because women stood up.

### *Afterword*
I see it all in a different light now; I do. I saw them [the opposition to my point of view] as the enemy, but with the wisdom of my fifty-two years, it would no longer be me against them. Now, I think, I would be able to go in and be more respectful of their position and of them personally. That includes all of them from the top down. From those that were just milking it for all it was worth to the lowest employee. That is my regret, but it was something I didn't know then. I had to journey more in my life before I could come to that point. They believed they were doing something right, just as much as I believe I am doing something right. But at that time I couldn't see it because I was trying to measure them by my own measure.

# CATHERINE HOLCOMB

Initially reluctant to join the group working to close Marine Shale, Catherine Holcomb had a change of heart when she looked around her community. A teacher, she was a founding member of the Atchafalaya Delta Society. Her mention of lobbyists is significant. Louisiana's industries have many paid lobbyists; environmental groups have one or two, mostly volunteers, in any given year.

### Narrative from Catherine Holcomb (b. Morgan City, Louisiana, 1958)

My mother is from Morgan City.[7] And my father is from Lafayette. His family members were all from Lafayette and Saint Martinville. They are Acadians or Creoles. Morgan City was a nice place to live and the schools were nice. We were outside all of the time, playing softball and swimming in the summertime.

Morgan City was starting to grow a lot in the late 1960s. People built houses, and the schools started to grow. We always had the oil industry here, which brought a lot of people into the area. When they were first married, my parents were in the oil industry, but my dad ended up teaching. He was a city councilman and a junior high school principal when I was growing up. I think he tried to do the right thing and the people that he worked with did also. When I was in junior high school, Edwin Edwards was running for governor for the first time. We all supported him because he looked like he was going to be such a good governor for the state.

I went to Nicholls State University in Thibodaux, Louisiana. I was always with kids, so I ended up going into education. I really do enjoy teaching, but it was just something that happened at that time. I started teaching in 1980. I got married in 1983. We had five children.

I got involved with environmental issues in 1986. I was pregnant with my third baby. Marine Shale was putting out all these fumes, and people were noticing that the company was not doing what they said they were going to do. They said they were not going to burn hazardous waste. They were supposed to just burn oilfield waste. So a lot of people complained and a lot of people were involved. The plant is just right over there. It is only about five and a half or six miles away from here. Everybody lives close to it.

Now I look back and think, "If only more people had paid attention at that point." However, I did not get involved. I remember people bringing handouts to work and saying, "You need to come to this meeting. You have children now and you have to be responsible and pay attention." I did not want to hear any of that. I just ignored it. And then, I don't know why, but something told me that I needed to get involved.

One of the little girls that died of cancer was my oldest daughter's age, and the other little girl was my second daughter's age. I had just watched a news story about Marine Shale. They interviewed Jack Kent, who owned Marine Shale, and they interviewed Miriam Price [also featured in this book] and some of the parents of the children with neuroblastoma. I watched and I thought, "Oh my gosh, so that is what my friend was telling me about. I am going to have to do something."

So I called Mrs. Mancuso [also featured in this book]. She had come over a couple of times and talked to me about doing some things. I told her I was ready to help and get involved, and so we started going to Baton Rouge. When I sat there and listened to the public officials and the questioning and the way things seemed in Baton Rouge, you just knew nobody was taking care of you. My eyes were opened and that was it. Ever since then I have been involved. My husband was very helpful. He teaches too, so he has always been there. The children were small then and you could put them on your hip and carry them somewhere and you always had someone willing to babysit.

Lobbying is very effective when you are there, but we couldn't be there all of the time. The people who get things done are the ones being paid to get them done. Individual citizens don't have those resources. When you realize that is how they operate, that's really scary. You would bring information to some politicians, and they would say the same thing, "If it's wrong the government is going to shut them down." Well, that's what I thought too. But, I think letters have an influence and telephone calls have an influence. Sometimes the results take a long time to see, but there were a lot of times when I saw things that proved to me that we were doing the right thing.

Congressman [Billy] Tauzin helped a lot in the beginning. There were hearings in Washington, and he made the Environmental Protection Agency (EPA) pay attention. That was the problem. No one was paying attention earlier. Governor Roemer really did a lot to help out also. He was a reform governor, and they don't last long. He was the kind of person that stepped in between, and if it had not been for him, things would not have gotten as far as they have. And Secretary [Paul] Templet, of the DEQ [Department of Environmental Quality]—all of those people helped us during Roemer's administration.

[Catherine, now fully immersed in her role as an activist, continued to lead both her children and her students—by example.]

At the time that I started to get involved, I taught history, and I can remember telling students to vote and get involved. You just always try to teach children that if something is very important get involved in your community. As a teacher, however, you have to be careful and really fair since I teach a lot of children whose parents probably work out there. I have always had my own children there with me. We participated in candlelight marches and cleanups. I wouldn't say at that time that I ever felt this work was too hard. I don't remember thinking, "This is so overwhelming." You just always have the strength to do things if they are important to you.

So you get consumed in it because it is all consuming. But I don't think I would do anything differently. We were going to hearing after hearing after hearing and we even went to the governor's office. Everything that we did made a difference. Every sign that we held up, every hearing that we had, every call that we made, it made a difference. It makes a difference with the legislature, and you could see it. You could see things happening with the DEQ. So many different kinds of people were working together doing what they are good at. That was in 1986.

I think people label others to cloud the picture and draw attention away from the issues. When you use the term "environmentalist," everybody pictures hysterical housewives. Well, you do get hysterical after a while when no one is listening. There were a lot of people who were speaking out against Marine Shale, but it was never really reported that way in the media. We didn't have money to buy a lot of media coverage.

## *Afterword*

Industry is important. Business is important. You have to have business to have jobs, to have income, to have schools, and to have education. However, I do not think that you need to sell all of the important things. I think if we charged more for people to use what we have, it would be worth our while in the end, instead of allowing people to come in and operate so cheaply.

## MONICA LAUGHLIN MANCUSO

Monica Laughlin Mancuso, the next speaker, was the school principal who Catherine Holcomb called after deciding to join the fight to close Marine Shale.

### Narrative from Monica Laughlin Mancuso (b. Hobbs, New Mexico, 1953)

My dad pretty much worked and was away a lot with the oilfield.[8] He was an assistant superintendent for Dixielyn Oil Corporation. He worked his way up from a roughneck. Mother was by herself a lot and raised us with an excellent work ethic. Saturdays were devoted to housecleaning. But, of course, the boys got out of it a lot. We were very close, and we still are a very close family. My father was transferred to Morgan City when I was twelve. My mother was a homemaker until after my dad died, and then she went to work at the hospital as a switchboard operator.

I went to a very small high school, Central Catholic High School here in Morgan City. Our senior class was forty-nine. I was very active and involved in just about everything. As long as we had a band I was in the band. I was the drum majorette. When we made mistakes we were taught how to learn from them, how to get along, and how to work things out. We were a close class.

I started college at Northeast and then went to Nicholls and ended up at LSU. My fiancé was there too. I ended up getting married before my last year of school. I graduated from LSU. Then I graduated from the University of Southwestern Louisiana with a second degree and then Nicholls with a third. I tried law school and now I am back at LSU. I am still learning.

In college I went into horticulture because I was told to major in something you enjoyed and I enjoyed growing things and taking care of flowers. I vowed I would never be a teacher, and I got out [of college] and that is what I ended up doing. I started teaching immediately. I taught fourth grade, and as a mother of five, I was involved in Boy Scouts for a little while. I also was a softball coach for my daughter's team.

[Monica became an environmental advocate after being appointed to a parish committee and asked to tour the Marine Shale facility.]

I do not consider myself an activist. I pretty much like conforming to what is expected. I think as far as this issue [Marine Shale], it was not handled right. I became involved when I was appointed to a parish committee of local people who were charged with the duty of addressing this issue. As such we were invited to the plant. They wanted us to come at lunch and sit down to a meal. But my husband and I said we would show up—on our time and at our own convenience. We happened to go by on a Friday night. When we asked to see the engineer on duty, the man there said, "I have got no college, but I know my job well and I am in charge of the plant tonight." He took us to the back and we saw them scooping the chemicals. Some of the chemicals were in the open vat and the drum would sometimes go straight through and they [employees] would get all excited and they would run and look at the video camera and say, "See the drum go through." They were also running a bag house test. They were testing the bags and they would put a dye through the stack and it was supposed to capture all of the dust particles. Well, it was not capturing them. They knew they had a problem and they were just burying the stuff in there. Well, with the small amount of chemistry that I had, which was sixteen hours, it really left a visual in my head that this was not the way it should be. I also studied horticulture, so I knew the benefits of pesticides and I was never one that hesitated to use them—but with caution.

Once I took the tour of Marine Shale, it was something I could not look back on. It was something I could not turn away from. If I had gone to Marine Shale that night and been pleased—but to go there and see that it was wrong, and then later on for something to develop with the kids, and to know I did nothing—I would not have been able to handle that.

Yes, it was the tour that night and then the haze on the lake. I was commuting to LSU. I had decided I was going to try law school, and so I would get up in the morning and drive out along the lake, heading to Baton Rouge, and the sun would be rising and you could see the haze on the lake. It meant pollution. It meant that the things that I had seen were now out in the air that was being breathed.

[Shortly after the tour, Monica learned that doctors in New Orleans had begun to question why so many children living in Morgan City had been diagnosed with cancer. Being conscientious about her work as part of the parish committee studying the problem, she telephoned the doctors to hear firsthand their concerns.]

I took a ride with Helen [Solar] and Miriam [Price, both grandmothers to one of the affected children] to Baton Rouge to talk to Martha Madden of the DEQ. Channel 2 and Channel 9 showed up. So the minute I get back I called the parish president, and I reported that we were there and the media was there, and everything now is a very public issue. All of a sudden the parish committee we were appointed to was no more.

[The international environmental organization named Greenpeace began actively challenging Marine Shale. In 1989, they staged an event where they put a raft in the water adjacent to the Marine Shale plant and proceeded to take water samples. Waiting nearby were Marine Shale employees armed with ax handles, and news broadcasters reported the event as it unfolded.]

Marine Shale had approached the Greenpeace raft and there was word in the community that they were at a local hardware store and they all had ax handles, so when the Greenpeace boat came up in the news footage, it came off that they [Marine Shale employees] had ax handles. At the next hearing Catherine [Holcomb] and some of the others had a banner that said, "Will all Marine Shale employees please check your ax handles at the door?" So, it put that imagery in your head, and then as you came in you picked up a yellow balloon with a frown on its face and as you looked out into the auditorium you saw all these blue shirts [Marine Shale employees], you saw all of these yellow balloons and you said, "Here is a cry that must be heard." And, of course, the public officials sat under a banner that said, "If the health department would have only gotten here sooner." And they are listening to all of this testimony, and it was just teachers breaking down the issues, saying, "Well it [the Marine Shale expansion] is going to be six times the amount of chemicals, and six times the amount of water pollution, and six times the amount of air pollution." You would just break it down into people's visuals so that they could understand, and they really did. They did not okay the expansion. Certainly it was because it [numbers] kept on going—that six, times six, times six.

So, they [teachers] had their balloons. They had their banners. And I had another teacher friend who wanted to do a demonstration. Now this is well into the issue, and when she gave her presentation she had this machine that blew smoke on all of the people. Everybody is intimidated, but she was gallant enough to get up there and say, "This is my response to that." These women were very gifted educators.

At another hearing Barbara LeLeux [featured earlier in this chapter] got up on a Wednesday night and walks to the podium and says, "There would be a whole lot more of us here, but everyone is home baking pies tonight." The hearing was held the night before Thanksgiving—thinking they would just be able to get it through, whatever it was that they were asking for from the parish government.

We really tried to do our homework. We began getting the statistics available from the Department of Health and Hospitals, and we would do the map and we would track things, but all of a sudden they stopped publishing those. And you would begin to really suspect something. Is it stuff that they don't want us to know?

They tried to get to us through the school system to some degree. One was the parish-wide memo that went out. I had eighth-grade science at that time, and I encouraged them [students] to attend some hearings, giving them bonus points one way or the other. It does not matter which way, just go learn about the issues. This is the way to do it. They will have people on both sides. You will hear both sides. The very next day, we had a parish-wide memo that kind of insinuated that any time this [issue] is brought up in class, you were to be reprimanded. It was a very subtle way of saying, "Don't do it." And, at that, more teachers came to find out what was going on—because they viewed that as a silencing mechanism.

### *Afterword*

I am a principal, and I speak in front of people all the time, but it is nothing that I am ever comfortable with. But, I will go to the front if I am not pleased with the way things are—when it is something that I feel strongly about. I call it gut-level feelings. It is your belief in what is right and what is wrong and your need to go with that. Inner strength comes from the way you were raised. The conscience, I guess, is what keeps talking to you. I really think it was a calling that day we visited Marine Shale.

I would like for my children to carry something with them, whether it is their experience at the capitol, accompanying me to Baton Rouge [for public hearings], or seeing their mom not afraid to fight the Goliaths. Until my children started talking about the trips to the capitol, I really did not see it from their perspective, but I think in the long run they appreciate and maybe learned something in the process about persistence or doing the right thing. I hope so anyway. I think it was time well spent.

# HELEN SOLAR

While these five women were fighting a battle on behalf of their neighbors and fellow citizens, the next two women here were fighting a personal battle. As grandmothers, they watched as their granddaughter was stricken with childhood cancer.

### Narrative from Helen Solar (b. Morgan City, Louisiana, 1946)

I have lived in Morgan City all of my life.[9] My parents had a jewelry store and were in the business here for fifty years. I was always impressed with the way daddy ran his business and handled people in general. He was outgoing and involved in everything. He was involved with the Shrimp and Petroleum Festival for years and years. He was also involved with Mardi Gras.

I went to Morgan City High School and graduated in 1964. I joined every school organization. I participated in pep squad, home economics, and the Future Business Leaders of America. During my time they had a lot of school activities for the students. That was a big thing in our day. By participating, I learned about communicating and being able to relate to people.

When I graduated from high school I got married. I worked at the jewelry store, but I was basically just a housewife. We have three children. I had a Cub Scout group for a year. And when the girls were in Girl Scouts, I did activities with them. I became a lay minister and did music ministry. I taught the kids music at the Catholic school.

[In the mid 1980s, Helen was enjoying the rewards of being a grandmother, but her life soon changed.]

One day I was talking to the grandmother of a child who had been very sick and asked what happened. She told me that they found a tumor on her grandchild's back. I went to my daughter's house and said I wanted to check Nicole. And God help us, I found a lump on her back. I called the local surgeon and he said that it was probably a fatty tumor and to watch it, but we went for x-rays at Ochsners in New Orleans. We were sitting out in the waiting room and we really were not too concerned. In fact, we were discussing where we were going to eat after the appointment. They were taking so long, and the next thing we know—here comes my daughter, and you could tell from her face that she was devastated. They found a tumor the size of a Nerf football on Nicole's back. I could not believe that this could be growing in this child and we do not even know it.

The doctor put Nicole right into the hospital. Dr. Black asked us, "What is near you? What is there in your town that could be causing this? We have two children from the same town with a very rare cancer, which usually occurs in only one in one hundred thousand people, and here you are in your community [population of fourteen thousand] with two cases." Well, we started investigating and came up with five children that had neuroblastoma within Saint Mary Parish. And this is a very small area.

Nicole's illness consumed my life. It really did while she was in treatment. It was hard watching her have her life zapped out of her with chemo and then having such a horrible surgery. And after that her heart being affected by it; she had to live on heart medication. Nicole died seven years ago. She didn't die from cancer; she died from a heart attack. The chemotherapy destroyed her heart muscles. Her little heart just gave out.

When we started we were very naive to anything like this. I did not even know what Marine Shale was. I thought our government took care of us. I thought this would not be allowed to happen. What about their own children? What about their own lives? Monica Mancuso [also featured in this book] was the first one that I talked to. She was already aware of Marine Shale. We started meeting with others in the community and we came from all walks of life. We started checking and we found out a lot of disturbing things. With my level of education there were a lot of things that I did not understand, but I did know that what they were doing was wrong. I am not technical, but it does not take a rocket scientist to figure out a lot of things that I have discovered on my own. As I went on, I found out that that is how they [some companies] operate. They get their foot in the door and get established before the citizens even know. That's why we don't know what's in our own backyards.

When I came home, the first time, from Baton Rouge and we were on television, my husband seemed worried because he has a business in the area. I told him,

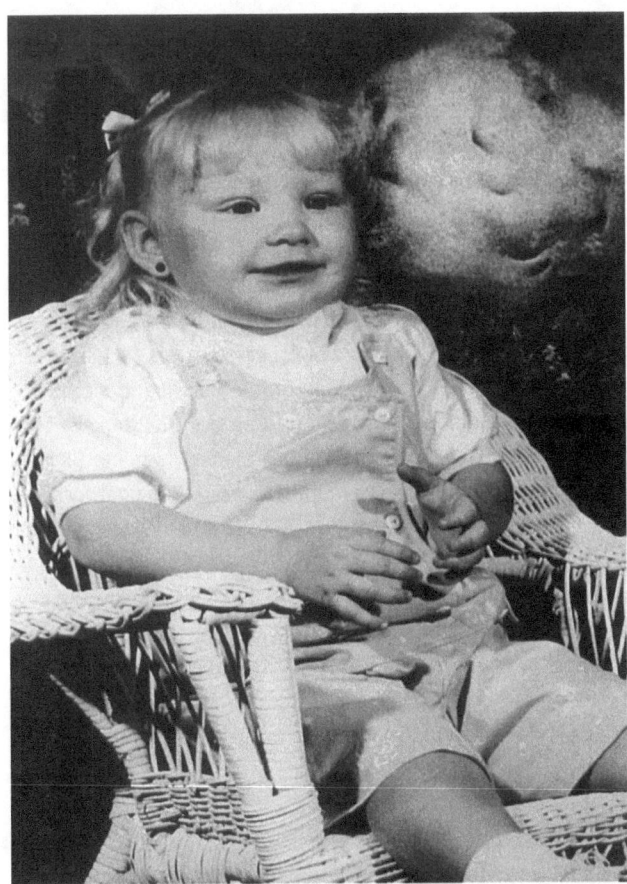

Nicole Price

"There is no price on Nicole, my children, or my grandchildren, and I don't care what it does to us."

We went to Baton Rouge many times and I was disgusted with what I saw. It's just big business. It's whose back are they going to scratch this time. You bring these children up there, that have been affected by this, and it's like a big circus. I think everybody ought to spend a couple of days at the legislature and see what goes on. Sometimes I felt like we were the only seven women in town fighting the company. They used everything they could against us. It was very lonely work because it affects your family and everything around you. But, I believe in God. I believe that with him you can fight anything and so you just had to turn your faith to him.

Governor Roemer was a very good governor. Had it not been for him, I don't believe the facility would be closed today. He helped us a lot and he fought for us. When we went to talk to him, he said that what had transpired was the fact that

Marine Shale had gotten a license as an incinerator. In other words, they didn't have a hazardous waste permit to burn the chemicals that were going into our atmosphere. They didn't have to have all of the regulations that would keep the stuff from going into the air. He said that Marine Shale has no different license than Delchamps [grocery store] has for burning cardboard boxes. Now think of that. Think of what they were burning.

When we got started there were so many people like me, naive to what was going on. And if you knew—you would rather not know because that was easier than facing the truth. Many of my friends that I approached, to help or to get involved, didn't want to get involved. They had all kinds of excuses such as, "Helen, you have an air conditioner and you run it don't you? Well, that affects the ozone layer." Some of my best friends were on the opposite side, and I always tried to keep that separate because that didn't change the way I felt about them. It was hard sometimes when I sat with them at church and had to hold their hand. You fight for what you believe in, and I guess that was the hardest thing—to still come together and be loving and neutral in those respects.

At that time Marine Shale employed a lot of people. Friends of mine would say, "How can you be against a company that's putting food on your table?" And I understand that. I realized what was happening, but I just did not know how to fight such a thing. I guess they had to be affected, like I was, in order to have the will to fight as hard as I fought. I think I would still be one of the naive ones today if it hadn't affected me on such a personal level.

## *Afterword*

It is frightening. If you took everything you know about the environment—I tell you what—I could not sleep some nights thinking of all of the things, such as the chemicals you clean your house with and what it does to your body. The more you know, the harder it is to live with. That is why there are many people naive to the problem. It seems so much easier to be naive than to face up to it and try to fight it.

I would like to think we were very effective in the end, but it took a long time. I fought hard for ten years. It was a constant battle, and physically it just wiped me out. Every day, every minute the phone would ring and you would hear more stuff. We fought day and night, and at that time we had no local political support. We had no businesses involved in it. We had very few people. I was fighting to try to save the environment for my children and grandchildren that were coming up. But they have always got the best lawyers and the best people on their side, and you are just a housewife that doesn't know a whole lot about it except what you see happening before your eyes to the people you love. Sometimes I didn't know whether I was going to be able to go forward the next day. You would get down and then all of a sudden you would read something else or someone would tell you something and educate you on another problem and then you would get all fired up and start again.

# MIRIAM PRICE

Like Helen Solar, Nichole's paternal grandmother, Miriam Price, never expected to become an activist of any sort.

### Narrative from Miriam Price (b. Morgan City, Louisiana, 1941)

All of my grandparents lived in Morgan City and raised their families here.[10] My grandfather, on my father's side, was the original owner of the meat market on Front Street, and his wife was a homemaker. My grandparents on my mother's side, my grandmother was a homemaker, and my grandfather worked for a railroad company. He had a garden and always had beautiful flowers. He used to give me flowers to bring to the church when we had special occasions. They [grandparents] all died in Morgan City and were buried in the cemetery here.

My parents are from Morgan City. My father was a butcher and was involved in political issues. He served sixteen years as a parish councilman for Saint Mary Parish. My mother worked at a dentist office until she retired. I was the oldest of three children, so I think my parents had higher expectations for me. I tried to live by their rules, and in turn I set up my own family based on the same rules they had. I went to school from the first grade through the eighth grade at Sacred Heart Elementary. From the ninth through the twelfth grades I was at Morgan City High School.

I got married in 1959. We were high school sweethearts. My husband is a retired police officer and currently serving as city marshal in Morgan City. We had one girl and four boys. I tried to be a friend as well as a mother to my children. That is about the only leadership role that I thought I was allowed to have because, when given a choice after high school in the fifties, most girls were either going to college or they were going to stay home and raise a family. That was the choice that I made, and I have never had any regrets about that.

It was always important to us, the beauty of the world surrounding us. We tried to teach that to the children, especially in camping trips and other outings. We tried to teach them that God gave us the Earth, and you have to be careful what you do with it because you have to leave it to your children as well.

In the 1970s and early 1980s, I was busy raising my family, so I never got involved in anything political. My issues were with my religion, the kids going to Catechism class, baseball, and swimming. Those were the things I was involved in. Social issues very seldom came into my mind. I just didn't think I would play a part.

Being a wife and a mother and staying at home, you do not always feel like you have that much to offer, but when push comes to shove, sometimes you are forced to do it. I think that is what Marine Shale did.

When my granddaughter Nicole took sick with cancer, I got really angry. I think that and the pain of seeing her suffer motivated me. That is when I became aware of the environment because the doctors were so insistent on the fact that it could be some kind of contamination that had caused her cancer. Helen Solar [also featured in this book] was with her at the time she discovered the lump in her back. Helen's daughter, which was my daughter-in-law, came and asked me what I thought. I really did not think there was very much to it. I thought it was a fatty tumor. We decided to have Nicole checked at Ochsners in New Orleans, and within two weeks she was diagnosed with cancer. And the first thing they asked us was, "Do the kids play on a hazardous waste dump in Morgan City?" After doing some investigating, we found out Nicole was the fifth child to be diagnosed with the same type of cancer. Some of the other children were being treated at Ochsners, so the doctors knew about it. It was not normal to find that many children with cancer in a small community like we live in. We should have had 0–0.5 cases, if any.

Coming back to find the cause, after fighting Nicole's illness, to me, the most obvious and the most blatant violator of the environmental laws was Marine Shale. I know now that there were a lot more environmental issues around here that we should have been dwelling on, but Marine Shale was the most obvious. In the middle to late '80s, I thought Marine Shale was a shell processing plant. I never realized it was there to incinerate hazardous waste. I did not know what the chemical benzene was. I didn't know what toluene was.

My house is three miles from the plant. It concerned me that the grandchildren either lived by me or they played at the house all of the time. I made it my business to learn what I needed to know about what was going on out there. I guess Nicole was the driving force. I never went anywhere without her. Nicole motivated me to do everything that it took to call awareness to what the plant was doing. It was her plight, I think, that drove me to do the things that I never thought I would do—like getting up at a public hearing in Baton Rouge to speak. And it seems foolish when you talk about people, like Greenpeace, who chained themselves to the bridge in Baton Rouge to [gain media attention], but we often said, "What would happen if we chained ourselves together and laid across the highway and the trucks could not pass?" I never thought I would see the day when I would talk about laying down on Highway 90 to stop the trucks from coming in, but I was that desperate if that was what it would take to close the plant. I just did not know what more to do. We were trying to find some way to make people understand.

I was not in favor of being radical, but sometimes I thought maybe that is what it is going to take, a grandmother chaining herself to the fence at the entrance. It

Miriam Price

never came to that, but there were times when I thought that was maybe what we would have to do. And I did not mind speaking out about how I felt, which was totally different from what I was before because I was a very complacent person.

[Mothers, grandmothers, and teachers often gathered around Miriam's kitchen table to discuss what could be done to stop Marine Shale.]

We talked about going to Marine Shale and standing on the side of the road showing our signs, which we did. We also went to Baton Rouge, and we went to public hearings and sat, and sat, for hours waiting to be heard for five minutes. We spoke at several hearings, for all the good it did us, because I honestly felt that nobody heard what we said or cared. These pompous people sit up there and pretend they are there to help the people, and you know darn good and well, when you go in, they aren't going to help. They are going to do whatever is politically right for them. We saw the lobbyists and big business pulling strings to get what they wanted in the legislature. Here we were, I was crying at the table, speaking before a legislative committee, and they couldn't have cared less. That attitude infuriated me because

I know if it had been their grandchild they would have been just as upset and they would want something done.

I do not understand how people's opinions and people's ideas are not more respected in the political system. Aren't "we the people" the government? Aren't "we the people" supposed to protect each other from places like that? What I didn't realize, I guess naively, was how corrupt the process of awarding permits was. I thought everything went by the law, and I thought the law was made to protect people. I had this perception that not just God, but the people elected were going to take care of us. It was a rude awakening for me when I learned that that isn't exactly how politics is played. I had to see firsthand that not everyone in Baton Rouge and Washington was out there to protect us. In the end, I realized we were responsible for ourselves. It was every man for himself.

I think it was the political system back then. It was well accepted that Edwards ruled Louisiana, and whatever you wanted you could get. With Governor Roemer we had hope. We saw some hope that maybe things would get a little better, but he was not in office long enough.

There were some threats. There was always the fear that if we didn't let the plant stay here, then everybody would go broke. My husband was an elected official, and he was told many times that he would never get elected again because his wife spoke up against the plant. He said that if that was how he had to win an election, he didn't deserve it in the first place. Someone even came up to him and told him, "You had just better keep your wife quiet." He said, "Whatever she says, she says for me as well."

Nicole was like a poster child for everything that was right about what we did. I think she was Jack Kent's [Marine Shale's owner] worst enemy. She was only a child, but I think he feared her more than anything because she got the sympathy we were looking for to make people understand what was happening to these kids. I mean, three of them are buried in the cemetery here.

## *Afterword*

I spent time trying to save Nicole in the hospital, and I spent time in Baton Rouge trying to close Marine Shale. It was like fighting two wars. I didn't think I had it in me, but I would have given anything to save her. A lot of the times Helen would go to the public hearings and I would stay home with Nicole. Or she would stay home with Nicole and I would go to the hearings. When Nicole was well, we took her to the hearings with us. I have pictures of her with Governor Roemer when we went to see him.

It was very tiring to fight Marine Shale, and finally I said, "You know what, Lord? I am giving it to you. If you want the plant closed, you close it because I do not know what more I can do as one human being to make people understand that this plant needs to close." Within two years it was closed. Nicole lived long enough to see the plant closed, and I was glad of that.

Chapter Two

# "WE ARE BLACK AND WHITE, RICH AND POOR"
## Crossing Boundaries, Remaking Louisiana

In Iberville parish of the 1980s, 23.3 percent of the population lived below the poverty level.

Oil refineries and petrochemical industrial facilities have released millions of pounds of chemicals into the air and waterways over the years. In 1980 waste associated with these industries was placed in 744 solid waste dumps, 1,000 hazardous waste dumps, 50 hazardous waste landfills, and 4,000 injection wells.[1] Approximately 1,300 orphan wells and 10,000 waste pits were created by oil and gas production facilities, and over 1,000 groundwater contamination plumes were documented.[2]

What would it mean to find that industries near you were evacuating their own workers because of potential dangers without telling you, a nearby resident, to leave the area as well? Let this question stand as a metaphor for this chapter, one that explores movement among people, some positive, some less so. The crossings take place within the soil of industrial waste, within races, religions, local and national governments, local and national news coverage. The women also talk about conversations over fences, neighbors in unison acting together, but also new fences going up in the estrangement that comes when there is fear of inadequate means of support.

Decades of racial segregation and the power of white elites, as well as the 1960s civil rights movement, formed the backdrop of such old and new divisions. Others have written on the ways that the environmental movement built a more inclusive community of citizens. The efforts of early and continuing activists extend the concept of justice to include attention to the production and distribution of information; encourage more heterogeneous groupings formed around specific, sometimes temporary, goals; and allow the creation, then, of new ties of people to one another.[3] More will be said of such work, especially in chapter 7 in the narrative by Will Collette. The women of chapter 2 tell of more subtle changes, the at-first-invisible changes in attitudes, the slow recognition of shared problems, and yet also the erection of ladders of assistance, one to another, older to younger, white to black, educated to uneducated, extrovert to introvert. The women's successes and their failures show, too, the lapse of time, a short time, actually, in which especially toxic waste dumping and incineration came to the state. The women are willing and even eager to tell of this as a period when the state had simply not learned to care for its resources, when the state had not yet learned to value people enough to take the time to study potential problems.

The chapter also takes us from times when New Orleans was the second largest port of debarkation for Europeans and through some of World War I, the Depression, and World War II. As in other sections, we hear idyllic memories of Louisiana as a place where shrimp could be eaten from the Mississippi River, where whole families lived on the bounty of their gardens, and where fish caught from a local river in the early morning could be cooked for breakfast. Oil was always known to be a part of the earth and water here, but it was not until the early 1900s that barrels of this black gold flowed. It would not be until the 1980s that jobs created by petroleum or related industries surpassed those linked to cotton, cane, rice, and soybeans.[4]

# ANN WILLIAMS

Ann Williams, of Buras, Louisiana, recalls such transitions. One of the earliest Louisiana women to take up the crusade to protect the environment, she became active in 1973 after her retirement from teaching. As the founder and president of Protecting the Environment and Ecological Resources (PEER), she worked tirelessly for the protection of the Mississippi River, and she successfully led the fight to stop a proposed oilfield waste treatment plant from locating in Myrtle Cove, Louisiana. On January 5, 1989, she received the Governor's Award for Outstanding Service and Dedication.

The Plaquemines Parish of her childhood and even her adulthood may seem familiar to other Americans. It was a place where farming was an integral part of life even for those who made their income in other ways. Yet Plaquemines Parish is also a very distinctive place, unlike almost any even in Louisiana. Its very name, so thick upon the tongue, derives from the Indian word for persimmon. The largest parish (county) in the state, it is also well known for its farming plenitude, for such delicacies as Creole tomatoes, satsumas and other citrus fruits, sweet potatoes, and okra. Moreover, in the period 1919 to 1969, political boss Leander Perez and his sons governed the parish in a near monopoly, gaining national attention for their election-fixing and their strict enforcement of racial segregation. This backdrop then makes both her narrative and that of Rose Jackson that follows all the more telling about the crossing of divides.

### Narrative from Ann Williams (b. New Orleans, Louisiana, 1920, d. 2001)

I grew up right here in Buras, Louisiana. I was an only child.[5] We lived with my grandmother down in Triumph, Louisiana. When her house blew away in a hurricane, we moved across the street from the school to go into business selling sandwiches to the schoolchildren. Mother and Dad sold sandwiches for a nickel a piece. The kid's favorite was corn beef hash and codfish. They could get a ham and a cheese sandwich for a dime. We sold ice cream for a nickel a cone.

My dad told me an interesting story about the last ride of the Ku Klux Klan when he was a small child growing up here. They came [and made] a circle around the house. Dad was a little boy and he was looking out the window and scared to death when all of these hooded men came. They took off their hoods and their cloaks and threw them in this huge bonfire. And that was supposed to be the end of the Ku Klux Klan because they had accomplished what they set out to do, and that was to get rid of the carpetbaggers and the scalawags and put the government back into responsible hands.

We lived, it must be, a block from the Mississippi River. I used to be scared to death when the ships would pass. It would shake the windows and then you could hear the waves breaking on shore.

When I was growing up, the people of Buras sold oranges. And they grew Easter lilies until something hit the lilies and wiped them out, and they haven't had any since. They sold cows. They grew sweet potatoes, which grew wild. And everybody had a garden. My dad had these large tomatoes that he was very proud of. Then along came those floods. We always had floods, you know, and one year they killed all his tomato plants. He also lost his seeds that he saved every year to plant. So that was gone forever. We didn't necessarily eat fresh meat. We ate pickled pork, which was used to flavor the turnip greens. There were turnip stews. We had green beans, black eye peas. Oh, the pea patch—that was a privilege for me to go to the pea patch. Planting seeds was a big job. The peas were planted in between the orange trees to fertilize them. They didn't put artificial fertilizer and nitrates on them. We had cattle because we sold milk. We had four cows: Amy, Sue, Betty Lou, and Friday. And we peddled milk.

I graduated from Buras High School in 1937. After high school I went to college at Louisiana State University (LSU). I didn't have a choice in the matter. My parents bought me a trunk and a suitcase and put my clothes in it, and Daddy drove me up to Baton Rouge and left me there. I survived. I took anthropology classes and a whole bunch of sociology classes. I graduated in 1941 and did a year of graduate work in social welfare. Teaching school was much more uplifting, so I continued with that.

[Ann met her husband in Buras; he worked for the Gulf Oil Company. They married and moved to Texas, where they lived for several years. They had four children and moved back to the family home in Buras, Louisiana, in 1958.]

I was teaching school when my daughter Martha graduated from Louisiana State University. When she went to Georgia University, she found out about the canals that the oil companies had dug in Louisiana, and how land was disappearing. She told me that they weren't telling people about that at LSU. Concerned about Louisiana's coastal erosion, she [Martha] wrote me a letter saying that I had an obligation to teach my [school] children about the environment. She sent me the information and on Earth Day I read the whole thing to my children. They were squirmy because there was a lot to read and I didn't see it all myself until about ten years later when this man was advertising that he was going to put in an injection well and dump oilfield waste into the Mississippi River. He had put a little sign in the paper. It was a little bitty sign and his address was listed as Post Office Box 621, which was Martha's box number, so I was curious.

I became involved shortly after that. I don't know how it happened. God was guiding me. I felt like that anyway when I went out and picked up thirty-five dollars in my front yard. The night before, I found fifty dollars. This [random money someone else had lost] all happened as I was ready to mail a letter to Luke Petrovich, president of Plaquemines Parish Commission Council. I thought, "Well, giving me all of this money, God must need for me to spend it on stamps." So I did, and after that I just got carried away. My first letter was written to Luke, complaining about the water intake. He publicly stated that the water was pure, much purer than it was in the olden days when you could get typhoid fever from it.

When I first started out, I called the DEQ [Department of Environmental Quality] and I said, "Tell me quick. What do I do? I don't know anything about toxic pollution." I got a phone call the next day, and the man from the DEQ said, "What you have to do is ask your friends and neighbors and they will help you. So, that is how I write and wrote all of my letters. I always say, "Dear Friends and Neighbors."

Then I started attending meetings and reading permits. If you read them carefully, they are a bunch of fakes. And at first, they would just make flagrant misstatements, and I would make a big hullabaloo about every mistake they made. They would say they had a permit similar to the one at the International Lab, and I would say, "I can't find any record where they had a permit." I checked every little miserable thing they said. I didn't realize that I was agitating, but I later read in the paper where they said I was this little bulldog. I would nip and not let go.

In 1988 there was a newspaper editorial and they were bragging on me for derailing a plant. It must have infuriated that poor man [Delta Environmental Service's owner], even though he had always planned to sue me right from the start. He was going to make a million one way or the other. Well, one thing led to another and I got in a big fight with him and he said, "I'm going to sue you for a million dollars." I didn't believe him, but he did.

I tried to get a lawyer to represent me, but I wasn't too successful with the local lawyers. I realize now that they probably had their fingers in the oil pot. I finally got my offbeat fellow. He's an ornery cat that likes the challenge. He lost interest after many years, though, and nothing was ever done. Then, many years later, I got in touch with the Tulane Environmental Law Clinic, trying to get the case dismissed.[6]

Once I got involved, I took up other issues, like the hazardous waste incinerator proposed for the small community of Oak Grove. It was in the 1980s and I started trying to stir up the people in Oak Grove [an African American community] about the incinerator proposed for their community. I went by with the letter I had written. I knocked on the door of this house and there were all of these sick people. They were in the stage of dying, really. I mean that is the way it hit me at the time. I was horrified.

I learned to know Rose Jackson [whose narrative is next here] at this time and to be concerned about those people that looked so sick. When I went by the house, it wasn't Rose that I was looking for, but she was the only one that would get up and fuss at the public hearings. We fussed together. Rose and I became great friends because of our involvement in the environmental movement. I love her now, but the first time she kissed me I was such a prude.

At the hearings I pointed out that they proposed building the incinerator over the landfill. I said, "You know methane gas emits from landfills and they catch on fire." I said, "It will catch on fire." I pointed out that this incinerator in Boston had the people worried that methane gas from the landfill would come up through the city streets and blow up the city. I said, "And you're going to build an incinerator on top of a landfill?" He [the owner] decided he would put the incinerator behind the landfill, but then he would be building in the marsh, where there would be marsh gas. At this point he didn't have a suitable place, yet the Delta Bank gave him a million dollars. He still hasn't built the incinerator.

[In the late 1980s, Ann Williams attended the national Citizens' Clearinghouse for Hazardous Wastes (CCHW) conference in Washington, D.C. Mary McCastle (also featured in this book) from Alsen, Louisiana, was a speaker at the conference.]

The landfill is bad enough, but to build an incinerator on it is even worse. You can't destroy matter—it might take another form, but it is still there. When you burn it you put it in the air and then you have to breathe it in. I thought that the best way to get people's attention in the community was to make it hit their pocketbooks. Around this place there are a lot of people who grow vegetables for a living, so I told them about Mary McCastle, who spoke when I went to Washington, D.C. Mary lives near the Rollins incinerator near Baton Rouge, Louisiana. And that's a very bad facility too. Mary said, "At first the vegetables didn't grow right, then the chickens were walking kind of wacky. And then the children, living next to an incinerator, started getting sick."

So I told the people in Oakville the story about Mary McCastle and the incinerator in her community of Alsen, but, you see, people forget. It has been long enough that they forgot my story. But Rollins is still with you all in Baton Rouge. You are breathing Rollins's garbage because they take it from all over the United States. The incinerator in Belle Chasse is constantly burning. Surely they are not creating that much stuff [waste] in Belle Chasse. They are taking it from all over the United States.

### *Afterword*

It takes stamina, and you don't ever win. You have just got to keep holding them off. You've got to outsmart those smart people. When it first started, they were naive and they would tell me how it was, but then it got so they wouldn't talk to me. They wouldn't return my calls.

I learned that most people are hesitant to say anything. Some of them will get me off to the side and say, "Oh, I am so glad for what you are doing." But they didn't want to be labeled as a kook. I still cannot get my bridge club to get into a confrontation about the environment.

## ROSE JACKSON

Rose Jackson, mentioned by Ann Williams in the previous narrative, worked especially for the protection of Oakville, Louisiana, a centuries-old majority African American community located approximately three blocks from the Mississippi River, also in Plaquemines Parish. Rose founded the Dakrill Community Action Group and, with her neighbors there, successfully stopped Industrial Pipe from building a pit burner incinerator at their facility. Her narrative, too, suggests the long reach of slavery in Louisiana, the French *arpent* system of dividing land along the Mississippi into narrow strips, and the subsistence farming of the area, as well as the vision of residents carrying water up from the river for all their needs. Rose served for many years on the Louisiana Environmental Action Network (LEAN) Board of Directors.

Rose Jackson

## Narrative from Rose Jackson (b. Ironton, Louisiana, 1942)

I was born and raised in Ironton.[7] My mom and my dad were also born and raised there, and so were my grandfather and grandmother. As far as I know, my great-great-grandfather came here from France. And we have a home in Ironton, built on that strip of property where my great-great-grandfather settled, about a block from the Mississippi River. I was told that my great-grandfather was a slave master on my father's side of the family. I knew my great-grandfather on my mother's side. He was in his eighties and he had been a slave. All of that area was plantation property.

When I was a little girl he used to tell us about how hard they had to work. They talked about how hard it was to get an education and work and try to take care of their families. And the families were pretty large. Both sides of my family were religious. My great-grandfather was also a minister. Back then they had to baptize in the Mississippi River. So I got baptized in the Mississippi River in Ironton. People are no longer baptized there because it is too polluted. For many years that is where we got our water supply. We filled barrels and rolled them down the levee.

We used to pick wild berries near the river and sell them. We would go out on the riverbank on the day the banana boats would be going up and down the Mississippi River. They [crew] would throw bananas and we would stay out until the waves would wash them in. We used to catch catfish from the river. We used to go crabbing. We would catch [river] shrimp. But you can't get that out of the river anymore because it is so polluted. Back then you didn't see oil slicks all over the place.

My grandfather had fruit trees and raised chickens. We had to pick up eggs every day. He had ducks, geese, and turkeys. He had two pigs. He raised bell peppers, peas, squash, cucumbers, tomatoes, cabbage, mustard greens and turnip greens, peas, and corn. So we had all of the basic foods we needed. My grandfather never used pesticides. The only thing I remember him using on his plants, to kill bugs, was baking soda. And for fertilizer he would take shrimp [peels] and mix them up with soil. My grandmother used to make her own preserves. She canned okra, green beans, and even corn. She taught me how to cook when I was seven years old. I can just vaguely remember her going to the grocery store. It wasn't that much she had to purchase. My dad used to fish, trap, and hunt. My dad used to trap for muskrats. I remember him fussing about these big nutria rats, but then he found out that he could sell the hides.

As far as trash, there was not that much that had to be thrown away. My grandmother always found some way that paper could be reused. We would get the newspaper and we cut it up in little strips and put it in the hen houses. All of the cold drinks came in bottles. We would wash them and carry them back to the grocery store and get the deposit. Then we would buy cookies and candies. My grandmother would cut the top clean out of cans. And she would wash them out and take the labels off. She would then go and buy these big pieces of wax and we would take those cans and make candles. And we would use those candles until we couldn't use them anymore. I had a work ethic instilled in me at an early age.

In 1953, Plaquemines Parish built three schools for the African American children. That eliminated the kids from going to school in churches, but church is where we started our education. My mom also went to school in a church. My grandmother went to school in a church. My dad went to school in a church, and so did his parents. They opened the public schools to us in 1955 [when I was thirteen].

One of the teachers that made a difference was Mrs. Nelson. She was the type of teacher that could put an impact on any child's life. If that child couldn't read, trust me, she took that kid in her classroom for a month and when that kid came out, he could read. That was the type of teacher that she was. She was dedicated. However, the one that really had an impact and influence with me was Miss Washington. She was my music teacher. I started singing at an early age as a small child in church, and it was something that I didn't want to continue to do. Miss Washington found out because she would take each child in the class and she would make them sing so many notes of a song, and she picked it up right away that I had a soprano voice. And she wrote my mom a letter. And she told my mom that she was going to train my voice. And she did.

I met my husband in church. When he heard me sing he told my aunt, "I want to meet that young lady." We dated for almost two and a half years and then we got married. We've lived in Oakville, which is eleven miles from Ironton, since we got married. We have four girls, and if my son were living now, he'd be almost forty-two. [Rose lost her son to an accidental drowning.]

Now, three weeks before my son died I almost lost my daughter too. She had a ruptured cyst and then about three months after that she got another one. A month after that she was back again. She had two that were side by side on her thigh. It was about two and a half months after that and she had two others removed. The doctor told me, "Your daughter has some type of bacteria that is in the environment where you live and whatever it is, she is allergic to it." He said, "The best thing that I can tell you to do is to keep her inside." I said, "You mean to tell me that I have to keep my baby locked up in the house?"

That's when I went after Industrial Pipe, I mean, much harder than what I was doing before because now it was causing my child too much misery. I found out about the five hundred transformers [containing PCBs] that were buried at the site and all of that toxic waste. And the Industrial Pipe dump was burning. During this time, 1986 or 1987, a lady named Mrs. Lois Lowery came to me and told me, "Something is going wrong over at that place." She said we had to do something because whatever was burning back there was poison. I went out that evening when it was getting dark, and you couldn't stand the odor burning your throat.

So I called the Plaquemines Parish Sheriff's Department and the firehouse. They had fire truck after fire truck trying to put that fire out. They told me they couldn't put it out because it was underground combustion. The sheriff's office told me to tell all the people to get their kids inside because whatever was burning over there was toxic and it was going to make a bunch of the kids sick. I told them it was their job and that they were supposed to notify the people in the community that what was burning was toxic. I also told them to tell the fire department to make a report. But three months passed and I saw where there wasn't anything being done about it. So, when someone told me about Miss Ann Williams, I contacted her. She gave me Willie Fontenot's number. He in turn gave me a number to call, which was the Tulane Environmental Law Clinic, and I spoke to Audrey Evans [also featured in this book] and they came out immediately. Mr. Fontenot also told me to contact the media, and I did.

Then I sat down with several other parents and we drew up a petition. We took those petitions out and we got them signed. I contacted the local government, which at that time was Mr. Luke Petrovich, who was president of the Plaquemines Parish Commission Council. He set up a meeting for the residents of Oakville. I went to the council meeting along with the Tulane Environmental Law Clinic, Willie Fontenot, Marylee Orr [also featured in this book], and Ramona Stevens. I didn't know that the Department of Environmental Quality had so many charges on the owner of the landfill. The Tulane lawyers pulled out all of this documentation of the extensions and fines that he had within a year's time. He had violation after violation. I couldn't believe that my local government knew this was going on, because it had been brought before them, and they wouldn't stop it. And that landfill burned for seven and a half years. It might still be burning.

During that time my youngest daughter had a baby girl and she was living here with me. And that baby broke out all the way up her back and under her arms; it was like somebody had scalded her. She would scratch, scratch, and scratch. It was to the point where I had to wrap her in Ace bandages and give her Benadryl. She was miserable. I sat down and talked to my daughter one day and I told her, "Look, you are going to have to move from here with this baby." The baby was having one asthma attack after another. And my other daughter Leslie has asthma also and my granddaughter. They all have respiratory diseases.

In my opinion, the landfill was causing harm to so many families. I have a neighbor that buried her only son. He had lung cancer. And this kid never smoked. My neighbor up the street had breast cancer. We had young women twenty-one years old that had to have their uteruses removed. There were miscarriages on top of miscarriages. I had one little girl that was working with me, only twenty-three years old and she had to have a complete hysterectomy—cancer. My youngest daughter ended up having surgery because they found cancer cells in the uterus and cervix. She was twenty-eight years old. As a young mother, when I was thirty-two years old, I also had to have a hysterectomy.

Linda King [also featured in this book] and I went through the community and did [an unscientific] medical survey. Linda sent the documentation to Dr. Legator, who found this community was overwhelmed with children with respiratory problems and cancer.[8] I went to my local government officials and I told them that I found a 49 percent rate of respiratory problems in the community. They told me that I didn't know what I was talking about. So Audrey Evans suggested they do a survey. When the Health Department did their own study, they found a 69.5 percent rate of respiratory problems in Plaquemines Parish.[9]

Anyone who figures that what comes out of smoke incinerator stacks is not going to come back down, then, there is something wrong with them. It is contaminated. This whole community is. I can remember planting flowers in my front yard and they would stand up so pretty for about two or three days and then I would go back out there and they were dead. And the ones that were not dead and had leaves on the plants were not green but white. It was like a white film or paint.

## *Afterword*

If I had had the chance to talk to Kenny [plant owner], I would have said, "Anybody that gives you a piece of paper to tell you that you can continue what you are doing, you can say that they have given you a loaded gun to kill innocent people. If you think that what you are doing is only going to affect the people in Oakville, you are sadly mistaken." And like I told them at the council meeting, "Don't come and say that there is nothing wrong with the children in Oakville because that is not true." The majority of young mothers around here have jobs, but they don't have the type of jobs where they have insurance benefits. So if you have to go give Meadow Crest Hospital $300 to go into that emergency room to have a child treated for asthma and you don't have any insurance—that is interfering with your budget. I think it is wrong for him [landfill owner] to sit back and make millions of dollars a year off the expense of someone else. He said I was a fanatic. Well, that is what they say about all environmentalists—that they are fanatics. But when you are messing with a mother's child and that mother knows that this is not the way that child is supposed to respond and react, and you get all of those mothers together that are having similar problems—then you have trouble. You have got a fight on your hands.

## MARIETTA HERR

Because her parents immigrated to this country from Germany, Marietta Herr, of Harahan, Louisiana, grew up speaking German at home. She believes her willingness to start fighting for environmental causes in the 1960s stems from her ability to look at issues with an objectivity her bicultural background afforded her. She and Mildred Fossier [also featured in this book] were instrumental in preserving Bayou Sauvage—the largest urban wildlife refuge in the United States—and in expanding the opportunities for activists to meet at a monthly gathering in a traditional New Orleans venue: a gathering given the name of the "mayor's environmental breakfast." In the last ten years, she successfully worked to have more than three thousand acres added to the Jean LaFitte National Historical Park and Preserve.

### Narrative from Marietta Herr (b. New Orleans, Louisiana, 1930)

My father was from a small town in Germany.[10] He was born in 1888, "the year of the three kaisers": Wilhelm I, Frederick III, and Wilhelm II. My mother lived right across the street from him in this tiny little village. They had a farm and were self-sufficient. They even planted flax. I have a picture of my grandmother on the spinning wheel, spinning the flax. Papa came to the United States during World War I, but not voluntarily. He was a barber on a ship, and the German government made the ship stay in New Orleans because there was warfare. This was before the United States got involved in the war. Papa liked New Orleans. He decided to apply for citizenship, and when war was declared, the rest of the crew was interned and

Marietta Herr

he, because he had applied for citizenship, was protected. So he stayed free during World War I.

He would make trips to Germany, and in 1928 he married my mother and returned to New Orleans. My parents had two children. During the Depression I didn't feel poor. We always had things to eat. Sometimes beggars would come and Papa would send them to Mama. I wasn't really concerned about the Depression as a child. If you have things to eat and clothes to wear, that was what was important to you. We lived there in my father's barbershop on Magazine Street until 1937. Then we bought a house and moved up to Arnoult Road. There were hardly any families on that road. Everybody had three and a half acres and that was from the highway to the river. I started at Live Oak School in New Orleans. In Jefferson I attended Jefferson Elementary School beginning in the second grade. I graduated from Jefferson High School as salutatorian. I went to college at Newcomb and was a sociology major. I also took a lot of German literature courses because I spoke German.

My future husband's aunt lived on River Road, and when he visited his cousin, I got to know him. We got married and had three wonderful children. In the 1960s we used to go to the Mississippi River and find river shrimp there. River shrimp used to be a delicacy. They were very seasonal and widespread then. They were like the filet mignon of the shrimp, but now they are gone. The last one I saw had a tumor on it, a third of the size of the shrimp. It was caught right out here and so I saw it with my own eyes. And this is at the same time the industrial corridor was being developed from here to Baton Rouge. Things were changing radically, but people weren't making any connections yet.

[Marietta's husband's job required the family to move to New Jersey in the 1960s. In 1971, when they returned to Louisiana, coastal erosion was already being identified as a potential problem.]

As soon as I came back to New Orleans, in 1971, I got connected with the New Orleans League of Women Voters and became environmental chairman. Governor [John] McKeithen had appointed a coastal advisory committee. [Edwin] Edwards continued it during his administration. Rachel Hamilton was chairman at the time of the League's Environmental Committee, and shortly after that I became chairman of the committee. We were the only environmentalists, the only lay people, to monitor these meetings. When it was all over they issued this wonderful report on coastal erosion, and somehow it fell to me to contact all our legislators in New Orleans. I contacted every one and told them, "This report has been issued and there's going to be a two-day seminar in Baton Rouge." I thought all these legislators would be so thankful because not only did they have the information, they also had a model piece of legislation to go with it. Well, you would have thought that we were trying to usurp their powers. They had nothing but criticism, and I think only one or two came to the meeting. It was just brushed off. Well, I was so disillusioned; you can't imagine. But it didn't stop me from being involved.

Dutch Morial, the first black mayor of New Orleans, recognized the environmental problems in his city and embraced the environmental movement. He served in that position [as mayor] from 1978 through 1986.

Dutch started the environmental breakfasts. When he started it, there were just four or five leaders of the different groups, Sierra, Audubon, and the League of Women Voters. We'd meet at the Quality Inn and order breakfast and discuss issues. At the time I was very involved in trying to keep New Orleans East from being developed.

When Sidney Barthelemy took office as mayor in 1986, Mildred Fossier became his volunteer environmental consultant and I was her sidekick. At first we were given a desk and part of an office in city hall. But that didn't last any time. They shoved us out, but Mildred knew people in city hall and we would go to this one to do the mailing list and we'd go to another one to do the typing for us. And we'd stuff envelopes. Mildred had all these connections and we were able to get what was needed accomplished. Also, as environmental consultants to the mayor, we could get appointments with the senators and the members of Congress. We marched in. I'd bring people from every environmental organization. Sometimes they'd tell us at the last minute that we could come and I could only scare up four or five people, but we got their ear.

When Mildred came on the scene, she said, "We've got to get more people going to the environmental breakfasts." Sidney didn't care who we invited, and a lot of times we were criticizing the administration. And so we broadened the mailing list. We began to have people from the Corps of Engineers, the Park Service, and representatives from Bayou Sauvage Refuge, all federal people. Then we had state people and local people. Our mailing list grew to over 135 people, and these were all people who were active in the environment.

We accomplished three things during Sidney Barthelemy's administration that he would not have done if we had not been there. One is the establishment of Bayou Sauvage—the largest urban wildlife refuge in the United States, which is not part of city government. It's a federal refuge, and it is under the US Department of Interior. I wanted to save those wetlands in New Orleans East because they had plans to develop the whole thing. I wanted to keep New Orleans viable. I'd just got back from New Jersey, and I could see what happened to a city like Newark.

The second thing accomplished during Sidney Barthelemy's administration was to stop the dumping of gypsum into the Mississippi River, which was Mildred Fossier's and Maureen O'Neill's issue.

And the third was the saving of Big Oak Island, a strange little place in New Orleans East. Waste Management wanted to make it into a landfill. And the area was ecologically different.

Under Governor Edwards's administration he continued the coastal advisory committee. He was not good on the environment, but he did appoint Pat Norton as secretary of the DEQ. And I will say this about Edwards—he was nice to everybody. He was a charmer. You know he did not make enemies and he was wonderful to the League of Women Voters. As a person you would like him. As a politician, he was brilliant. In Louisiana you can't get elected without funds, and the people who have funds are the petrochemical people, and they donate to the politicians, so what can you expect?

The progress we made astonished us because we don't give money to anybody. However, if you get all the environmentalists speaking with one voice, maybe 1 or 2 percent of the population, that 1 or 2 percent is very important in local elections. If legislation gets passed, it's because we're on the side of the angels.

Governor [Buddy] Roemer did a splendid job. There has never been a good governor for the environment since. He was a really different kind of person. He was not a real politician. And that's the reason he didn't get re-elected. He lost out to Edwards and David Duke [former grand wizard of the Ku Klux Klan who ran against Edwards in a gubernatorial run-off election]. I think the era in which we worked together the best was when Roemer was governor. Absolutely!

### *Afterword*

I was always a little bit different. I'm a second-generation immigrant, and that puts you where you never actually fit in well with the culture. You've got one foot in this culture and one foot in the other one. My parents were both German immigrants and we spoke German at home. I lived over there for nine months before World War II. Then World War II came and all of our relatives were in Germany. I always felt that gave me a more objective view of things—rather than a provincial view.

You see, I feel this way: nobody knows about the afterlife, but we do know about this life—this marvelous creation. This is an infinite universe and it is up to us to figure out how we can live to appreciate it. The air and the water and the land, we have to treat these creations with care. We can't abuse it because this is what we are dependent upon

## RUTH SHEPHERD

Like Ann Williams and Marietta Herr, Ruth Shepherd of Sulphur, Louisiana, was an environmental activist who began her work in the 1970s. She was a founding member and secretary of the High Hope Road Committee (1978), one of the first groups to cross the boundaries of race. Ruth also served as board member and president of the Calcasieu League for Environmental Action Now (CLEAN). This organization was founded in 1982 and was one of the earliest environmental groups in Louisiana. At its peak, CLEAN had five hundred members, including doctors, lawyers, students, and housewives.

Some of her story we have read in the introduction since she lived in the same community as the author and worked with the community of Willow Springs. She, too, witnessed the health problems of both people and animals, the leaking of chemicals into ponds, the death of whole groups of chickens over one night. As she notes, too, one neighbor there, Harvey Miller, "had a bull that fell in the pits and lost all of his hair and died. When Harvey complained, BFI took him a five-gallon bucket of soap and told him to wash his bull." This type of disregard and near mockery made her all the more aware of the need to fight for the creation of a different type of permit process to govern waste industries.

### Narrative from Ruth Shepherd (b. Thayer, Missouri, 1922, d. 2006)

My parents married and had three children.[11] My father worked one year for the railroad in Iron Point, Nevada. Then they went back to the 340-acre family farm,

Ruth Shepherd

where he was born, in Thayer, Missouri. He farmed the rest of his life there. My grandfather had homesteaded the farm when he returned from the Civil War.

My father loved the outdoors. I loved being outside and followed him everywhere. I fed the horses and the cattle, milked the cows, and worked in the fields doing regular farm work. He taught me the name of every tree. I would go to the fields in the afternoon, where my dad was working, and beg him to let me drive the machinery, which was horse drawn. My father also taught me to be independent and truthful, not to cheat anybody or be wasteful.

I was told I couldn't date until after I graduated from high school, so I didn't have much of a social life. Also my parents didn't think it was important for a woman to get a college education. And there would be a problem financially. After high school I went to work first at the jewelry store in town and then as a telephone operator. When World War II erupted, I went to Kansas City, Kansas, and worked in the Defense Department.

In May 1945, I married my husband [Leo], who was a locomotive fireman in Kansas City. I worked for a while, and then my two sons were born. In Kansas City, I was active in church, and I sang in the church quartet. I was president of the Women's Missionary Society and taught Sunday school. I was also president of the Parent Teacher Association. We moved to Sulphur, Louisiana, when my husband was transferred. We bought a place out in the country and I loved it. There was a large pond on the property and it was full of fish. I liked all the greenery and the wildlife.

After I moved to Louisiana, I became more aware of what was going on because of all the chemical plants. Leo would come home after work in the plant's switching yard, taking railroad cars in and taking empty cars out. He told me the employees were emptying stuff in the ditches behind the plant and setting fire to them. I could smell odors in the air, and I also remembered Rachel Carson's book, *Silent Spring*, warning about the dangers of pesticides such as DDT. She made me well aware of what was going on. I admire her for her courage because she was criticized when she wrote the book.

In June 1977, my son and I were riding down Willow Springs Road in a community I had never been in before, even though it was only two and a half miles from my home. It was a narrow dirt road and we drove to the river. I didn't know this small African American community of Willow Springs existed. It was pretty back there, and it was new territory for me to explore.

Returning home from the river, we encountered two or three tank trucks on the dirt road. We turned around and followed them to see where they were going. They turned off onto a narrow road that was hidden in the trees. I saw them take a hose off the back of their truck and dump its contents into a big pit. The odor was terrible and I knew immediately what was going on. The next day I went back to the same area and started counting the trucks going in and out of the facility. They averaged one truck per hour. The truckers were not happy when I parked my car near the entrance to the facility. One of the truckers threatened me, so I moved my car. He was in a big high truck and his engine was running. He stopped his vehicle beside my car, and I knew by the look on his face and the tone of his voice that I was not being well received. So I moved to Willow Springs Road, where I could continue to count the trucks. I have also sat at the Willow Springs churchyard and counted the trucks.

I used to spend a lot of time at Willow Springs. I went there and watched them take a bulldozer and dig a hole and fill it full of liquid chemicals. It would be leaking out at the bottom and running onto the ground. I observed that more than once.

I also talked to some of the neighbors in the area who lived on a farm across the road from where they were dumping. I found out that this had been going on for a long time. I also heard that when the company moved into the area, they told the citizens they were building them a resort and a fishpond.

I came home and called the president of the Calcasieu Parish Police Jury and he told me there was nothing he could do and suggested that I contact the Louisiana Department of Health. I contacted someone in New Orleans and they didn't give me any information at all.

In researching the site, I learned that the small rural Willow Springs community was primarily [composed of] African Americans who had settled in the area in the 1800s. The property where the facility was located had been owned by Gus Anderson. He owned a grocery store and a hardware store in Westlake, Louisiana. When people couldn't pay their bills, he would acquire their property or land. A lot of the colored people in the area traded at the store. That is how Mr. Anderson got the forty acres at Willow Springs that he sold to Mud Movers, Inc., in 1969, and they operated until 1972, when Brown and Ferris Industries Incorporated (BFI) acquired the property.

BFI dug seven open pits and filled them with hazardous waste, which eventually leaked. In addition, they constructed a four-thousand-foot injection well in an abandoned natural gas well. And they continued to acquire property, and by the 1980s, the site had expanded to eighty-five acres.

I think there were thirty-nine chemicals dumped at the site. There were a lot of phenols dumped there. I have been up there when I couldn't breathe and had to leave because the odor was so terrible. I don't know how the people around the area survived, especially those people who lived close by and were breathing the many chemicals in the air. One time Mabel Jones and I counted twenty-two people in the immediate area who had died of cancer, and this is not a thickly populated area.

Ruth Duhon and I [two white middle-aged women] went to a NAACP meeting in Mossville around 1978. We thought it was important that they realize what was happening to other people around the Willow Springs site. We were told that we could not attend the meeting unless we joined. So we did. The little group that was there was very nice to us that night. Then they disbanded and joined the Lake Charles group and I went to a NAACP meeting there. We were not received very well with this group, so we didn't attend any other meetings.

At some point in time, I discovered there were no laws governing the dumping of hazardous waste in the state of Louisiana. I contacted Mike Tritico, a local environmentalist, whom I had read about in the local newspaper. Together we called a meeting of the residents from the Willow Springs Community. We had our first meeting at the Willow Springs Baptist Church in April 1977, and we formed the High Hope Road Committee to stop the dumping of toxic chemicals into the open pits at the Willow Springs facility. About two hundred people attended the meeting. The next day someone from BFI called on the pastor of the church and donated $200. They reached an agreement that we could not use their facility for a meeting place any longer.

In 1979 we [eight of us from Sulphur] made an appointment with Governor Edwin Edwards to ask him to implement some rules governing the dumping of hazardous waste. We had seventeen ideas that we wanted to propose to the governor. Our spokesman had read maybe three of our ideas when the governor took a ring off his finger and threw it to his friend who had arranged the meeting. His friend was also a jeweler. The governor said, "What will you give me for this?" It was a yellow diamond, and I did not think it was very pretty. The ring was passed around for all of us to admire. I couldn't believe what I was seeing. I thought it was very unbecoming of the governor to treat us that way. We had traveled 152 miles one way, and after the ring incident we were dismissed and that was the end of any communication.

After CLEAN was formed in 1982, more people became active. The organization held public meetings to educate and inform the public of what was going on in the community. For the first time, people learned about certain chemicals and how dangerous they were, and how bad the air was in the area. We also made industry aware that they could operate more efficiently without harming the environment. They have improved somewhat, but they have a long way to go. Industry had to be pressured into doing this. They did not do it voluntarily.

We held two protests. We did one when the young man who was hauling hazardous waste died while emptying his truckload of waste into a pit at Bayou Sorrel near Baton Rouge, Louisiana. We paraded from Lake Charles to the Willow Springs site with placards pointing out the dangers of hazardous waste with the young man's name and his death on the posters.

Another time Hixson's Funeral Home loaned us a hearse and a baby casket and we had a protest at Willow Springs, which drew the attention to the dangers at that site. The following day Shirley Goldsmith, Peggy Frankland, and I went to New Orleans with a champagne bottle of water drawn from the Rigmaiden's shallow water well to present to Supreme Court justice Jack Watson. At first, we were not going to be able to give it to the judge. The media was there. They knew we were coming. Shirley asked the representative from the judge's office, "Well, what will I tell the media?" At this point the judge's representative took the water. He was admonished and told not to drink the water. That was funny. I have retained my sense of humor and once remarked that I am a sixty-two-year-old woman, and old women shouldn't have to do things like this.

### *Afterword*

I don't believe that God meant for us to destroy the Earth. Chief Seattle once said, "All things are connected. Whatever befalls the earth befalls the sons of the earth. Man did not weave the web of life. He is merely a strand in it. Whatever he does to the web he does to himself."

# THERESA ROBERT

Theresa Robert of Gonzales, Louisiana, also tackled a community problem that crossed the divides of race, class, and, ultimately, parish, and state lines. In 1979, she made the decision to organize her community to stop a California company, Industrial Tank Corporation (IT), from building a hazardous waste disposal plant. After years of effort, in 1984, Theresa and her allies took their case to the Louisiana Supreme Court. In its ruling, the court issued the landmark IT decision [*Save Ourselves v. Louisiana Environmental Control Commission*], establishing that the government of Louisiana has a constitutional obligation to protect the natural resources of the state in making permitting decisions. This ruling was one of the most important of its kind for the whole of the United States.[12]

Theresa and members of her community also founded the environmental group Save Our Selves (SOS) in 1980. SOS helped generate momentum for creating the Louisiana Department of Environmental Quality (DEQ) in 1984. She was a founding member of the statewide environmental group, the Louisiana Environmental Action Network (LEAN). She has also served on many local and state environmental committees and has lobbied at the state legislature on many issues related to the environment.

### Narrative from Theresa Robert (b. Vicksburg, Mississippi, 1953)

My dad worked at an industrial plant most of his life but always kept up with community and world events.[13] We moved to Louisiana in 1968 because he was transferred. He worked at Agrico in Donaldsonville, Louisiana. He understood the political system, which was such a big part of going through any kind of battle.

My mother is a very spirit-filled Christian. She was secretary at the Catholic school we attended. In fact, her paycheck paid for our tuition. She also raised five children. She prayed with us regularly and reminded me that this battle was in God's hands. She also helped me to stay focused and to remember that, no matter what was against us, there was always someone more powerful.

I went to Saint Francis Xavier Academy in Vicksburg, Mississippi, my freshman year. When we moved to Gonzales, I went to East Ascension High School because they didn't have a Catholic school on this side of the river.

My husband and I met in August after I graduated from high school, and I started college in 1972. We got married in 1975 and raised three children. I was in elementary education in college. I always loved caring for small children. It was an opportunity to have an effect on future generations. I taught for a couple of

Theresa Robert

years and then chose to stay home with my own children. After marriage I wasn't involved. I didn't read the newspaper. I really didn't know what was going on in my community until this happened. I didn't realize the amount of industry we had. I didn't understand that we had hazardous waste in most of these plants in addition to hazardous by-products. I just assumed that what they did out there was safe.

[In 1979, Governor Edwin Edwards held a press conference and announced that the largest hazardous waste plant in the world would be built in Burnside, Louisiana, literally next door to her home.]

It was for a one-thousand-acre tract of land, which had been farmed for generations, where they [IT] were going to incinerate waste. They proposed to solidify the waste after they incinerated the ash, and then they were going to bury it on site. All of our representatives, including Governor Edwin Edwards, who brought this in, all the way down to our senator, state representative, and our local politicians, were in support of the IT proposal.

I had a cohort named Ruby [Cointment]. We both believed that this proposed facility was catastrophic for our community and that God would bring justice to victory. We stood on our faith. In the beginning we really didn't have a lot of community support. It took us a number of months because, when IT first made their announcement, much of the community supported it. They thought it was going to provide jobs, making a big contribution to the economics of the parish. However, as time went on IT officials came to public meetings and made presentations. And at each presentation they would bring up different things [issues related to the site]. After a number of meetings we realized the major discrepancies and the ramifications that such a plant could bring to our community, and so we decided to organize. We formed an environmental organization called Save Our Selves, Incorporated [later Save Ourselves].

We had no idea how to participate in the permitting process until we met Willie Fontenot, with the attorney general's office. Willie showed us how the process works. He took us to the Department of Natural Resources and showed us how to go through records. He helped guide us through the process of hearings. We found an attorney, which God sent, named Steve Irving from Baton Rouge, and he represented us. We started going to governmental meetings not only in Ascension Parish but also in our neighboring parish, Saint John Parish, [and] in New Orleans. We knew those parishes would also be affected. Our own police jury had gone on record supporting this issue before we even knew anything about it. We had to go before our police jury and literally demand that they take a stand against IT, which they did do eventually.

It took us ten years before IT was completely turned over. We lost in every court until we reached the Louisiana Supreme Court. The lawsuit was *Save Ourselves, Inc. v. the Louisiana Environmental Control Commission*.[14]

The IT decision also opened the door of the Department of Environmental Quality. A secretary that is concerned about the environment and looks at the complete picture now has the power to reject these permit proposals that should not be going into our communities. Until this landmark decision, our state environmental agency believed that as long as industry met the minimum criteria of state rules and regulations, they had to issue companies a permit.

The Ecology Center of New Orleans raised some ethics questions regarding the IT proposal.[15] The Ethics Commission came back charging IT with wrongdoing in obtaining permits to build the $90 million hazardous waste treatment plant in Ascension Parish. The Ethics Commission charged Research Associates, a Baton Rouge firm working for the Department of Natural Resources [with ethic violations]. At the same time that the firm was being employed by the state, IT hired them to help them to do a pre-study.

The study was commissioned by the state, with Governor Edwards saying, "What can we do about our hazardous waste problem here?" And they came back and said, "We need to build a regional facility." Guess what? "IT is the one that should build it." And then when IT came back for the proposed permit, guess who was there judging whether or not all of their information was correct? These very people who had helped them do their original pre-application study. So, both of these people and the firm were charged [with ethics violations].

The other thing the Ethics Commission said was that IT received state money to conduct the study on where its plant could be suitably located. IT received $365,000 from the state of Louisiana to do the study. And before the study was submitted to the state, IT was already trying to buy the land. The Ethics Commission charged IT for that also. It is also our understanding that they were charged a fine of $5,000 and ordered to pay back the $365,000 that the state paid them for doing the study. It was another interesting part of our ten-year battle.

Edwards admitted publicly that he sold out our environment for jobs. I think he had a devastating influence on our community as far as the environment. When we went through the adjudicatory hearings, David Treen was governor, and we really didn't get too much help from him either because he had a lot of oil and gas people that headed his environmental agencies, although he had some concern about the environment compared to Edwards.

Without a doubt Governor Roemer was my favorite governor because the environment was a very important issue to him. I think he cared what the people in each community thought and that they should have some say-so of the quality of life that goes on there.

One of the important things that he did was appoint good people in key positions throughout state government. When the IT permit was questioned in court [Louisiana Supreme Court], Governor Buddy Roemer was in office and Dr. Paul Templet was the secretary of the Department of Environmental Quality. He was the one and only secretary that was technically qualified, and he had a true sense of protecting the environment.

When I first got involved I was shocked that there were very few rules and regulations on the books and little or no enforcement. Unfortunately, today we still do not have much enforcement from our agencies. That is why I became involved. I realized that I had to take some responsibility for the condition of the state that we were in. I felt if community activists participated, they would realize that we weren't a bunch of radical and crazy people. Instead, we were educated, somewhat articulate, and capable of understanding the proposals and the effect it would have on our environment and our community. That was important for the final decisions that would be made.

Environmentalists, in the beginning, weren't very well accepted. People thought of them as radicals and anti-industry, but I am not anti-industry. My father worked for industry. Our industries provide many jobs, but we need responsible industry. In the beginning years industry said, "If you put these rules and regulations on us, we are going to leave and you are not going to have jobs." Actually, cleaning up the environment has created more jobs. We also have more industry and a cleaner environment.

### *Afterword*

If anyone had ever told me that I was going to fight this battle for ten years, I would never have believed that I could because it truly takes over your life. In fact, my children still talk about the amount of time that I spent going to meetings. I also drug them to meetings, and I was always on the telephone.

I have fought many battles since my first with IT. The interesting thing is that the organizing of a cause, the investigating of the facts, the gathering of the data, and the lobbying of your political representatives, it's all the same process. It doesn't matter what the battle is. Unfortunately, in every incidence and every battle that I have been involved in, our political representatives are all aware and usually supportive of these things coming into our community. And usually they've already made a commitment before the community even hears about it.

In the beginning I got involved because it landed in my own backyard. I was the mother of two children when this proposal first came about, and I was very concerned about the health of my children. I was also concerned about the air, the land, and the water. However, once I got involved and understood that I had to be involved and the community needed to be involved, things changed for me.

We women have a strong bond with our children and the next generation. We are emotional, and nurturing—the very assets that make us most effective. I have become very close friends with many people in my community. We are black and white, rich and poor. I think that is what is special about the environmental movement; it crosses all boundaries. We are all God's children and these are bonds that will never be broken.

# KAY GAUDET

Kay Gaudet's drugstore in Saint Gabriel, Louisiana, became a focal point for community activism in the late 1980s. Although she worked on a number of issues, she is best known for collecting data about the high miscarriage rates in her community. As she began speaking out, she gained the attention of

Kay Gaudet

the state, local, and national media. In 1986, Kay was invited to Washington, D.C., to observe the Clean Air Action Committee hearings and meet with Senator John Breaux and other legislators. Kay's story illustrates both the setbacks and the triumphs of Louisiana's first environmental activists. Her narrative tells of the cost of fame and the integrity necessary both to remain where she is and to cross into different ways of living.

### Narrative from Kay Gaudet (b. Baton Rouge, Louisiana, 1950)

My mom was a housewife, a homemaker, and a mom.[16] My dad worked for Exxon Plantation Pipeline. I have five brothers and sisters. When I was growing up dad was president of the Parent's Teacher Association (PTA) and served on the Democratic Executive Committee in Baton Rouge. My parents instilled in us success through the importance of education and service to others. My dad always said, "Be a leader. Don't be a follower, because anybody can follow. If you think something is right, stand up for it." I am a Roman Catholic, and my maternal grandparents were Catholic. My dad's parents were Protestant. Both had a strong religious influence in their lives, and we likewise. In that respect, I would say that they inspired us from religious convictions, moral convictions, and being cognizant of how to treat other people.

I graduated from Northeast Louisiana University and was married in 1974. We bought our first house in 1974. My mom and dad moved here from Baton Rouge. And my grandmother lived right down the road. I graduated from college as a pharmacist, and in 1976 we opened our own pharmacy.

Before we moved in this house, we lived right at the Mississippi River. It was not unusual, in the night, to hear the plants being evacuated. I lived between the railroad tracks and the river. So, to get away from the plants, the cars had to go in front of my house. Normally, it is a quiet little area, but when the plants were evacuated it was bumper-to-bumper traffic. It got to the point where we had this sign in front of the drugstore that said, "Did we have a leak today? Check the six o'clock news," because that is the only way you are going to know.

They [industry] never notified the community [about a release]. It got to the point where me and my neighbors were frustrated over the plants being evacuated, because what if there was some big hazardous leak and nobody tells us? So, I guess, we kept the community pretty well stirred up with the sign outside the drugstore. We did depend on the plant afternoon traffic at the drugstore because they would stop and pick up stuff. And so, I was probably cutting off my nose to spite my face. But it was a life-and-death situation when you are releasing chlorine or ammonia, or whatever. And it was not unusual, at that point, that we would smell ammonia and chlorine. There was no way I could close them down because they were up and operating. And I did not want to close them down. I just wanted them to clean up their business. Then I found out Ciba-Geigy had hydrogen cyanide. And that was like, "Okay. We are selling this house"—and so we moved.

[Like most of the women featured in the book, Kay did not expect to work on additional issues related to the environment. But because she was vocal and passionate about what she thought was wrong, people began to rely on her to assist with other environmental issues in the community.]

In the 1980s, there was a proposed solid waste landfill in the community that was going to be very close to our pharmacy. I noticed in the newspaper that there was going to be a public hearing. I cut out the notice and put it on the door of the drugstore to make sure that our community was aware of it because, until that time, I had not heard anything about it.

The proposal was to put waste in the old Shell Oil oilfield and then build it up and make it into something that, probably in the future, you could put homes on top of. I was interested because I didn't want one more thing in the neighborhood that we were going to have to fight after they got going. For one thing, I didn't know the number of trucks that would be coming and going. And the oilfield is in a flood area and our floodwaters are diverted somewhere else. We have enough industrial facilities around here, and I didn't think we could sustain one more thing put into the land, air, or water. It wasn't something that I thought we needed, knowing what had gone on with Lois Gibbs at Love Canal in New York, where those homes were built on top of landfills.

From my understanding of the permitting process, they wanted to haul in non-hazardous solid waste. I asked the DEQ how they could guarantee that there would only be non-hazardous waste going into the facility. They said, "They [owners] promised they would not violate their permit." But there is no way that you can keep hazardous waste out because almost everything is hazardous. If it's not hazardous, it's toxic. Paint and anything that people throw in the garbage can be hazardous. So there was no guarantee, in my opinion.

At the same time this issue was surfacing, there was an environmental organization formed across the river in Plaquemine.[17] Les Ann Kirkland [also featured in this book] had come across the river to make our community aware that the landfill was being proposed. She and the Iberville AWARE environmental organization existed on the other side of the river. So we teamed up and now called this side of the river East Iberville AWARE. To stop the landfill, we had a letter-writing campaign. I was in charge of making sure it happened.

[The Spanish Lake landfill proposal was eventually defeated thanks to the work of Kay and other activists. But other concerns soon surfaced. As one of the main health providers for Saint Gabriel, Kay was in a unique position to monitor medical trends among the residents of this heavily industrialized area.]

My sister suffered a miscarriage, and in a letter [protesting the Spanish Lake landfill] she wrote that she thought the environmental conditions under which we lived and the eight or ten industrial plants that we have in our community had contributed. And, off the top of my head, I could start naming women who had miscarriages. We would have them back to back to back, and then you would have a period of time where there would be none. Then we would have another cluster. I started keeping information on that [miscarriage] data.

It had come to candidate Buddy Roemer's attention that I had been discussing miscarriages in Saint Gabriel. And then it caught the media's attention and everybody started calling—women that I knew and women that I didn't know. Gynecologists were having women call me. We were seeing clusters, and then at the time that it caught the press's attention, we were hearing more and more about additional miscarriages. By the time I counted, I think there were sixty-three over a two-and-a-half-year period, and for this area that was significant. And that's just the ones that I knew about.

I was concerned about the miscarriages, yes. But I was also concerned about the cancer. The number two drug [Nolvadex] dispensed in my pharmacy, for this community, was used for breast cancer. And that drug was not, at the time, in the top two hundred drugs dispensed nationwide. Local pharmacists were saying, "Yes!

It is over here too." Not only did we have breast cancer, we also had lung cancer. And the vets around here will tell you that we have lung cancer in the cows on the levee. And how many times have you seen a cow smoking a cigarette?

So we were lucky enough to have candidate Roemer take our cause, and we got some national attention and funding to start addressing these issues. The Sierra Club called and asked if I would mind going up to Washington to talk to our legislative group to make sure they understood how important the Clean Air Act would be for Louisiana. So I did. I went to D.C. and actually saw the committee discussions. The national Sierra Club allowed me a national forum. And from there, a *New York Times* article and a *Washington Post* article [were published], and the *Oprah Winfrey Show* came to Saint Gabriel. A lot of national press was here to discuss the Clean Air Act and the conditions under which we lived. It has gotten better as a result of that publicity.

In one of his debates for re-election Governor Edwards called me this "irate housewife" that was going crazy. I didn't even get called a pharmacist. When I went to Washington, it was on every television channel in Baton Rouge, and Edwards tried to discredit me as best he could. When I came back from Washington, he discredited me at a press conference, saying I was a loose cannon and that I had nothing backing me up.

My husband and I felt pretty segregated for a good while. Our friends at church would not even talk to us. That was so difficult. To this day I have not gone back to Saint Gabriel Catholic Church except when my mom makes me. We changed our membership.

We ended up closing the store in 1990. There were a number of factors, probably, with HMOs and everything, but the plant workers were customers of ours as well. And one afternoon I had a friend of ours come in saying, "You know, I like you-all, but I like my job. Some people came in today and told us we should not be shopping in here."

I knew most of the community. I was in the store from eight o'clock in the morning to five o'clock in the afternoon. I was accessible. And if somebody had a child with a red ear and they didn't have money to go the doctor they would ask me. The rich can drive ten miles to another pharmacy or doctor. But ours is a poor community. And I guess if there is one way I would want to be remembered, it would be in making a difference as a pharmacist. I don't see those people now. And with this closing a piece of the community is gone. So, that was the hardest thing for me.

And when I told you that I don't go to Saint Gabriel Catholic Church anymore, I do go to the Catholic Chapel out at Carville. The pastor is a Franciscan priest more in-tuned to the Earth. He discusses stewardship of the Earth. And we feel at home there. And he has certainly made my transition from being a pharmacy owner to being a pharmacist in general easier because he does address environmental issues.

Catholic traditions have been rich in our family for many years. He has helped us keep that tradition strong.

When I came back from Washington there was a reporter here waiting to interview me. He called me an environmentalist, and I resented it. I am a mom. I am a wife. I am a pharmacist. I am just a normal citizen. Of course, I had a picture of an environmentalist in my mind that I did not fit. But now that we are fifteen years down the road, yes, I am an environmentalist. I wear that proudly now.

At some point I said, "I have had enough." People were calling me for every problem they had. I had to tell them, "I can't help you. I can tell you how I have learned to handle this particular situation. I can help you handle it, but I can't take it on myself." I was shot. I had expended all I had. Chris and I had talked about moving, and, of course, we could have picked up our two kids and left the state. But then we thought, if we leave, then we leave my parents and my grandmother. And then there are the older people that have their roots here. And so, for me it goes way beyond grandparents. It's a community thing.

## *Afterword*

If I made a difference, it certainly wasn't a big victory. It was probably challenging friends to look at the situation, where their paycheck was coming from and who exactly is feeding their family. Finally, people are starting to question some of the decisions made on a governmental level, and maybe it [a decision] was made because of money and not because of what was best for the citizens.

I will tell you the truth—my dad having worked for Exxon for forty-three years, I am sure he got some grief at work over me. My brother, employed by Dow, told me he has gotten grief over me. But they never asked me to stop doing what I was doing. Some friends have, but the family—never. So I have got to tell you that the inspiration and the courage, all of that comes back to family.

Chapter Three

# "I KNOW THAT IT WAS A REVELATION FROM GOD"

## Religion and Environmental Action

*By the 1990s, knee-jerk support for local industries had become less prominent in some communities as citizens and elected officials came to embrace more nuanced positions. Media outlets began carrying more environmental stories, and a few churches began to explore the spiritual aspect of environmental stewardship. The women thus helped pave the way for their communities to consider more balanced economic options and values.*

*"You were just literally living in your home and watching it fall down on you while trying to keep it up. Trying to keep it painted and fixing the boards, but nailing them back doesn't work because the emissions in the air would rust them and the screens. And if it is eating up the screens, the fence, the nails, the boards, and the roof, imagine what it's doing on the inside of people." (Debra Ramirez)*

Louisiana, like other southern states, is known for a conservatism often framed by evangelical practices. Unlike other southern states, it is also known for the predominance of Catholicism, whose members make up 30 percent of the population, and an even larger percentage of residents in the coastal areas of the state. It is not surprising, then, that among the women in this book, twenty-two are Catholic women, alongside fourteen Protestant and two Jewish women. All of them speak of some attachment to religion, and most speak of considerable attachment.

They do not, however, emphasize their work as Catholics, Protestants, or Jews, but as believers in the universality of care for the Earth. In the words of one of them, Shirley Goldsmith:

*The environment is everyone's responsibility. We live in this world. Our feet touch this ground and we can look up at the heavens, but there is nothing up there that we can be assured of. We do know we have this, so let us take care of it. I feel this world was given to us for us to take care of. We are not the ones that should be destroying it. I have a very strong belief in God, and it was God's message to me that you do not tear up my Earth.*

Two practices unite the women to whom we spoke, practices both ancient and local, seamlessly part of their lives, which have also stood with organized religion since the time of Saint Augustine. First, these women consider the place of the church primarily as a change maker, or at least a support, in assisting communities to remain vigilant in protection of the environment and the health of residents. Various markers in the chronology of the modern environmental movement confirm this centrality of the church as reformer, including the 1972 publication of René DuBois's *The God Within* and the 1987 United Church of Christ Commission for Racial Justice's *Toxic Wastes and Race in the United States*.

Second, the women in the Louisiana movement also often spoke of prayer and the need to call upon a higher power. For them, everyday worries as well as care of the world have always meant, literally, attention to silent or shared supplication, and sometimes attention to voices that they perceived as holy guides. Likewise, faith itself sustained many of these women as they trod the difficult, often lonely road of environmental activism. Sometimes the beliefs they saw as religious, as spiritual, led them down paths they had never expected to follow. Some of them changed churches, crossed, as we have seen in the previous chapter, to different churches; others remained socially and politically conservative but emerged as liberals in terms of the environment; still more eschewed categories and continued praying as they had been taught to do as children.

## LORENA POSPISIL

Lorena Pospisil, of Libuse, Louisiana, represents the attitudes of mainstream religion of most of the United States, as well as the work of various religious denominations in the Louisiana Interchurch Conference to address environmental concerns. She started one of the first environmental organizations in Louisiana in 1980, called Concerned Citizens of Cenla (CCC). In 1983, she stopped a proposed solid waste landfill from being built in the small rural community of Pollock, Louisiana. She helped prevent two other commercial solid waste landfills from being built in Rapides Parish. In 1987, she started the first recycling program in Alexandria, Louisiana. Concerned about the aerial spraying of pesticides in her parish, she organized an informational conference in Alexandria, Louisiana, to educate citizens about pesticides

Lorena Pospisil

and their effects on humans. She has participated on many state and local environmental committees and has served as president and board member of the state environmental group Louisiana Environmental Action Network (LEAN). Lorena tells forthrightly of the "good girl" impulse, the influence that arrived with her intact from Juliet Low's admonition to be "honest and fair, friendly and helpful, considerate and caring, courageous and strong, and responsible for what I say and do, and to respect myself and others, respect authority, use resources wisely, make the world a better place, and be a sister to every Girl Scout."[1]

## Narrative from Lorena Pospisil (b. near Lost Springs, Kansas, 1923)

My father immigrated to the United States and was raised here.[2] I was born on a small farm near a very small town on the Santa Fe Trail. My parents were farmers. I was the youngest of six girls and one brother, so I learned how to get along with others. We had to bring in the wood, milk the cows, separate the milk, and help in the garden. If the stock tank got low on water, we had to pump and get water in the tank. We gathered eggs and fed the chickens. We did whatever there was to do on a farm. We also worked in the fields when we were needed. Many evenings we sat and shelled corn for seed for the next year. We carded wool for our comforters and blankets. We planted flowers in tin cans. Jars were used over and over again for canning. We didn't throw things away.

My folks stood up for the things they believed in. They taught us to be independent. We were always involved in the community. It was something you did just because it needed to be done. We lived through the Depression, which was a great influence because you didn't have, and you did with what you had. But if we were living in poverty, we didn't know it. We always had food. We always had clothes. The clothes were homemade. We wore hand-me-downs, and since I was the sixth girl down—you know what I got. A very special time was when school started and you got three brand-new homemade dresses. Those were yours, made especially for you.

We went to a country grade school. Then we went to Lost Springs High School. There were fifteen in our senior class. Being a small school, everybody participated in everything. I went to American Business College in Wichita, Kansas. You either went to school for nursing, went to business school, or became a teacher. My first full-time job was as a secretary.

I got married in October 1946. My husband had just come back from World War II. We came down here to Louisiana right after we were married. I didn't work until we opened our retail furniture store in the fall of 1947. We started the store on a broken shoestring.

When my daughters were old enough, it was Girl Scouts, and then things just snowballed. I started out as a Girl Scout leader and ended up president of the council. I was involved in the organization called Church Women United and Christian Women's Fellowship. I ended up as both local and state presidents of the two organizations. Church Women United was the first program that I was involved in with the environment. That was in 1971. In the 1980s, when I was president of Church Women United, we also did something on environmental issues. It was about not throwing away things and about not littering and using things instead of trashing everything. When I was state president, we passed resolutions regarding Styrofoam. This was during the time that McDonalds was using it for cups.

It was in the Louisiana Interchurch Conference that we started an environmental committee. When Bishop [William Benedict] Friend was president, we started doing a study to inform the churches of the environment. It was interesting to learn that most churches had papers regarding the environment. It seems like they had the information on a national level but not on a local level. This committee was formed in order to bring it to the local congregations, to get them active and participating.

[Lorena's involvement in environmental issues intensified when she heard about a landfill proposal planned for a neighboring community, Cenla, and heard that the people there had not been informed about the proposal.]

That is what community is about. It's about knowing what is going on in your community so that you can take care of the issue. Several of us went to a meeting being held in reference to the landfill proposal. When I heard what was happening I got up and spoke. And guess who was at the meeting? Willie Fontenot, who was employed by the Louisiana attorney general. He asked if we were willing to support the people opposed to the landfill. I agreed to help. That was the reason Concerned Citizens of Cenla (CCC) was formed. And we have gone from one issue to another ever since then.

An attempt was made to place three solid waste landfills in Rapides Parish. All three areas were not suitable for landfills. Our latest project was where they wanted to store hazardous waste near three schools in the Tioga area. We fought that issue. You just don't endanger children like that. A permit was granted and we had to go through court. We finally won and settled that issue. It has been interesting working with the different communities, informing them as to where they can get legal and technical assistance. We also brought in other people to assist them.

Another issue was recycling. We had two meetings and decided we were going to set up a recycling center. We placed the signs in Pineville and in Alexandria, the two sites chosen for collection centers. We also had articles in the newspaper with drop off dates. On the first day we just hoped that someone would show up. To our surprise, we had a steady stream of people dropping off their recycled material. It was very successful. This was an all-volunteer group and we had more than we needed. It was wonderful. We brought in schoolchildren, and some of their teachers gave them credit for working at the centers. We felt like the recycling center did a lot of good for the community. Right after that, Alexandria set up a collection system.

In the late 1980s Waste Management wanted to put a landfill in Rapides Parish. The site they had chosen was bad, and so we protested. I was sixty-six years old. I wore a railroad cap to the protest because we had talked about the company trying to railroad their landfill in our parish. We were receiving reports that Waste Management, at one of their other solid waste facilities, was receiving things brought into the landfill in the middle of the night. We wanted the landfill to be publicly owned so that we would have control over what was being dumped. We ended up not having a landfill in Rapides Parish because there were so few good sites.

Since I have been involved in this movement, my concept of government has changed totally. I used to be intimidated, but I am not anymore. I do my homework, and if an issue comes up that I feel strongly about, I will get involved. Women were considered not to have the knowledge that others do on issues. You have to convince people you know what you are talking about. Commitment by women can overpower the money part—but it takes commitment.

Oh the foes! These are the people who run for office and are your friends, but instead of reaching out to their constituents and meeting their needs, they coerce with each other to get their own issues across. To me they become the "fellowship of the elective," and you don't see them again until the next election. Women are at a disadvantage, working with elected officials, because so much is done behind the scenes. They will have a meeting just before the regular meeting and decide what they are going to do. We got pledges from different public officials who said they would do one thing at the meeting and then they would do something else. Some of the men in our environmental group attended some of the sessions that these public officials had at bars, and they have told us what happened. It is much like the cocktail parties in Washington, D.C. It is all done ahead of time. Women have to work twice as hard to get their point across, and you have to do it publicly. I have found that unless you stand up and say something publicly in a meeting, it just often goes by the way. If other people have heard it, then they have to pay attention.

I have received many of the same comments that everyone else has. I have been told to go home and bake cookies. Comments have been made that when women speak on an issue, we are doing it from a purely emotional standpoint and with no reason behind our action. But when you start talking about an environmental issue—it is emotional. You love your family, your home, your country, and love is an emotion. Women, I think, work on an issue primarily from intuition, looking at an issue from a family's point of view.

Industry has the money to spend on good public relations that citizens don't have. They will question your creditability on all levels. That is why you have to be prepared in relation to the issue you are addressing. If you are prepared you can handle the situation. One of the first things we do when we go to a community, to help citizens, is ask them to form their own environmental organization. By doing this you protect individuals. If you have one individual going before a public agency or company, you don't have the same impact. There is also a physical danger working alone against some companies. Every community we have worked with we asked them to form a group. You then have a group working with a group. That gives you creditability and safety.

My favorite governor was Buddy Roemer because he appointed Paul Templet as secretary of the Department of Environmental Quality. That was the time we were fighting the landfill in Rapides Parish. He told us that he needed to hear both sides of an issue. He also told us to feel free to visit his office any time. I never went to see him that he didn't grant me an opportunity to visit with him, even if it was only five minutes. I admire him fantastically. [Governor] Edwin Edwards, I think, was just so-so on the environment. He was not helpful, but he was not harmful in the dealings I had with him. As far as our present Governor [Mike] Foster, he seems to have no respect for the environment.

### *Afterword*

When I first started we wondered if my activism would hurt our business, but we found it did just the opposite. It helped business because people got to know me. Industry is always arguing that environmental restrictions will hurt business, but John Adams once said, "In the long run, every job in this country depends on our natural resources." And so it bothers me that we hold ourselves in such low esteem that we allow people to come to Louisiana and pollute, and we pay our people the lowest wages. We are telling the world we aren't worth anything more. We have a beautiful state and we shouldn't allow people to come in and trash it. We have to think about what we are leaving the next generation. That is part of my Girl Scouting. You always leave a place better than it was when you got there. I guess that is what I am trying to do.

## SHIRLEY GOLDSMITH

Shirley Goldsmith's words quoted in the introduction to this chapter reflect upon the conviction she brought to her work. Her narrative begins with the childhood influence of the Depression. She also evokes the memory of a good citizen, surrounded by a stability anchored in her attachment to the Jewish faith. She was founder of Calcasieu League for Environmental Action Now (CLEAN) in 1982, another of the earliest environmental groups in Louisiana. Under Shirley's skillful leadership, CLEAN helped stop a proposal to burn hazardous waste in the Gulf of Mexico. Shirley also helped other activists close the Willow Springs landfill.

### Narrative from Shirley Goldsmith (b. Niles, Michigan, 1928, d. 2007)

My father had owned three clothing stores, which he lost during the Depression.[3] My mother was a housewife. When I was five we went to Corpus Christi [Texas] to visit my aunt. While we were there, my dad lost his job. He didn't have enough money to go back to Michigan, so he stayed in Corpus Christi. He had $2,000 to his name and ended up buying a motel on the beach, the Edgewater Beach Motel. I don't remember a whole lot about it, but I knew that times were hard.

My mother got very ill when I was fifteen. It was during the war and my brother was overseas. And they told us that the Red Cross needed to get my brother home because he might not be able to see my mother before she died. He was a tail gunner in the Air Force and was getting ready to do a mission over Tokyo when the Red Cross stopped him from getting on the plane. She died from a burst appendix three years later.

Shirley Goldsmith

That is when my dad moved to San Antonio. He built the first drive-in theaters in San Antonio. He also built the first shopping center in Corpus Christi. He did all of that on his own and with us working hard and pulling together as a family. It seemed like a struggle then, but when I look back and think what he did—I am very proud of him.

I had an old patriarchal father, though. When I came home crying that I was going to fail a math test, Dad said, "Girls don't need to know math." So consequently, I never became very good in it. They only had one high school in Corpus Christi at the time. I graduated when I was sixteen.

[Shirley continued her education for two more years at the University of Texas at Austin. She married in 1951 and raised two children.]

At the time that I married, my husband was a rancher. I had never been on a horse in my life and had not been around farms or cattle or anything like that. It was a cultural shock for me to be in the middle of forty acres of land in Ragley, Louisiana.

As a family we participated in our temple. I was a member and president of our temple sisterhood. I was chairman of the women's division of the United Jewish Appeal, and I taught Sunday school. I also was active in the Junior League.

Then in 1982, it just happened that I needed braces. My teeth were beginning to shift, so I had started seeing an orthodontist whose name was Dr. Casey. After my first appointment he became ill, and they sent him to Houston [for medical treatment]. They thought something was wrong with his pancreas. After they spent three months trying to heal the infection they let him go home. He called and said he could get back to working on my braces. I had had two visits with him when I opened the paper and there was the news that Dr. Casey had died of cancer.

When I went to his funeral I heard everybody rationalizing that "This was God's plan." I looked on the front row and saw his wife with six small children and I thought, "That is not the God I know that would want this man to die and leave six little children." This voice began speaking to me in my chest and I knew, but I would not say this to many people because I was afraid they would belittle me. But I knew it was God saying, "You know this is not true and I want someone to do something about it, and I have chosen you."

I went home that night and I called local environmentalist Mike Tritico and I said, "Will you help me? I have never done anything like this, but I can try to organize people and get it [a group] started." He agreed to work with me, and that was the beginning of Calcasieu League for Environmental Action Now (CLEAN).

It also seemed like the timing was right in that people were getting concerned. They were shipping all of the toxic waste in from the Livingston, Louisiana, train derailment because the Livingston community's city council voted against them burying it in the Brown and Ferris Industries (BFI) landfill there. That made me angry and I thought, "Well, how can they refuse it and we can't?" You just saw truck after truck bringing the toxic waste to our area. At the time I didn't know what BFI was, and I didn't know what a landfill was. The inspiration had come from the death of Dr. Casey, and it just began to expand into so many avenues, and before I knew it, I was knee-deep in waste. I also knew there was so much cancer in Lake Charles, and I felt like there could be some connection. I wanted to find out about it. I think it was time for people to come out of denial.

We were extremely close to the Strauss family when their son started fainting. He was a medical student at the University of Texas when he became very ill. They [parents] took him to some doctors and found out he had a brain tumor. He was raised in Lake Charles. He visited his grandparents, who had a home on the lake, where he frequently fished and water-skied. As a teenager and early adult his parents built a home on Contraband Bayou, which is where they were living when [all] three in the family were diagnosed with cancer. I don't know how to exactly say one person could get cancer from the lake or the bayou, and another one couldn't, but in this family the son was the first to get cancer and then the mother got lung cancer. Then the father got lymphoma. The three of them died within five years of each other. They were a young family and very well thought of.

Then there was my street. It's like you can't get away from it. I lived on a street that was only a block and a half long and at the time that I went to Washington, D.C. to testify [on ocean incineration] there were five cases of cancer on this short street, adjacent to Contraband Bayou. [Five years later, Shirley recalled there were five additional cases of cancer.]

Then there were the odors. Every night at three o'clock in the morning these fumes and odors would come right through the brick wall into the bedroom and would stay in the house during the day. When that smell was in the air you could not go outside, and you could not be inside without that hanging, creeping odor. I knew it was coming from the plants because everybody was using the expression, "It's the sulfur crude and nothing to worry about."

Oil meant money, so you had to be careful with whom you were talking. It was too political. No one wanted to talk about it. You were not to talk about anything that may be affecting us from the plants. You were not to talk about anything environmental. I have never seen a community with such a blackmail mentality. If you talked about it, you would not be putting food on the table for your family. But I was free to say what I thought was the truth and that is what I did. I spoke the truth.

[After getting a commitment from activist Michael Tritico, Shirley contacted state and local public officials, neighbors, and friends and invited them to an organizational meeting to be held in her home. Shirley was surprised when fifty people attended the first meeting and made a commitment to get involved.]

I called two hundred people that I knew and said that we needed to start doing something about the environment. I invited Margaret Lowenthal, who was then our state representative. I said, "Margaret, I don't know how to do this, but I need help." She said, "You get the people, and I will be there to speak." I invited Leonard Knapp, who was the district attorney. Former Governor [David] Treen was helpful with BFI. Governor Buddy Roemer was very helpful, and he turned things around toward our advantage. Edwin Edwards—I don't think he cared.

[At Sea Incineration (ASI) was a company that wanted to load commercial hazardous waste on a ship at the Port of Lake Charles and other sites on the Gulf Coast. The ship would then take the waste, including PCBs (polychlorinated biphenyls), into the Gulf for burning. Although Senator John Breaux and other officials supported this plan, the American Medical Association, fishers, and a broad cross-section of residents opposed it. Their opposition eventually killed the project.]

ASI was a large fight, and we networked from Brownsville, Harlingen, and Laredo [Texas], all the way to Newark, New Jersey. Senator John Breaux invited me to Washington, where I testified against it. I was fortunate enough to sit next to

Jacques Cousteau, who backed me in one of my questions against the ASI ship. I questioned the US Coast Guard as to what they would do during a hurricane. Their mouths fell open, as they had not even thought about it. I asked if they would jettison the cargo to save the crew. Jacques Cousteau said, "Now this lady knows what she is talking about." He also said that the people working on the ship carrying the waste during a hurricane would be so sick in their moon suits that they could care less about the cargo. My testimony also stated that all of the people who lived up and down the Gulf Coast, particularly Lake Charles, could be influenced by the fallout and ash coming back into the town due to the prevailing Gulf winds. That was what caused people to really wake up and listen. Then we had all the help we needed to influence the police jury to make the right decision

In the very beginning people in the community treated me great, but as it began to get closer to people's income, then their commitment to me would change. One friend of mine wanted me to know that her husband told her that he would divorce her if she began to work with me. I was not the social belle of the city doing what I was doing. In fact, I lost many friends because of my activism. I later began to realize that the ones that were really interested in the environment were the ones affected in their backyard. When the ASI ship was going to bring dioxin and PCBs (polychlorinated biphenyls) to the best fishing spot in the Gulf of Mexico, there was a certain element of people who wanted to work only on that issue. When it was some place else, they were not interested.

## *Afterword*

The most frightening part to me was getting up to speak at public hearings. I have to tell you I was the shyest person that you could ever meet. I had a very nervous stomach and I couldn't get up, like in high school to read a paper, or I would throw up. So I had to believe that what I was doing was important. I mean, before I knew it I was standing up against Governor Edwin Edwards and going to Baton Rouge to lobby and testify. It happened so fast that often I didn't have time to get scared, but I was plenty scared a lot of times.

But the environment was bigger than me and that's where, I think, the challenge was. It's the mother instinct in women to take care of this world. And we have to feed the planet the right things, just like we do our children. In order for the species to survive, mothers have to be there to see that everything is taken care of. I think it's a God-given instinct.

## GERRY ARDOIN

Gerry Ardoin, of Iowa, Louisiana, challenged local and state public officials and one of the most powerful landowners in Calcasieu Parish—and won. After a six-and-a-half-year fight, she stopped a major corporation from building a municipal solid waste landfill, five hundred feet from her property. Gerry also formed the environmental club called Iowans for a Clean Environment (ICE).

### Narrative from Gerry Ardoin (b. Welsh, Louisiana, 1930)

My father was a baker and my mother was a housewife.[4] Together they had seven children. My grandmother lived with us, so there were ten in the house. We all went to work when we were very young. I was eleven. The reason was because my father had tuberculosis (TB). He was a baker, and at that time there was no ventilation in the shop. He inhaled all of that flour and it caused him to have TB. He died, in 1943, at forty-three years old.

    The boys hunted and fished a lot. When they were old enough to shoot they would hunt rabbits, squirrels, and birds to put food on the table. They would bring them home and clean them, and Mama would cook them. Daddy would buy groceries at the store, and we always raised a cow for milk and a hog in the wintertime. We didn't have a refrigerator, so it was salt meat. We had chickens. And we always had a garden. I think the most important thing I learned at home was that you had to work. You really had to work and help out at home. And you had to look out for yourself.

    [Gerry finished high school and was married at age seventeen. She and her husband raised four children. In 1985 they purchased property between Iowa and Lake Charles and built a retirement home there. Four years later, Gerry's activism would begin.]

    I had the same dream every night for four nights. I dreamed I was standing before a group of people and speaking. I couldn't understand why I would have that dream since I had never spoken to a group of people before. On the fifth night I kneeled on the side of the bed and told the Lord that if this was coming from him, and there was something he wanted me to do, I would do it. There is a scripture in 1 Samuel that says, "He will go before his people and fight their battles for them." I stood on that scripture.

    Six months later, I read in the *Lake Charles American Press* where Western Waste wanted to rezone a tract of land, which was five hundred feet from my property, for a commercial solid waste landfill. Six hundred and forty-eight acres were

Gerry Ardoin

going to be designated for a landfill, if they could get it rezoned from A-1 agricultural to I-2R heavy industrial (restricted). It was five weeks before the date for the rezoning hearing, and I knew then that I wouldn't want to live with a landfill across the street from me.

At the time, I didn't know that much about landfills. I didn't know how dangerous they were. I didn't know about leachate problems. All I knew was that when I went to Lake Charles, the parish landfill on Broad Street would smell terrible. If the wind was in the north, it was terrible. I knew I couldn't have a landfill there because I would have been north of it and would have gotten the odor most of the year. And with the smell of it, my property value would depreciate. We bought this land and we put all of our savings into our home, to pay it off, so we wouldn't have a house note after retirement. We had only been in our new home for four years. If the waste company succeeded, we wouldn't have been able to sell it.

Two weeks after this article came out in the paper about the proposed landfill, I got a call from a man in Lake Charles. He said he had a lot of respect for my husband and me, and he knew that I was going to be up against a hard battle. I went to see him, but he told me that I couldn't use his name. He told me that in 1980 [nine years earlier] a prominent businessman in Calcasieu Parish, who owned the land where the proposed facility was going to be built, took several politicians from Lake Charles to San Francisco for a meeting. While they were there they drove to Sacramento to the corporate office of Western Waste, Industries. They told Western

Waste that they had a piece of land on US 90, a mile from Interstate 10, that would make an excellent landfill. It was 648 acres, and they would guarantee that they could get it. All or most of the politicians in Lake Charles wanted the landfill.

I was told that I had to get Mayor [Lawrence] Toups and the town of Iowa behind me because we were too small of a community [population of seventeen hundred citizens] to fight something this big without backing. So we drafted some petitions and went door-to-door collecting signatures. When I got thirteen hundred names, I called the mayor and made an appointment to see him. Then I called the people on the petition and asked them to meet us at the Iowa City Hall. About seventy-five people showed up. I approached Mayor Toups and told him I was going to fight this landfill. I said, "I have thirteen hundred names of people from Iowa who signed a petition in opposition." The mayor told me he would support me and he did. From day one until the final day he was with me.

I didn't have any money to fight the landfill issue until I formed Iowans for a Clean Environment (ICE). I needed $150 to rent a building but did not have it, so I prayed. And then, the day before the scheduled meeting, a lady knocked on the door and told me the Lord had told her to give me some money. She handed me a signed blank check. I never charged any dues. I collected $3,000 in donations and that is all the money I ever collected.

And then, one day, I heard about a secret meeting to take place about the landfill in Governor Roemer's office. There were about ten men from Lake Charles that met with Senator Jack Doland, also from Lake Charles, asking him to set up a meeting with the governor. It was the local attorney for Western Waste, the mayor from Westlake, the mayor from Lake Charles, a state representative, a Calcasieu Parish police juror, and the Calcasieu Parish zoning commissioner. Somebody called and told me about the secret meeting, and so I called Senator Doland. I told him that I was the opposition, and I didn't think it was fair for these politicians to meet with the governor because he would hear only one side. He agreed.

Representative Tim Stine [acting as mediator] from Sulphur, Louisiana, was the one setting up the meeting. He called me and said I could go, because Senator Doland wanted me to go, but that I could not say a word. I had to sit there and listen. So I agreed to do that, but when we got inside, Mary Ann Miller, who was with me, knew the governor personally. So when the group from Lake Charles started talking, the governor told the men that he felt he should listen to both sides. Well, I had everything to prove my point about the geology of the land, the flooding of the land, and the fact that there was already a landfill in Jennings, Louisiana, and we didn't need another one here. I had all of that information, so every time the opponents opened their mouths I would say, "That is not correct. Here is the right information." I had it all. They did not get what they wanted from the meeting with the governor that day.

[In December 1989, Western Waste's attorneys approached the Calcasieu Parish Zoning Commission about rezoning the property for the proposed landfill on David Road from A-1, agricultural, to I-2R, heavy industrial. Also attending this hearing in opposition were nearly three hundred people from Iowa, Louisiana.]

Western Waste was first to give their presentation, and the zoning commissioners were quiet and listened, but the minute the citizens got up to speak they were totally disrespectful. They were talking between themselves and leaving to go get coffee and Cokes. It was a farce, and we felt it was already a done deal. The zoning commissioners never listened to anything we said.

The following night the zoning issue went to the police jury. They brought police in because the people got so rowdy at the zoning board meeting, the night before, because of the way we were being treated, that they didn't want us giving them any more trouble. It was upsetting to know that they thought we would stoop to that level—when all we were doing was voicing our opinion. The jurors knew they were going to approve the rezoning of the land on David Road because the Zoning Commission had already rezoned it to heavy industrial, and the jury usually accepts their recommendations. They have a process to go through whether it's a done deal or not. They [police jury members] were not interested and didn't listen to what we had to say in opposition to the landfill zoning. They just wanted the meeting over with.

The jury voted to rezone the property but attachèd a resolution, with conditions, to send to the Louisiana Department of Environmental Quality [DEQ]. In the resolution they listed fifteen conditions that Western Waste had to abide by or the property would automatically revert back to agricultural zoning. Well, they broke three or four of those conditions. Yet every time I would go to the police jury and try to get something done about it, they would say, "The way it is worded, it doesn't necessarily mean what it says." Well, I learned one thing about lawyers and politicians. They have a way of playing with words. They will write something that says one thing, but it means something else.

Western Waste's permit was denied three times. The second time, the DEQ denied that they made a settlement agreement with Western Waste. In their rules and regulations, the DEQ cannot have a settlement agreement without the attorney general's approval. However, they had reached a settlement agreement that the attorney general didn't even know about. When I went to see him, he agreed that it sounded like a settlement agreement and that if it was, something would be done. When I walked out of his office, a Western Waste representative was sitting there. About five weeks later I received a letter saying there was no such agreement, and I never did hear anything else from the attorney general.

Western Waste's plan was to have the landfill in operation within a year and a half and here it was five years later and heads rolled. March 30, 1993, DEQ secretary [Kai] Midboe denied Western Waste their permit application for the landfill on

David Road. He denied it because the company had failed to respond to the Solid Waste Division's requests for technically complete information and the department was unable to conduct a proper technical review of the application.

### *Afterword*

I am proud of the fact that I did what everyone told me I couldn't do. People told me that it was so political that I would never be able to do anything, and I did. With the grace of God, I did it. It took me six and a half years to defeat the landfill proposal, and I defeated them with only $3,000. The last time I went before the police jury, when they reverted the property back to A-I agricultural, they stood up and gave me a standing ovation.

Mayor [Greg] Marcantel of Jennings told me he admired me for being persistent and not giving up. The Iowa aldermen congratulated me on the victory and several others did also, I just can't remember their names. Toward the end I had gone to a Lake Charles City Council meeting on recycling. I got up to speak and I used the wrong word and someone on the city council corrected me, and Mayor [James E.] Sudduth stood up and said, "You leave that young lady alone. She knows exactly what she is doing and she does not have to listen to anybody. She knows what she is doing and she is doing a great job." That surprised me.

# JANICE CRADOR

We hear next from Janice Crador, of Grand Lake, Louisiana. Janice put her community's health ahead of her own immediate needs when she spoke out against a landfarm and injection-well facility proposed by Big Diamond Trucking Services, Incorporated, which already owned and operated a waste pit and injection-well facility in her community. Her attention to schoolchildren is almost buried in the narrative, so seamlessly is this care a part of her life, a part of a small place with one school. At the same time, this united place stands strongly as the basis of her activism.

### Narrative from Janice Crador (b. Lake Charles, Louisiana, 1944)

My parents were from Grand Lake, Louisiana.[5] However, I grew up in Lake Charles, Louisiana, twenty miles north of Grand Lake. I was a war baby. After my dad returned from the war he was a house painter, and my mom was a homemaker. I have three brothers. We were regular churchgoers, and faith in God was encouraged at home. It was a gift and it's one that I cannot ever remember not having. One thing instilled in me in elementary school was to be an individualist. Don't follow the crowd. Stand up for what you think is right.

I graduated from LaGrange Senior High School and married when I was a senior. We moved to Grand Lake in 1962 and we've been here ever since. I started having my four kids in a row, so my social life wasn't much—it was to go to church and back. At different times I have taught Catechism and also been involved in retreats. When my daughter was one month in kindergarten they said they were going to need a secretary at Grand Lake School. I went and got interviewed for the job. I have been working there twenty-nine years now.

This is where my husband was raised. He also went to school and graduated from Grand Lake School. Most of our relatives are from here. This year it will be forty-two years we've lived in this community. The most important advantage of living in a small community, to me, is that you know everyone. You just get to know what community is all about. You have support when something goes wrong, and to me, that's important. I like the fact that we have one school that goes from prekindergarten through high school.

I lived in this community. I had my friends and family members living in the community, and I was beginning to worry about their health. People were getting sick. It seemed like there was more cancer in this area, and in Lake Charles, than many other places in the state or in the country.

For years, we felt the Big Diamond waste site was affecting our drinking water and could possibly be linked to an increasing number of health problems. However, we didn't know a single thing we could do about it. This company already operated waste pits and injection wells and was a dumping site that had been in operation since 1979. It was located next door to our only school, recreational center, and Black Bayou. It was reported that trucks were lined up along the highway at night for dumping. We were told that when the pits were full, sometimes the contents were released directly into the bayou.

Then we heard about plans for a new gigantic site to be opened by the same company just across the bayou from the old site. The company owned a lot of acreage that they were going to use to dump the waste. They were going to dry the waste in the sun, stir it up, and then sell it to people for their yards and gardens.

We heard that in October of 1985 the president of our water board sent a letter to the regional vice president of Amoco saying that he was sure that after Big Diamond explained their project, that no one would object, including the water board. This letter made it appear as though everyone was for the project and that Big Diamond should go ahead with it. However, not everyone knew about the project. The people were not told about a public hearing because there was no hearing. Big Diamond tried to grandfather the site in.

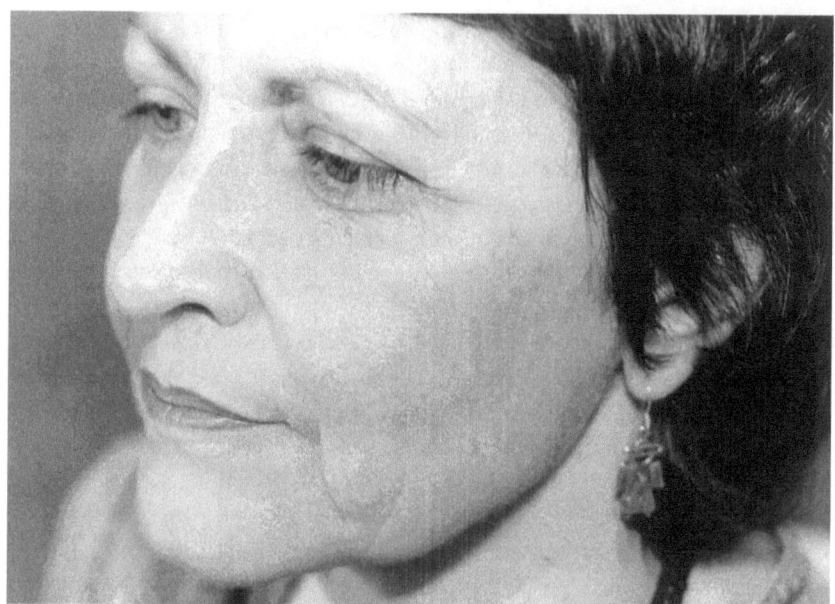

Janice Crador

Well, let me tell you about some problems I had already documented at the school where I have worked for twenty-nine years. On July 3, 1984, when Grand Lake School first connected to the community water well, school personnel repeatedly complained about the bad taste and discoloration of the water. The school was instructed to flush out the lines and every faucet inside and outside the school was left on for an entire weekend. Then when the principal, Mr. Delmus Hébert, turned on a faucet in the teacher's lounge, the water was completely brown. He immediately put the entire school on bottled water for consumption, except for cooking, for a period of nine days. On November 20, 1984, the school was put back on the community system. But in January 1985, Grand Lake School went back on the school's water well because there were so many complaints of discoloration and yellow particles found in the [community] water. And an orange blob was collected from a faucet and put into a water jar and sent to the Cameron Parish School Board. On April 16, 1985, the community was switched to well #3, and on July 17, 1985, the school was again switched to the community system.

The community water system well was a few acres further away than the school's water well. And in our opinion, we thought that the community water well might be polluted, because Big Diamond's injection wells were never tested for integrity. The Conservation Office never tested them because they said it was too much for them to monitor. They just continued to hand out permits.

Our friend James "Pete" Kjerulff said that there was going to be a Calcasieu Parish Police Jury meeting to discuss the new facility because the road to the new proposed site was under the jurisdiction of Calcasieu Parish. The [police] jury was concerned because there would be heavy traffic on the parish roads that they had to maintain. When I went to the meeting on April 3, 1986, I met Shirley Goldsmith [also featured in this book], the president of Calcasieu League for Environmental Action Now (CLEAN). She suggested that I get in touch with Willie Fontenot, who worked for the Louisiana attorney general, and he could help us get organized. This was the first time that it dawned on me that citizens could do something. I contacted Willie and we set up an informal meeting to discuss landfarms.

I knew that the principal of Grand Lake School had been very concerned about the drinking water, so I got permission from him to send a letter home with the students. I quickly composed the now famous "What is a landfarm" questionnaire.

[Landfarming involves mixing contaminated waste with soil, bulking agents, and nutrients and then tilling all this together and aerating it. The process is not unlike composting, but landfarming often takes place in underground clumps. Various conditions must be controlled, such as run-off pits for rain and flooding and possible leaching of harmful substances into water supplies.]

I figured since we had so much trouble with the water at school, the other people in the community might be interested in learning about this issue. The note ["What Is a Landfarm"] went home on Friday for the meeting on Monday. Well, it was like sending each child home with a lighted firecracker, timed to explode upon arrival. My phone began ringing immediately with Big Diamond sympathizers. They said I had a nerve sending home a letter from a public school. They assured me there were many people upset with me.

At the meeting Monday evening, Big Diamond employees showed up in full force and they were very angry. They felt like I was making accusations and threatening their livelihood. The turnout was incredible. Willie Fontenot calmly tried to answer the accusations and questions of the enraged employees who monopolized the entire meeting, while others with concerns quietly listened. When they finished saying their piece, the employees left. I tried to apologize to Willie for how everything had turned out. He said, "This was a great meeting. Now you know which side everyone is on and you can form your committee or group."

It was not long after this meeting that we formed the Concerned Citizens Committee. There were about twenty-two people that showed up. We elected Mike Savoy as president. We formed the group to have a voice and to find out the facts and then present them to the Office of Conservation, the governor, or anyone who would listen to us.

From our first "What is a landfarm?" meeting where we met Willie Fontenot and Wilma Subra, some of us were threatened. Pete Nunez, a Concerned Citizen member, was approached by a state official saying that people in high places were "getting stirred up" and that it was best not to get involved.

The owner of the facility began to take us very seriously. People in the community that worked at various plants in Lake Charles were called on the carpet and their involvement in Concerned Citizens was discussed. Some people felt their jobs were in jeopardy. My own school board member, originally responsible for hiring me, was unhappy with our environmental committee because of a situation where the community water board president resigned. He suggested that if I continued to be involved with the Concerned Citizens, I should be dismissed from my job. But this was more important than any job because it could affect the quality of life for every man, woman, and child in the community. In every situation, each person was forced to make decisions about priorities.

[On April 1, 1986, the Cameron Parish Police Jury, aware of the citizens' concerns about the new facility, unanimously adopted a resolution asking the Department of Natural Resources (DNR) to hold a fact-finding public hearing in reference to the site. The DNR scheduled a meeting for citizen comments for May 15, 1986.]

When we started Concerned Citizens in 1986, we had less than one month to prepare for the Office of Conservation's May 15 fact-finding hearing. Before that date, we needed to pass a petition and have a fund-raiser to enable us to pay our bills, such as analytical lab expenses. We divided the Grand Lake community into sections and volunteered by twos to petition every house. We even went to houses of those we knew did not agree with us and gave them an opportunity to sign or not to sign and state their opinions. There were 852 registered voters in our community. In the short amount of time we had we were able to get 498 people to sign in opposition to the facility. We also had 19 people sign the petition in favor of the facility.

At the hearing, the Office of Conservation couldn't believe how many people were in attendance and speaking out in opposition to the facility. Almost all of the citizens of Grand Lake were in attendance at the meeting. And everyone from the company also showed up. We told Mr. Herbert Thompson, commissioner with the Office of Conservation, that they didn't know all of the facts because the material we had gathered indicated that there was a big problem with the expansion of the facility. Carroll Wascom [also featured in this book] and James Welch of the Department of Natural Resources [DNR] sat with their mouths open in awe of the mountain of facts presented to them at the hearing—to be entered as public record.

From the very beginning, when we learned that we were entitled to see the records of Big Diamond, we asked for those records and the Conservation Office provided us with that data. At the May 15 hearing, Concerned Citizen member Carol Savoy [also featured in this book] presented to the DNR a document from the company's files that stated that a conservation official had approved the injection of acids and xylene into their well in January 1985. However, on the next trip to the Conservation Office those records had disappeared.

The fact-finding hearing started at 7:00 p.m. By 9:30 p.m. things were not going well for our opposition when the hearing was mysteriously interrupted with a power outage. What was funny about the electricity going off in that building was that it was the only one in the community that had a problem that night. It stopped nothing, however. The hearing was simply transferred to the fire station next door, where the meeting lasted until 1:30 a.m. After the hearing started, twenty-five people who had been undecided asked to sign the petition in opposition to the landfarm.

The experience was wonderful. Nearly everyone in our community supported us. We banded together and worked hard. We hardly got any sleep because we knew what was at stake and we had very little time to do something. We ate, slept, and lived the fight against Big Diamond. Those were some of the best times of our lives, getting close to the people in our community who have become lifelong friends. We knew most of the people by name in our community, but we had never been very close to many of them before this issue came up. We united in our efforts, and we won.

We were very fortunate to have the support of our Cameron Parish Police Jury and the Cameron Parish District Attorney's office. When walls were thrown up in front of us, the police jury threw up walls of their own and stopped the company. And the new Big Diamond landfarm was abandoned. Old pits and injection wells could no longer be used. The owner died of cancer and most of his family left the community. Those whose only concern was losing their jobs found they can survive with new ones that are even better. When William Guste was the attorney general he actively supported us and stood up for us and gave us publicity that helped our cause. And our committee wouldn't even exist without Willie Fontenot and Representative Randy Roach, who also supported us.[6]

Governor Edwards was against us. He had an excuse when you tried to show how the people were sick and needed the environment to be considered. He said, "It was because people in Louisiana liked to season their food a lot, and that is what caused the sickness." He repeatedly went against everything we did even though we wrote him numerous letters about our issue.

## *Afterword*

At the time of the Big Diamond issue I was spending an hour a day in prayer in the morning and that was my strength for the day. I felt God leading me through every letter that I wrote, every time I got up to speak, and in everything that we did. One of the first scriptures that God pointed out to me was Isaiah 45:18, which says, "For thus says the Lord the creator of heavens who is God the designer and maker of the earth, who established it, not creating it to be a waste but designing it to be lived in." I believe it was my faith that motivated me because this was a good cause. People were hurting. They were sick, and they were dying. God made a beautiful world and named it Louisiana. He expects us to take care of it.

## DEBRA RAMIREZ

Like others in this chapter, Debra Ramirez started her environmental work close to home, for her, Mossville, Louisiana. Her involvement began in the 1980s after Condea Vista announced that ethylene dichloride (EDC), a suspected human carcinogen used in the production of PVC, had leaked into the groundwater beneath the neighboring Mossville community.[7] In 1995 local attorneys filed a class action suit against the companies responsible for the contamination, and in 1998 the lawsuit was settled for $32 million, including a $13.9 million property buyout fund for two thousand residents.[8] Debra's memories also relate to the previous chapter on crossing boundaries. Her memories make apparent how rural African American communities were often singled out as sites where industry could take advantage of Louisiana's permissive attitude toward environmental regulations.

### Narrative from Debra Ramirez (b. Lake Charles, Louisiana, 1954)

My dad's great-grandfather came out of Mississippi.[9] He had the slave name Higgenbothem, but when he became a slave of a family called Sullivan, he took up that name. His son, William Sullivan, went to Bird Nest, where he met my grandmother, and from there they moved to Mossville and lived on the Old Spanish Trail. My grandparents did a lot of things in order to help people, such as feeding someone if they had nothing to eat.

My mother is originally from Moss Bluff, Louisiana. My dad was from Mossville. When he met my mother he was singing in a quartet. Eventually, they married and moved to Mossville. My mother did a number of jobs from cleaning houses to being a maid. She went back to high school, after a number of years, where she got a degree and then worked for McNeese State University for twenty-six years. I went from kindergarten to eighth grade at Mossville. It used to be K through twelve, but after integration came in and segregation went out, I was in one of the classes that was integrated into another school.

Growing up, my parents and grandparents grew our own food. We had a garden and plenty of fresh vegetables to eat. The men hunted and fished and whatever they brought home my mom or grandma fixed. There was always fresh meat and fish.

Debra Ramirez

My parents and grandparents were also very religious. You had to get up and go to church on Sundays, and you had to have God in your life. I remember going to Grandma Lonnie's after church on Sunday and sitting on the front porch. She had a swing on her front porch and it faced the east, where the chemical plant was. And I would hear this noise, "umm, umm," coming from the plants, and that swing would swing me and I would get sleepy and fall asleep. So if the chemicals were there causing harm, I didn't know it.

We had been having problems early on—when they would have a chemical release. We didn't have an alarm, but the whistle would go off and the police would come in and tell us to hurry up and get out. Or the sheriff would come by and he would tell us to evacuate immediately. They didn't give us a ride. So we ran! And when we ran, now that I know better, we didn't run far enough. We would run to the corner of Trousdale Road and Old Spanish Trail and wait for the all-clear signal. And to get to the old Trousdale Road it was like a quarter of a mile from the house. Sometimes we were in our sleeping clothes and barefoot, running on the Old Spanish Trail. They had alligators and water moccasins [poisonous snakes] in there. Don't forget! We are talking about swampland.

Sometimes the whistles were going off all times of the night, so we got to the point where we were sleeping in our clothes. That way, if the plant exploded, we wouldn't be caught with our sleeping clothes on. Little girls had nightgowns sometimes that were thin, and when they told us to leave, we didn't even have time to grab a housecoat. And often when we would get back home after we had to leave our house and we had to go to school the next morning, sometimes we would be very tired.

[Debra raised two sons and a daughter. She was still deeply rooted in her connection to the Mossville community. Industries had arrived there in the 1930s, before Debra was born. By the 1980s, more companies found this community well suited for their needs, and it was this growth to which she responded.]

We were about, I guess, maybe a half a mile from Conoco. And I remember Vista moving behind us. They were going to be an alcohol plant. Miss. Hazel Verdine sold them some property, along with the Richardson and Campbell families. There was already a [petroleum] coke plant in the Mossville community.

There was an odor every day. Sometimes you could smell sweet alcohol in the air, or rotten eggs, or a sulfur or acid smell. And sometimes all those smells were combined. There was also flaring that went on in the community, and you could read a newspaper because the flares would be so high. Some of the folks said that their roofs were decayed from the emissions and heat that came off some of those stacks. You were just literally living in your home and watching it fall down on you while trying to keep it up. Trying to keep it painted and fixing the boards, but nailing them back doesn't work because the emissions in the air would rust them and the screens. And if it is eating up the screens, the fence, the nails, the boards, and the roof, imagine what it's doing on the inside of people. My mom went to the doctor one time and he asked her if she smoked. She didn't, but she had the stuff in her lungs. He also asked her about her respiratory problems. I remember her talking about the little black specks on her sheets and on her white clothes when she would hang them outside.

I know that it was a revelation from God that I would be active and involved in helping people. I was always a prayer person, and let me tell you I prayed a lot. I remember taking my children out on the back porch one evening, and I looked up and thought to myself how beautiful the sky was. I might have even spoken it out loud. I remember a beam of light coming down off the side of the moon. It was a very bright light I had never seen before and it went around me and the children. And when I asked the oldest daughter if she saw it, she said, "Yes, Mommy." And I looked at my sons and they said, "Yes." And I know it was God letting me know that he was with me and my children.

About a week or two after that, I was sitting in a chair and I remember this stream of smoke that came up from the floor. It amazed me, but I didn't get scared. That was the second time something had happened in such a strange way. I looked at the adjoining lot, where there were high bushes and tall pine trees, gum trees, and other shrubs. I asked myself, "Why is this smoke settling between these trees on such a clear day?" So I got nosy, wondering if my neighbors were burning anything. I began to look around and I saw no one burning. Then I walked to the VCM plant road [on the west side of the road, where they made vinyl chloride monomer]. I looked both ways and no one was burning. I thought about Vista, so I called them. Vista blamed Conoco. Conoco said to call PPG. It just went back and forth. And I said to myself, "Something is wrong here."

Soon after my phone calls, industry people started contacting me and asked if they could meet with me. I told my mom about it and I told some of the community folks and they all went with me. We met twice a month in the Normandy Room of the Sheraton–Chateau Charles Hotel. I told them [industry representatives], "Our ground is contaminated, the water that we drink is contaminated, and our air is contaminated." I was just opening my mouth and all of this stuff is pouring out. I am looking at these people and all of these men were white. And I was telling them about the cancer and the people dying and the people that were sick and the young women who were having hysterectomies. I was pouring out all of this knowledge I felt they already knew and were hiding. I knew it stunk in the area real bad, but I never really knew they were killing us.

[In 1986 Debra formed the Mossville Steering Committee in order to support efforts to clean up the community. She and her mother were attending a local government meeting when a new issue arose.]

As we sat there I remember the gentlemen saying that the next thing on the agenda would be to permit Conoco with that hydrocracking unit, or something that they were trying to get as far as permitting was concerned. They asked, "Is anybody here from Mossville?" He looked out in the audience and he knew it was only these two ladies left here. So I am sitting there and this man is saying this and I am refusing to raise my hand at this particular point and time. And just as they go to vote on it, the spirit in me got me up. I got up and I said, "I am from Mossville, and I know all about it." This man like was so in awe. He didn't know what to do. The whole panel was like that. So he said, "Well, come to the microphone." I went to the microphone and things began to roll out of my mouth about the condition of Mossville folks and what they had to endure and live up against. I gave them the same lecture that I had just given to the folk at Vista and Conoco at the committee meeting at the Normandy Room at the Sheraton. So I am standing there and I am talking and these people are looking at me with their mouths wide open. They go to vote and I put a freeze on the permit being passed.

We were supposed to go back to another meeting with industry, so I am rushing back and I am trying to get a little letter typed up to inform the community. I left here walking around 7:00 or 7:30 a.m. that morning, and I remember not returning until about 11:30 p.m. that night. I was so determined to see this thing through and let my people know what the issue was. I felt it was God's will and I was on a mission again. I was going from door to door in the neighborhood, spending sometimes anywhere from fifteen minutes to two hours with each household in the area. It was hot and I was walking those hot roads in all of that heat, sweating and getting a headache, and thinking I was going to get a heat stroke from the sun. But I never did. I never did. I sat there and I talked, talked, and talked, trying to educate them by telling them that we needed to get out of there and that we needed to get organized.

I had to learn it all. You are talking about a person that moved off the porch and looked at something and got nosy and it ended up here where we are now.

## *Afterword*

Before we learned the groundwater was contaminated, there was never any awareness that people would cause other folks harm and you could die from being exposed to these chemicals. We just thought folks got old and died, or some misfortune happened. And don't forget black people didn't have a set place to go. They couldn't go and move anywhere in the parish that they wanted to. They couldn't do that in those days. So eventually industry moved toward us.

Chapter Four

# "WHAT A FEW PEOPLE CAN DO"

## Learning to Advocate for Others

> *Fighting the establishment became especially difficult for these women in the mid-1980s, when the bottom fell out of Louisiana's oil and gas industry, devastating the state's economy. Thousands of people lost their jobs and were forced to leave Louisiana to find employment. These changes were particularly disruptive given many extended families' penchant for living in the same neighborhood over several generations. In this climate, businesses that promised jobs gained a great deal of power, even if they were polluting the environment. People's fears fed the view long held by many elected officials and business leaders that improved environmental protection measures would drive away industry and further harm the state's economy. At the same time, other voices began to question whether Louisiana's reliance on lax enforcement of the petrochemical industry was an appropriate way to meet the demands of the twenty-first-century marketplace.*

Louisiana's first environmental activists encountered numerous obstacles as they sought to protect their communities' health and way of life. The political and economic climate in Louisiana pitted these women against individuals and companies wielding a great deal of power and not afraid to use it.

As almost all the narratives have made apparent, the petrochemical industry was the state's economic engine, but older industries, such as the timber business, were also revered and, at times, sacred. Most state leaders wanted to ensure maximum regulatory flexibility for businesses, and citizens had long been taught that such a hands-off policy would be best for their economies. In addition, the environment was not yet a well-known cause in Louisiana; and until 1987 and 1988, with the advent of the federal Toxic Release Inventory (TRI), there were no public data on the amounts of chemicals being released by industry.[1] Not surprisingly, the link between chemical exposure and human disease was barely acknowledged.

The state's political culture posed obstacles as well. Most Louisianans were not accustomed to taking an active role in shaping public policy. The so-called Bourbon alliance of planters and merchants of the late nineteenth century and the legacy of autocratic Huey Long in the early twentieth century led to some belief that citizens had little control over the types of economies that grew up in their communities. In addition, the traditions of a patriarchal climate were pervasive and women rarely became involved in governance issues. There were a few female elected officials and appointees in state government, but women outside this circle were not expected to take part in debates about how industry should operate.

Nevertheless, women of the late nineteenth century had been at the helm of reforms of sewage, drainage, and various industrial health concerns.[2] As discussed throughout this book, by the 1970s, several women emerged from these traditional concerns to be leaders of the first local environmental groups. Out-spent but not out-maneuvered, the women proved to be remarkably effective adversaries. Their stories have a distinct David and Goliath cast, reinforced by the women's ability to achieve seemingly improbable victories.

The women especially created techniques that purposively propelled their messages to decision-makers. We have seen how they formed coalitions across racial and class boundaries in ways that defied the conventions of small town life in Louisiana. What can be less easily seen is how they gathered around kitchen tables, kept in touch by phone (or, when no phones were available, by walking to neighbors), and worked often in pairs. Competition was not often on their minds. Networking was a powerful tool, whether it was with other activists or with allies who could provide technical and legal support. The women also learned the ins and outs of permitting and mastered knowledge about the requirements of the regulatory process.

Tenacity was another essential ingredient. Many of the struggles evolved over several years, and the women had to sustain their campaigns even when it seemed they would never be won. Lawsuits, appeals, public meetings, marches, petitions—the women used all of these tools, not just once but over and over again. In so doing, they rewrote the rules of political involvement in Louisiana.

## JESSIE PRICE

Jessie Price of Bentley, Louisiana, displayed just the kind of stamina to make such change. An avid outdoorswoman, she waged a battle, at age sixty-five, against a paper mill that she believed was polluting Little River. In addition, public officials in Ruston also credited Jessie with the building of a modern sewage plant for the city. Finally, at age sixty-six, she ran for state

Jessie Price

representative in District 22 on an environmental platform. Although she was defeated, she considered her run for public office a victory because it brought attention to her concerns about river pollution.

### Narrative from Jessie Price (b. Grant Parish, Louisiana, 1920, d. 2003)

My dad was a railroad engineer until retirement.[3] He worked as a brakeman on the railroad during the war [World War I]. My mother was a housewife and a surrogate nurse. Back in those days, if somebody got sick, everybody went to tend to them. And my mother did that a lot. My dad, too. He helped out by doing things like potato digging or something that they needed. My parents were also church members.

    I loved everything about nature. I loved Little River and spent all the time I could there. My mother used to cook a little pan of cornbread every morning when she cooked breakfast, and sometimes we would take cooking oil and salt and pepper and go catch fish and cook them on the banks of Little River with cornbread and potatoes. So from childhood to adulthood, Little River was always on my mind.

During the Depression, businesses started to close. When it first started my dad was driving an engine at the gravel pit. When the gravel pit closed, we were lucky enough to have forty acres of land, and so we moved back there. My mother was a farmer. She had cattle and milk cows. She had hogs, and she raised a few for pork. During the Depression, she helped people with gardens harvest their vegetables. We didn't have refrigeration back then, and in order to keep food from spoiling we had a spring for the milk. My mother would put milk in jars, and we would take it down to the spring after breakfast.

The first thing I can remember about the river having environmental problems was in 1928 when the first black water came down the river from the Hodge Paper Mill (Southern Advance Paper at the time). I was eight years old. The black water was caused by the boiling of pulp with chemicals. For their first release, Huey P. Long gave them a permit. It killed an estimated seventy tons of fish. We had to move away from home for a while because of the odor, the flies, and the dead fish. My parents and grandparents attended meetings and called politicians, but it never did any good. Back in those days, politicians weren't fighting big companies.

I went to school in Selma, Louisiana, which was a sawmill town, and I learned to respect people and the way they did things. My first job, after I got out of school, was working in a restaurant. I made three or four dollars a week. I got married in 1934, and we raised six girls and two boys. We've lived in this community of Bentley for thirty-six years. My husband worked for a road construction company.

Little River has never been out of my mind. I had a lifetime of friends that lived on the river, and my mother and daddy. The river has been a way of life for many people. It supplied food, at times badly needed. All up and down the river are Indian sites. Several times, I put my boat in the river and would just float along. I imagined the Indian children running along the banks. I thought about how it must have looked to them during that time. It was a beautiful river then.

[The people living on Little River lost their livelihood when the pollution became so severe that it eliminated land use, fishing, and tourism.]

There was not one river-related job left. There was no tourism. There was nothing. People were suffering. They didn't have the fish and some of those people lived on fish during the Depression. My mother and daddy and all of my friends lost food and the use of their land. To me, that is one of the main things—the loss of food on that river. At one time, Little River was the largest freshwater catfish market in the state. It was also the best bass fishing area in the state. It is critical to the waterway system in the area because it drains into Catahoula Lake and then Black River.

I started attending meetings as early as 1976, regarding the river contamination. They would have a meeting and someone would bring a jar of black water they had collected. The politicians would be there and that was the end of it. However,

I always went to those meetings and put in my two cents' worth. Your mouth is the biggest force you've got. If you have got a mouth, you can do anything you want to do. I believe that. I stood up and told them to their face that they were lying.

I formed an environmental group in 1985. I called all the people I knew and told them we were going to form a club and call it the Restoration of Little River. I put out petitions and eight thousand people signed the petitions that wanted Little River cleaned up.

One particular hearing that I went to was an EPA meeting. There were five of us against the paper mill and three hundred that favored the company. They booed us. Dale Givens [from DEQ] got up and spoke. He was talking about dissolved oxygen and I had proof that he was lying. And when they [EPA] came down here two weeks later, I took out the documents and showed them. At this same hearing there were four younger men sitting nearby, and my son heard them saying they were going to shoot me. It scared him to death, but I didn't have sense enough to be scared. When we went out to the van, two of the men were sitting in the car and two were sitting on the fender. And as loud as I could I said, "You see why I told you to bring buckshot instead of squirrel shot?" I wanted them to hear it, and they didn't follow us. I used to travel quite a bit, coming home late at night, and several times over the years somebody tried to force me off the road. So I carry a gun all of the time now.

[For years, Jessie's efforts were centered on the local paper mill and their activities. She was shocked when she accidentally learned that raw sewage was also being dumped illegally into the river.]

I found out accidentally that Ruston didn't have a sewer system. They only had an aeration pond. Aeration waste is not treated. You just blow it up and air it out, and they were hauling the waste to Stone Container and putting it in that pond [Shepherd Creek], where they turned it right out into the river. At one time, when the high water would come up and it would stand in the swamp like backwater and then it would go back down, everything looked like Christmas trees—white hanging on the trees—even the blades of grass were white. Well, I sent that off and had it analyzed and it turned out to be fecal chloroform and paper. It was Ruston's sewage. I never ate another fish out of Little River after that.

I went down the riverbank once and I found the big old pipe where they turned it [waste] out into the river. In fact, I was standing at the pipe when a trucker from Stone came by and saw me taking samples. I guess he reported me, and they [plant officials] called me over to the office of the City of Ruston Water Sewage Plant. When I got there, the gate closed behind me and a man told me, "We are going to arrest you for entering without permission." So I said, "You can't do that because you have a sign up that says welcome to the plant." It scared me, but I thought about the editor from the Ruston newspaper that had written a story about me. And so I said, "Call him [the editor] and let's tell him what you're doing. And, we will also call a policeman for you also because it's against the law to move sewage from one body of water into another body of water." I said, "You are in this too." So he hem-hawed a little bit. Then he said, "Mrs. Price, we are just going to let you go, but just be careful what you do."

I was always looking out for Little River's best interest. I remember one time when the DEQ was going to do a fish study on the river and I asked if I could go. They said yes, so I went. They had put out a net the evening before and I counted the fish in the net. There were only five fish. When he [Dale Givens] wrote up his report, he said there were twenty-three species caught that day. Well, I counted the fish as the DEQ took them out of the net and I had DEQ sign my count. In the yearly DEQ report, that tells the results of all those tests, there it was—twenty-three species. At the next public hearing I stood up and told them to their faces that they were lying and I had records to prove it.

### *Afterword*

I guess my involvement stemmed from wanting to protect families. If I had been working outside of the home, I would not have had time to focus on the environment. I was somewhere all of the time doing something related to the environment. My husband always supported me and he wanted Little River cleaned up. I guess you could say that he was proud of what I did. When I would tell him about the money and that we were spending too much, he would say, "Don't worry about it. It will help our children and our grandchildren someday if the river gets cleaned up." The best reward I received was I went to Sunday school and this old, old lady came up to me and said, "Jessie Mae, I didn't have any money to give you when you were fighting Little River, but I have got this." And she handed me a little thing of hairpins.

# GAY HANKS

Gay Hanks, of Kaplan, Louisiana, started her environmental activism in 1978, eventually founding the Vermilion Association to Protect the Environment (VAPE). VAPE helped close down all of the oilfield waste sites (fifty-five identified by DEQ) in Vermilion Parish and proved instrumental in placing three of the sites on the Superfund list. Gay also helped research and rewrite regulations governing oil and gas exploration and development, giving special attention to the safe disposal of oilfield waste in the state.[4]

Gay Hanks

## Narrative from Gay Hanks (b. Kaplan, Louisiana, 1931)

This house was built the year I was born.[5] I came home from the hospital to this house and have lived here ever since. It has remained in the family all of these years. My father was the mayor of the town, a state representative, and a police juror, but most of all he was a great humanitarian. I met a ninety-three-year-old man the other day, and when I told him that I was Mereist's daughter, he said, "You had a wonderful father and during the Depression he gave us all jobs. We knew if we went to the door of that house there would be money at the end of the day to feed our family." My mother was a housewife. She prayed a lot and cared about people. She also brought food to the hungry. We grew up seeing the corporal works of mercy being encompassed in our everyday life.

I went to a Catholic boarding school for girls, the Academy of the Sacred Heart in Grand Coteau, Louisiana. I then came to Kaplan High School for two years. I got married at nineteen. My husband was in the service and we traveled a lot. He was a paratrooper. When he was discharged, we moved back to Kaplan. We had six children.

[Gay continued her family's work, helping to form Christians Who Care, an organization that assisted people in need. When her daughter, Angela, became ill with leukemia, Gay learned how prevalent the disease was among southwest Louisiana children.]

My daughter, Angela, was a beautiful little girl that fell victim to leukemia in 1963. One day, while at Saint Jude's Hospital in Memphis, the doctor came into our room and said there were too many children from southwest Louisiana with leukemia (at the time there were five or six children from Kaplan).[6] That statement sparked my interest. Why do we have too many children from the area with cancer? The damage had been done to my child, but I was out to see that it didn't happen to other children. So, beyond the obvious sadness, it [Angela's cancer] became an important part of my life.

I was really young and idealistic when I started fighting for the environment in 1978. It had been brought to my attention that there were many dump sites being established in the Kaplan area and in rural areas, where people didn't know how to stop it. They would come by and complain about how bad the smell was coming out of the pits, and they would ask me to please go and see what they were having to put up with. There were so many people being affected that had never been inside a lawyer's office, and some had never been to a public hearing. Some didn't even have telephones, but they found their way to my door, saying, "We can't sit outside of our homes anymore. The fumes are overwhelming." They came to me because they knew if my father had been alive he would have helped them. That's how I became an environmentalist, actually, in an effort to help people who had no defense.

Many of the waste pits had pipes dropped right into public waterways from one lagoon to another, to a canal where farmers picked that water up for rice or crawfish. A lot of times, during the process of excavation, the clay barrier was broken, and the seal was broken, and the contents of the pits went straight into the Chicot Aquifer, which supplies water to southwest Louisiana and parts of east Texas.

In 1987, the EPA designated the Chicot Aquifer the sole source for drinking water for southwest Louisiana. Approximately seven hundred thousand people depend on the system for drinking water. The affected area includes fifteen parishes or eleven thousand square miles, extending west to the Sabine River, east to the Atchafalaya River, south to the Gulf of Mexico, and north to Vernon and Rapides Parish.

They [polluters] were telling people in the neighborhood that they were digging a fishpond, but the next day there would be eighteen-wheelers waiting to dump their loads of toxic waste. Most of the dumping happened at night and on weekends when there was no one to notify. I don't know where it was all coming from, but it ended up there in big trucks. I would always go and see if I could help find a solution.

Out of that need the Vermilion Association to Protect the Environment (VAPE) was founded. I was president, vice president, and chairman. It was a loosely knit environmental organization of people throughout the parish. When it was at its peak there were four hundred or five hundred members. We identified, closed, and had cleaned up three Superfund sites. We also stopped new ones from being formed. We were instrumental in rewriting regulations that govern the disposal of oilfield waste in Vermilion Parish and the state of Louisiana. These made it more difficult and costly for the polluters, and they had to be more careful in disposing of the byproducts of oil wells.

There was a key moment in my life when I testified before the National Superfund Committee where all the CEOs, of all the companies, were meeting in New Orleans. I had no prepared statement. I was sitting in a room with forty of the most influential people in the United States, and I said, "I am not easily intimidated, but I am intimidated by you-all because you are influential men. We are not here to point the finger. We are here to look for a solution. We are here to ask you to help us so that our children can keep on living." Every one of the men came up to me after the meeting and said, "We want to help you." It was a key moment in my life. After that everything took a different turn.

It was gutsy to take on polluters in the late 1970s because the people you offended spent a lot of time trying to fight or discredit you. Through the years I noticed certain families that were going to open a pit and then didn't; [they] have changed their attitudes towards me. They didn't want to be a part of hurting the environment, but there was an opportunity to make money and they felt like I had deprived them of that. It didn't feel very good because it was people I know. I spent many years not knowing what kind of reception I would get if I walked into the feed store or a drug store and one of the polluters was there.

But even today, we still have a very high rate of cancer. I lost my own husband to cancer several years ago. And Saint Jude's still has more children from southwest Louisiana than from any other part of the country. People will tell me, "I really wish I had helped you more because my wife has cancer or my son has leukemia, and maybe if I had helped you we could have put an end to this sooner."

### *Afterword*

I began to have stomach trouble and will always think that was a byproduct of stress. Having to show up at those meetings, where you knew you were not welcome, and appearing before the public was stressful. I had a family that had been neglected because of my ten years of activism in the environmental movement. And I don't think they really understood. My husband wasn't that much in favor of it because he worked for the Vermilion Parish Police Jury. I was always away, attending meetings, testifying before committees, going to Baton Rouge and attending different activities, which I took on as part of my role in the movement. It took me away from my family, so after ten years I chose to stay home and see about my children and my husband. I had to say, "I can't do this anymore."

# MARY BRASSEAUX

Mary Brasseaux, of Crowley, Louisiana, describes an early life in which sharecropping, a common practice among African American and white southerners, steeled her for later fights. In the 1980s, she began to notice severe health problems developing among members of her community. These problems seemed to stem from environmental pollution. In the Rice Capital of America, all was not quite right. In 1988, indignant about plans to build a medical waste incinerator facility within the city limits, Mary sought assistance from other environmental activists as well as members of her community. Together they prevented this facility from locating in Crowley. Mary then led a campaign in opposition to the Laidlaw hazardous waste processing facility, a few miles from Crowley, which was closed in 1990. Mary was also instrumental in the passage of a landmark parish ordinance regarding the landfill. In April 1989, she became a founding member of Help Our Polluted Environment, Incorporated (HOPE). She saw this group as a means to provide the public with information and solutions to environmental problems.

### Narrative from Mary Brasseaux (b. Acadia Parish, Louisiana, 1934)

My father was a sharecropper.[7] We did cotton picking, dug potatoes, and harvested corn. We had our own meat and grew all of our vegetables and practically everything that we ate. Of course, we had no refrigerator. We always had chickens, and my father hunted for birds and rabbits. It was just those things that we couldn't produce that we had to buy at the store. I remember shucking the corn and putting it through the machine in order to grind the kernels off the cob. We had wood-burning stoves, so we had to bring wood in. Everybody had to share in doing the chores. There was very little that you threw away. If you peeled potatoes, the peelings were fed to the animals, so you didn't have all of that type of trash to throw away. And there wasn't the pesticide use like it got to be later on. We used to pick the bugs off the Irish potato plants. We made a lot of vegetables, so I guess it worked.

We traveled by buggy. I think I was about fifteen or sixteen when my dad bought a car. We were always poor, but we did get the basic necessities. There was not much cash because it took everything you made and worked for just to provide for the things you had to buy. It was not that easy for us, but I think that is the better way to go. You learn to depend on yourself.

I went to Church Point High School until the eleventh grade. I was not quite eighteen when I got married. My husband was in the service. When the war ended we moved to Crowley, where we live now. We have three daughters. Where we live

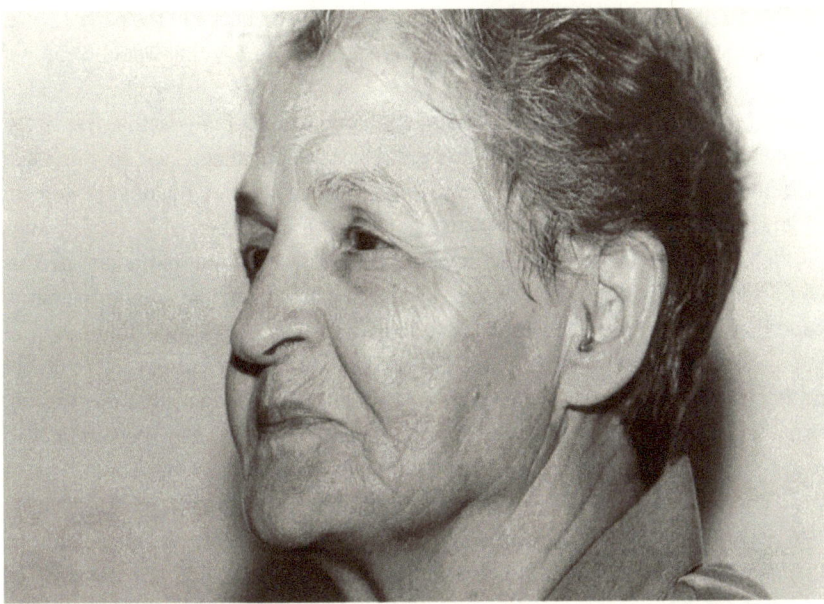

Mary Brasseaux

[Crowley] is where they plant rice. Of course, the development where we built our home had been a rice field. Our backyard is where the fields ended. They used to do aerial applications of pesticides, and when these crop dusters would go over you would have this smell. I didn't really know all that was involved, but I was never comfortable with it. Then besides that I worked at a fertilizer plant in the office. They would unload these big old boxcars with all types of fertilizer. There was one particular fertilizer that when it was unloaded you would get this kind of sick feeling. But it never dawned on me that this could be harmful. I was so trusting and naive. I just felt like people would not use anything that would be harmful to you.

On the block where we live now, and we have lived here for forty years, we've had at least nine people that have died from cancer—in eight homes. Those were the original people living on our block. They were the early ones. I could have been one of them because I live in one of those homes. Some of the people moved away, but they had been exposed in those early years. There is no telling what they sprayed forty years ago.

I was just recovering—it might have been after my breast cancer. That was my second cancer, by the way. I had one earlier, which was a different kind. I have been dealing with cancer for about twenty years. The first one was on my face. Nine years later I had breast cancer, and twelve years later I had it in my spine. That experience motivated me that I had to do something.

[Mary completed her high school degree and entered college in the early 1980s. Her graduation day was a milestone achievement and the day that would begin her activism.]

My father was more for higher education than my mother. My mother was of the opinion, I guess, because none of the girls had an education—just so you could read and write—you know what I am saying? There really were no jobs for women. At any rate, I decided to go back to college in the early eighties.

Well, it was graduation day, December 18, 1988, and I still remember it. This was a very important occasion for me. I was going to my graduation and the newspaper had a story that we were going to have a medical waste incinerator right at the city limits. I was shocked. I couldn't believe it was proposed right here on our doorstep. When I read this I just knew, in my gut and in my heart, that this was not right. I started calling. I called the mayor. I do not know how many people I called to get more information. I called Robert Istre and he knew of Wilma Subra. That is how I got in touch with her and found out all that I could. In the meantime, someone else called about the proposed medical waste incinerator. And, of course, we had friends who lived fairly close to where the proposed site was, and they were not too happy about it either. So we started meeting, and in time ended up giving ourselves the name Help Our Polluted Environment [HOPE]. I started going to every police jury and city council meeting. I had never attended these meetings until the issue of the medical waste incinerator came up, but if you go, then you know what is happening. I even had them put the group's name on the agenda for every meeting.

Then I started going around with a petition. My husband went one time, and it was cold and the people at the houses said anybody who would come out on a night like this has got something important and they would sign the petition. Some of the other members got signatures as well.

After we received a number of them [signatures], I went to the police jury meeting and turned them in. I think that was a mistake because once you give it to them—it's public record. We were driving down the street one day, and one of the opponents was coming out from the courthouse and he had the petitions in his hand. He would walk a couple of steps and look, and then he would stop again and look at all the names of the people who had signed the petitions.

One of the big arguments in the medical incinerator issue was that the hospital in town incinerated waste, and there were odors coming from there. Even the newspaper people asked about it. Our argument was that waste would be transported here from all over the country, and once you let them put their foot in the door they can add on and have more volume to handle. Can you imagine what it would have been like burning twenty-four hours a day? It seems that instead of transporting waste all over the country and contaminating everybody, they could take care of the waste where it originated. It's expensive to do this, but how much is life worth?

The *Crowley Post Signal*, in the beginning, was not necessarily supportive of our cause. But once more people came out, they were more willing to jump in. Anyway, our little group met for a number of months and more people got involved. In the end, we had everyone from the police jury, city council, area groups, and men's organizations supporting us. It was unbelievable.

### Afterword
It was not necessarily something I cared to do. I did what I had to and then I just moved on to the next step. I had never felt so strongly. It didn't matter what anybody thought. It didn't matter if they said anything bad about me because I knew what I was doing was right. Any time you tell me that I can't do something, you better believe that is when I'm going to work the hardest. I still don't understand it today—to not have had more knowledge than I did and to do something that I had never done before, like speaking publicly and all of the other things. I just feel that when something is not right you have to speak up and you have to do something about it. I think one of the things you can clearly see is what a few people can do. And it just takes one to start.

# FLORENCE ROBINSON

Florence Robinson, of Baton Rouge, Louisiana, a retired biology professor, worked tirelessly to reduce pollution in her community of Alsen, a rural, African American settlement north of Baton Rouge. She has served on numerous state and national environmental committees, including the Louisiana Environmental Action Network (LEAN) board of directors. In the early 1990s, she was awarded the Heinz Foundation Award for her environmental activism. Florence first noticed environmental problems in 1974 when members of her family came to visit and their baby got sick. Soon other signs made it clear that ash from a local incinerator was having a negative impact on the community's air quality. Florence recalls that Kai Midboe (whose narrative is also found in this book), then with DEQ, told her that the "air quality [in Alsen] is consistent with living in an industrial zone." She found this explanation unacceptable and poured her energies into putting a stop to further pollution in her community.

### Narrative from Florence Robinson (b. Monroe, Louisiana, 1938)

My grandfather lived in Alabama, but shortly after the Civil War he moved his family to Pensacola, Florida.[8] I think there were twelve children. He had I don't know how

Florence Robinson

many acres of land that he farmed. And he built a little homestead, which had no running water or electricity. My grandfather was educated at Tuskegee and Harvard. My mother met my father at Tuskegee. She went there for high school because the school for black youngsters in Monroe only went to the eighth grade. When she graduated, she came to Louisiana and went to Southern University. They married shortly afterward. I am the third child of that union.

My father got a job as a principal in a place called Mound Bayou, Mississippi. He was supposed to get one hundred dollars a month, which was an incredible salary for a black person in those days. "When you got it," he said. My mother was supposed to get forty or fifty dollars a month, but she said she got a check after one month and then didn't see any more money for a whole year. They basically got paid in sweet potatoes and pork chops and things like that. And the town provided them a house to live in. They weren't destitute by any means. There was always a strong emphasis on education in my family. My grandfather himself taught at Tuskegee. He worked along with George Washington Carver. My grandmother was a great storyteller, and some of the most delightful moments of my childhood go back to sitting on the front porch listening to my grandmother tell stories.

All of these experiences helped to make me what I am today because I think I have interests that were, often times, a bit different from mainstream black America. I went to the University of California, Los Angeles (UCLA), to get my master's degree in zoology. I was the only black in my area. Later I went to school at Cornell in upstate New York.

I left Cornell in 1971 and came to Baton Rouge, where I had the opportunity to buy a house on the edge of Devil's Swamp. I had known about it since I was a child and had always loved it there. When I was a senior in college I had a project in Devil's Swamp. Here I am a twenty-one-year-old girl going out in the swamp by myself. I was the only girl on campus allowed to wear pants, and that was when I was going out in the swamps. I had my jeans on and I was out there checking the range of animals. I had traps and I would run the lines and set them. I had to go out every day and check, and if an animal was caught I had to mark it and let it go and then check to see whether or not I caught it again.

When I came back in 1971, I had quite a menagerie of animals, and knew I wanted a place of my own. And so I bought this little piece of land on the edge of Devil's Swamp. It was two acres with a little house on it. And for me it was absolute heaven. It was a place where my son could have lots of room to play and lots of fresh air. He and I used to go out on forays in the swamp. Every spring we would get bags full of berries. The land was incredibly fertile. I had a garden. I had tomatoes and would go out every day and get a shopping bag full. I gave tomatoes to everybody I knew. We loved cooking outdoors. It was an excuse to get out in the evening. I would watch the hummingbirds. It was so peaceful and quiet.

But that summer—I think it must have been in 1974—I began to be aware of environmental problems. My brother's wife was sick, and his three children, including a six-month-old baby, came and spent the summer with me. The baby was the canary in the cold mine—the sensitive agent. There were things in the air that were obviously affecting this child's health. Later, I saw an article in the paper where people claimed that ash had come out of the Rollins incinerator and was falling on their gardens and when they ate the vegetables they got sick. And so they sued Rollins, and I think they won, or there was a settlement. Well, those people are dead. And I think Rollins ultimately bought up their land.

I have had the tops of my cars ruined with that stuff. People would wash their clothes and hang them on the line and have to wash them again because they would get covered with that stuff. The whole road back there and the side of the road used to be totally black. There were times when I was driving home and I would hit a certain place along Scenic Highway, and I would have to pull off to the side of the road and throw up. By that time it was the late 1980s and people were doing a lot of complaining. As a matter of fact, I was even on TV one time. Some of the odors that we got would come from their [Rollins] mixing building. Every now and then you would see a puff of blue smoke come out of that thing, where they had mixed something together, and you had some kind of chemical reaction and all of this stuff would come out.

The worst times were at night and on weekends. One weekend my eyes, nose, and throat started burning. The next day I felt raw from my nose down into my chest. I felt like that for several days, and when the rawness went away there was this dryness that I have never overcome. I was at the hospital and I had a full-blown asthma attack and I had never had symptoms before. That is how my asthma was finally diagnosed. The people in Alsen started having meetings. I think that was after a particularly nasty spill, where plumes of smoke went through the community and the children at the Head Start center were made sick by them.

I had cancers with my dogs. I don't know how a dog tells you, "I can't breathe." I had three bitches that had breast cancer. One, two, three—and they were all different bloodlines. I had to put my dog down for liver cancer. I took one of my puppies to the vet and I showed him her stained teeth. And later, where they were stained, they became pitted. He looked at that and said, "I have seen this in cattle where they grazed close to an incinerator or a chemical plant." What was interesting was that was a litter of eight puppies. I kept two of those puppies for more than four months. The others were placed by the time they were four months old. The two I kept both had the pitted teeth. Those that were placed, before they were four months old, did not. If it were a genetic problem, you would expect it to have shown up in at least one of the others from that litter.

I started calling the DEQ and was very insistent. The regional air person sent me data from Baker's Station, in Alsen, and there were columns and columns of figures of chemicals. They seemed to be small, but each one of these were being released over a twenty-four-hour period. Anyway, [in the mid-1990s] I got a letter from Kai Midboe, secretary of the DEQ, and his exact words were, "Your air quality is consistent with living in an industrial zone." And I thought, "This place was made an industrial zone when the people of this community couldn't vote and were systematically denied the right to participate in a government making decisions about their lives and future." But nobody wants to hear that story, and even if it is an industrial zone, is that acceptable in America?

[Rollins applied for a permanent permit in 1989, after operating on temporary permits for twenty years. Rollins also applied for a permit to expand their landfill operation to become the largest hazardous waste disposal facility in the country.]

Rollins would have pumped out smoke twenty-four hours a day, seven days a week, if there were three incinerators. So we formed an environmental organization in 1989, basically to fight that permanent expansion permit. We had a big public hearing in November, and I did this health survey in the fall of that year to try to get evidence that we had a problem. I asked a lot of questions. I was going at this kind of blind. I was asking, What kind of illnesses have you had? And I had questions about respiratory problems also. I knew of the problems the people had, such as emphysema, bronchitis, asthma, and trouble breathing. I remember something like 80 percent of the people reported respiratory problems.

A second survey was done on the other end of Alsen, and I think they came up with a 22 percent asthma rate. I was trying so hard to be objective. I designed the survey and I got a class of graduate students in toxicology to do the interviewing. I didn't go to anybody's house. They did it. And I took the survey and went to another community that I felt was ethnically, culturally, economically, and pretty much the same and did the survey and got an asthma rate of somewhere around 3 percent. Rashes that could not be contributed to fleas and mosquitoes and other insects or poison ivy was less than 1 percent. In Alsen we got a 5 percent rash rate. There were some interesting differences, but nobody would follow me up on this.

### Afterword

Alsen is a good community and I had friends there. I loved my place—two acres of land in the country. However, I finally got to the place where I just absolutely had no interest or physical ability to keep it up. I stopped cutting my grass and I hired somebody else to do it, and then I just lost heart. It was hard for me to move from Alsen, financially, but also I didn't want to move because this is home. I really loved where I lived. I had some wonderful times there.

# MARY ELLENDER

Although content with being a homemaker, Mary Ellender, of Carlyss, Louisiana, began working outside the home once she understood the threat a landfill and toxic waste incinerator posed to her community's health and well-being. Although Mary did not stop the landfill permit from being granted, her group did prevent the same corporation from expanding the landfill, from barging toxic waste through the Calcasieu Ship Channel, and from building a commercial hazardous waste incinerator to burn PCBs. Mary was instrumental in the cleanup of two abandoned hazardous waste sites in Calcasieu Parish: Pit #1, north of Moss Lake, and Pit #2, at Ellender Bridge near Hackberry. Because of Mary's involvement and work with Estelle Doyle, fifteen homes located near the Pit #1 site were bought out and the citizens relocated in 1986 through 1990. She also helped conduct a citizen-based study of the people living near the BFI/Willow Springs facility. Mary has served on many local and state environmental committees.

### Narrative from Mary Ellender (b. Wichita, Kansas, 1942)

My [maternal] grandpa built oilrigs for the oil industry when it was starting in Oklahoma.[9] My other grandpa worked for Cities Service in Oil Hill and Eldorado, Kansas. When the Depression hit, he continued to work for Cities Service. It was

Mary Ellender

after the recovery when he heard about Cities Service starting up down here, and so they came down.

My daddy was a pipefitter. He was with the Plumbers and Steamfitters Local 106 here in Lake Charles for about forty years. My parents raised five children. Growing up, I was allowed to just be a kid. We had a tree house. We played baseball and basketball. We had a large field beside the house and Daddy fixed us a basketball goal, a bag swing, a seesaw, and a merry-go-round.

Growing up, I was always active as far as voting and that sort of thing and tried to keep up with the issues, but I was not a protestor or demonstrator. I didn't know really what black people had because I grew up in a segregated situation. But as time went on you learned more about things. I remember two water fountains. One would be marked white, and one would be marked colored. You saw those things and you didn't really question it—but it was unjust.

The first thing I remember about any kind of a chemical was in 1957, when Hurricane Audrey hit and the eye passed over our area. We lived in a white, wood-framed house, and after the storm was over, we went outside and did a survey of all the damage. The south side of our house looked like it had been painted orange. Friends passed by and asked, "Did you all paint your house?" It turned out that it was the chlorine from Olin [local chemical plant] that was released and settled on that one surface, just like it had been painted.[10]

[Mary graduated from high school in 1960 and went to work in Lake Charles as a bookkeeper. She married a Louisiana State University graduate in 1963, and they raised three children in Carlyss, Louisiana, an area where her husband's family has lived for six generations.]

There are a lot of family roots here. I want our children to feel that connection. The little church, around the corner from us, was Vincent Settlement Baptist Church. The land for the church, as well as the land for Vincent Settlement School, was given by my husband's great-grandfather.

My life was uneventful. I was involved in the women's organization of the Methodist Church, and I taught Sunday school. I was home baking cookies, being a mother, and doing all the things you are expected to do for your family. I never suspected that anything was going to turn our world topsy-turvy, but just two miles west of our house was Mr. Moss's pig farm. He raised hogs. Well, he was getting up in age, so he sold this land to the Héberts. The Héberts then started getting contracts with Firestone Rubber Company. And they were taking what they called the "tank bottom." They [Héberts] would take that down to the field and put hay over it and disk it into ground. I have been told that tank bottom is some of the most toxic stuff because the heavy contaminates have settled to the bottom.

Shortly after that we were told they were going to make a hazardous waste dump on the Héberts' property. Chemical Waste Management, Incorporated (CWMI), bought the 280 acres in 1978, but before Chem-Waste bought the land from the Héberts, their attorney instructed the Héberts to plant a wheelbarrow full of waste on all four corners of the property. When they did that, they were able to "grandfather" the site in as a hazardous waste dump—the whole 280 acres. Calcasieu Parish has never to this day granted any kind of [new] hazardous waste zoning for any facility.

After CWMI purchased the property they wanted to dig a forty-foot pit, and with the water table and the way everything is around here, they built a slurry wall around the perimeter of the property and then put up a chain linked fence. A bulldozer, in the pit, looked like a Match Box toy. Then they started hauling liquid hazardous waste in. There were eighteen-wheelers coming in, I would say, four, five, and six at a time—day and night.

My brother's house ended up closest to the site. It was a dirt road where the trucks would go in, and they were having a lot of dust. He complained to the company, and so they sprayed water with tank trucks on the road. Jim could climb on top of the barn and count trucks; he was that close to the facility. So when he could he got out of there, he sold his property to the company—who else would buy it?

In 1979 we started going to hearings related to the site. All of the hearings were held in Baton Rouge. They never held the hearings here, and we had no idea that you could request that they be moved to Calcasieu Parish. We would get forty or fifty people and rent a Greyhound bus and go to Baton Rouge. We went before the Environmental Control Commission (ECC), which was before you had a Department of Environmental Quality (DEQ). There was one elderly man on the committee and he used the time to take a nap. The other committee members would come and go and drink coffee, and you felt like you were talking to a brick wall, and in some ways we were. It was difficult all the way really. I mean, every issue has obstacles, but you have to figure out what they are and work around them. And so I went from recipes for cookies to an alphabet of chemicals.

In the 1980s, the same company [CWMI] wanted to barge waste into the port of West Calcasieu, just south of the facility, to cut down on their expense of transportation. Also, people would not have been able to monitor what was going in, and if you had an accident on the waterway, the aquatic life would be endangered or killed.

Cathy Norwood, a neighbor, and I decided that we would circulate petitions. I don't remember how many hundreds we had signed, but we covered probably 98 percent of the community. We also had the telephone numbers of the dock board members and the police jurors, and we asked people to call them, and they did. That was probably the first time that we had fishermen in the area speaking out against a local hazardous waste facility. We were able to defeat that issue and stop that [waste] from coming in.

In 1983, Peggy Frankland, a concerned housewife and mother who lived near the Willow Springs area, called me because I had just finished the petitions with the dock board, and she asked me to help her collect petitions to close the Willow Springs facility. After collecting the signatures and presenting them to public officials in Baton Rouge, we decided to do an unscientific health study because Peggy kept hearing her neighbors talking about problems with their health. When we went to the people around the immediate site [Willow Springs], there was not a home that didn't have some kind of illness or respiratory problem.

[In 1984, Home Box Office (HBO) produced a documentary about the health study at Willow Springs, entitled *America Undercover—The Toxic Time Bomb*. The documentary focused on three polluted towns in the United States.]

Shortly after the health survey, we also learned that the two-hundred-foot sands of the Chicot Aquifer were contaminated near the Willow Springs facility. The Chicot Aquifer doesn't only supply water for southwest Louisiana, but it's for about 75 percent of the state and a large portion of east Texas. So we were talking about millions of people being affected

The Willow Springs landfill was closed in 1984. We had just finished working on the Willow Springs issue when CWMI wanted to build an incinerator at their landfill facility site near my home, to burn PCBs. We brought in Willie Fontenot from the attorney general's office to inform the people as to what PCBs are. We had a public hearing and three hundred people attended and we were able to stop them from building the incinerator.

In 1992 CWMI started talking about expanding. They went before the Zoning Commission and the people came out in numbers against it, and the zoning to expand was denied. They pulled their application before it went to the jury. After we defeated the expansion, the company pursued buying the undivided interest out of the 370 acres. They had bought the other 97 percent for about $700 an acre from the other heirs. Then they forced a sheriff's sale for the remaining 3 percent.

It went before the sheriff's sale on the courthouse steps October 2000. I went with my banker and bid against them [CWMI]. I went with the determination that they were not going to just walk off with the property for $700 an acre. That day they were forced to raise their final bid from $50,000 to $950,000. However, all it cost them was something like $27,000 because all they had to buy was 3 percent interest. Standing on the courthouse steps that day, I was scared to death. I was afraid if the bidding did not go the way I expected, we would end up losing everything we had.

You kind of do what you feel you have to do. Things that you thought were radical maybe do not seem so radical whenever they are in the context of the goal. I might have thought that was some kind of a radical thing, years ago, whenever I was home baking cookies. Now it is for the point, and when that point is well taken, people listen.

### *Afterword*

Something that keeps coming up is this saying: "If you don't stand up for something, you won't know what you stand for." One person can make a difference, but many people united can make a big difference. Don't let politics and politicians stand in your way.

## CAROL SAVOY

Carol Savoy, of Grandlake, Louisiana, was among those who joined forces with Janice Crador (see chapter 3) to found the Concerned Citizens Committee in 1986. The group secured the closure of four uncovered oilfield waste pits and ponds owned by Big Diamond Trucking in their community. Big Diamond then proposed a new site, nearly six times larger. Concerned Citizens helped to stop this expansion as well.

### Narrative from Carol Savoy (b. Lake Charles, Louisiana, 1958)

My daddy worked for the City of Lake Charles, and my mother was a bank teller.[11] I have two sisters. We cleaned house, cooked, dusted, mopped, cut grass, and fed the chickens. My dad took care of things. When something needed to be done he did it right away. We felt safe whenever he was around. I still call on him. And my

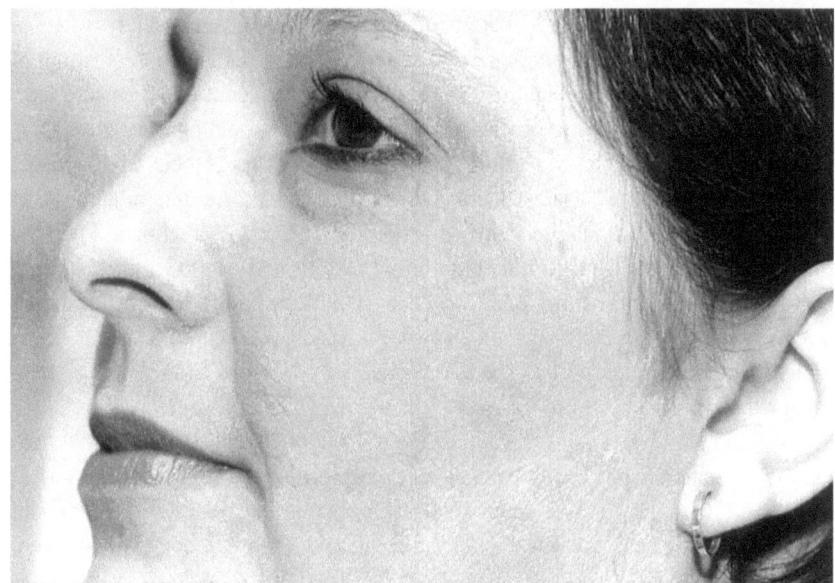

Carol Savoy

mom was the one who taught us how to respect our elders and how to care for the sick and dying. You learned to go out of your way to take care of people.

After graduation from high school I worked at Kroger's [grocery chain]. That was my first job. Then I went to work in a bank. I got married in 1978 and we started a family right away. We had three children. We lived in Lake Charles but wanted to get out in the country, so we moved to Grand Lake in 1980. My parents were here and that's why we stayed. Everybody knows everybody here, which is maybe a good thing, and maybe not. But you feel like everybody looks out for each other. Here in our community the kids stay in one school from kindergarten through the twelfth grade, and so they all hang together. When we got involved with the environmental issue, we found out where the community stood on a lot of things. You expected certain people to support you.

In the spring of 1986, we became concerned when Janice Crador [also featured in this book] called and said that the community water well was contaminated [along with] the groundwater in a large area around the facility [Big Diamond]. We found out later that the water board had done some testing and found that some of the people's wells were not even fit to bathe in—much less to drink. Here we were, a whole community drinking contaminated water and we don't even know it. We also started to hear the older people in the community talk about the smells and the burning of your nose whenever they were dumping this stuff early in the morning.

And these people were walking on the track at the school, which was by the site. So we decided it must be a serious problem.

Since 1979, the old Big Diamond facility had open pits where they put oilfield waste. They were just big holes—and what was being put in those pits, some of it the state knew about, and some of it they didn't know about because it was being dumped at night. Nobody was there to see what it was they were dumping in the pits at night. The old people in the community said that you could see trucks lined up on the highway, with their lights out, waiting to get in to dump. There is no telling what went into those pits. We couldn't imagine that the state knew that this kind of stuff was going on and they weren't doing anything about it. I really thought that everybody did their job and cared. The agencies that I thought were looking out for the people—like the [ones to come before the 1984 founding of the] Department of Environmental Quality (DEQ)—well, it didn't turn out to be that way.

In April 1986 we formed the environmental organization Concerned Citizens Committee to shut the old site down and get it cleaned up. The state told him [the owner] that he couldn't have any more waste pits, and he had to clean up the site, which was contaminated. The remedial action for cleaning up the site was to open a new landfarm operation, where they would haul the waste from the old site to the new one, which we thought would be adjacent to the old facility. Then we heard the owner was going to build a new place across the bayou from the old site. The proposed facility [a landfarm] was a process where they pour the waste on the ground and then wind row [aerate] it so that it dries out. That would save the company money in cleaning the old site up and then they would have this new landfarm operation.

We actually got to go visit a landfarm, and we saw the equipment that they used. We were expecting a big, elaborate setup to be able to test this stuff, but it [the equipment] was like a little briefcase. So we knew then that it wasn't going to be a good deal for our community. So we wanted to stop the new site from coming altogether.

We had our first public meeting at the community center in April 1986. That was the meeting that some lady referred to as the "poison pen letter" meeting. Janice Crador had sent "What is a landfarm?" letters home from school with the students. That's also when we first met Wilma Subra and Willie Fontenot. At first we didn't know if they were the good guys or the bad guys. They told us that the chemicals used in landfarming and injection wells could eventually cause things like cancer. In oilfield waste, we learned, they put chemicals in it when they are drilling to make the mud do what they want it to do, and some of those are hazardous. And we found out they were injecting acids and xylene. I don't even know what they are, but I know there were other chemicals they weren't supposed to be injecting.

Someone from the DEQ told us at a meeting, "This is off the record, but I would get out of there because when they start pouring that waste on the ground and it dries, it's going to get airborne." Heavy metals adhere to that dust and, with the site less than a mile from the school, wherever that dust settled would be dangerous for the kids. In addition, there was no way to do air monitoring. If nobody had gotten involved, this would have happened and we would have never known. It would have been permitted and that would have been it.

[Without a public hearing, the Louisiana Office of Conservation issued Big Diamond a permit to operate three new injection wells. When the citizens learned about it, they demanded a hearing.]

Wilma did this outrageous job in preparing for the public hearing. She had gone through all of the old records and pulled out the times where they [Big Diamond] disposed of the acids and xylene. That was one of the many reports presented by citizens at the hearing. Another issue was how close the facility was to the school. There was testimony about their [company's] past and the things they did wrong, such as integrity tests on the well. There was a lot of testimony pro and con. But most of the people were against it.

[Here below is one instance where the churches took a stand of non-involvement. There were other times when churches began closing their doors to activists who wanted to meet in various parish halls (see "Concluding Remarks," by Wilma Subra).]

It was a big deal organizing the community because we had churches that wouldn't take a side. We had people scared because some of them worked in the oilfields and they didn't want to lose their jobs. And then some of them were leasing land from oil companies. Some were afraid that Odell Vinson [Big Diamond's owner, now deceased] wouldn't buy their kids' 4-H pigs. It sounds so small town, but that is the way it was. Vinson would go to the Future Farmers of America events and buy somebody's pig and then they would say, "I can't go against him."

You could tell people, "There's nobody looking out for us. The state doesn't care what is going on here." But they were too busy, or they would give [money?] to us, or support us by signing a petition, but they wouldn't do anything like working on the issue. Maybe we cared because we had kids in school and the facility was so close to it.

There were a lot of older people that didn't know exactly what was going on, but they knew it wasn't good. They would hear things, so they were more informed than the younger people, but they didn't know what to do about it. So whenever somebody came along to do something, they were supportive. In fact, most of our group was older people.

No matter how much good information you had and when you were thinking this is going to be enough information—it wasn't. You would think the site being right by the school would be enough, but it wasn't. We didn't know enough about politics at the time to know all that he [the owner] was involved in and to whom he had contributed. Everybody thought he was a big deal, and people were scared. We actually got threatening phone calls that we had better be quiet, but we weren't that scared. I am proud that we didn't back down.

We could have moved, but we wanted to stay here. Even if I hadn't had children, I would still have gotten involved because it was affecting people. It was affecting me. And if I moved away, then all of these good families would have been left with no voice. People in the community would say, "I'm glad you-all are hanging in there." They weren't involved, but it made you feel good to know that people cared. There was a job that needed to be done and I was one of the fortunate ones able to do it. The facility wasn't technically in my backyard, but it was in the community. And it is my community.

## *Afterword*

I don't think I would have changed anything. Obviously, it affected my children. My son was real little, and I have pictures of dragging him on my hip to the bayou when we protested. They stayed with babysitters a lot, so it wasn't the most fun they could have been having, but I hope they learned something from it. And I think they did. I want my grandchildren to have a nice place to grow up. I want them not to be afraid to jump in and do what needs to be done. That is important to me. I want them to have pride in where they live.

Women should not sell themselves short because they are homemakers. Or just because someone is wearing a suit doesn't make them any smarter or more important than you are. I am proud of how far I have come as an individual and for standing up for what I believed in. I don't take intimidation like I used to. I am not afraid to learn how to change what needs to be changed. I used to put people on a pedestal because they were attorneys or they were some big deal. It took a few meetings with them and seeing that this guy is the head of the DEQ or whatever, and he doesn't know what's going on—and I can tell him.

Chapter Five

# "YOU ARE NOT SOMEBODY PRETENDING TO BE A MAN"

## Success, Politics, and Gender

*As so many of the women featured in this chapter have pointed out, the biggest beneficiaries of the Louisiana grassroots environmental movement are children and subsequent generations. Holding fast to their vision of their state as a place where both industry and nature can thrive when strict environmental regulations are enforced, these women provide hope for the future. Their courage, their willingness to take personal and financial risks, and their steadfast efforts to educate themselves allowed them to succeed when conventional wisdom said they would fail.*

*"Industry can intimidate a man with a job, but never a woman with a child." (Ruby Cointment, fellow activist to many of the women in this book)*

Five decades separate the oldest of the activists in this chapter from the youngest. Like the other women in this book, the activists also come from vastly different backgrounds—from homes that propelled them into an elite education, from homes where the next meal was considered first upon the day's agenda, and from homes in-between these two extremes. Yet, again, as in all the chapters in this book, their work *as women* often informed them, motivated them, and connected them. In this chapter we take note then of how traditional roles of caretaking, always extending out into communities, came to travel much further.

In this section, we also remind readers of how much all the narratives of this book show networks that built upon earlier reform movements of women, those overtly concerned with the improvement of the education, legal rights, work, and social roles of women. Sometimes these were the connections of reform and sometimes they were those of the churches and schools. Like other places in the United States, Louisiana had its nineteenth- and early-twentieth-century women progressives of the upper middle class who sought to work especially with health and city officials to ensure a safe water supply. First among such change-makers were nineteenth-century New

Orleans women who worked against child labor, who sought to clean up drainage canals, and who worked to care for those orphaned by successive yellow fever epidemics.[1] Also in the twentieth century came the League of Women Voters with chapters across the state. Again, many of the women in this book mention the League as giving them the power to emerge as leaders in various battles. The League's educated women are significant to this mapping of the past, this connecting of advocates for clean water and air, before such issues were even named a part of the environmental movement.[2]

In turn, when we consider the first narrative, that of Mildred Fossier, and her link to Newcomb College, the women's college of Tulane, and the last in this chapter, Mary Tutwiler, and her link to another coordinate college, that of Barnard of Columbia University in New York City, we also consider the influence of education for women. Newcomb taught generations of early reformers, such as the aunt of Willie Fontenot, Anne McKinne Robertson (cited in chapter 7), a city planner. Fossier may have indeed been among the students to hear, in 1936, an invited speaker to Newcomb, Alice Hamilton. This woman scientist had worked with the state of Illinois to reduce industrial poisoning in the 1910s, shaming the legislators there by stating that their laws were equal to those of nineteenth-century France. By the time of her visit to New Orleans, she was the first female professor in the graduate school at Harvard and an internationally recognized expert witness in cases involving the health of workers.[3] By the early 1970s, when Mary Tutwiler went off to school, she was encouraged to leave the state, but she was also taught to love Louisiana and thus chose to come back home with her education.

This affection for the state is a very real sentiment running through all the narratives. It is a testament to the many family members who teach younger generations what they have loved: the bounty of strong family ties, the bounty of natural resources, the cultural climate of rich regard for French, Spanish, African, and other settlers—and the advantages (as well as disadvantages) for women found in civil law, which remained, in part, in Louisiana.

Their affection is also a testament to the obligatory Louisiana history courses, requisites for graduation in public and parochial schools. Not to be forgotten then also are other types of education. Two schools for girls mentioned in the narratives stand out: the Academy of the Sacred Heart in both New Orleans and Grand Coteau (besides Fossier, see Marylee Orr in chapter 6 and Gay Hanks in chapter 4), but so too do other Catholic schools for girls, and those for both sexes. The nuns and other women administrators at these institutions instilled possibilities of expanded roles for women in urban and rural Louisiana communities. We hear also in Mary Brasseaux's narrative (chapter 4) of education delayed and then put to good use later, another traditional path for women after their children are grown.

Finally, there are those women who went to vocational schools or began to work early and learned quickly what could be changed and what could not, what was right and what was wrong. From all these women, we see "social housekeeping" transformed to include as decision makers the very people affected by policies. Indeed, the women from whom we hear drew the boundaries of community larger. They enlarged, then, the concepts of citizen action.

## MILDRED FOSSIER

Mildred Fossier, of New Orleans, Louisiana, proved especially adept at working within the male-dominated political system. In 1963, she was made director of the city's Welfare Department, and in the 1970s, the head of the Parkway and Park Commission. In the 1980s, she served as Mayor Sidney Barthelemy's volunteer environmental consultant.

### Narrative from Mildred Fossier (b. New Orleans, Louisiana, 1913, d. 2011)

My first ancestor came to New Orleans from Combrey, France, in 1719.[4] My father's father had a factory that he started after the Civil War. They were planters prior to that time. They had a plantation, but they lost it after the Civil War, and so he started a shirt factory. He then invented power-driven sewing machines.

My father was a physician and a historian, researching local history. At sixteen he got his bachelor's degree. He read, wrote, and spoke English, French, Latin, Spanish, and Greek. He had an international reputation as the one who determined that the human heart was the size of a fist. He taught medicine at Doctors' Tulane. He was head of the cardiac wards of Charity Hospital for both blacks and whites, where they had a very active medical society. Doctors would present papers about things that they discovered, and Papa often read his. We'd all dress up and go. When he read, the older doctors would say, "Well, we've always done it this way." And my father would say, "And therefore it is suspect, doctors; it is suspect." And some of that rebellion, I think, rubbed off on me.

My mother had inherited money and would buy land in this area of Uptown, which had been farms. She'd subdivide the land and build houses on it. She built about seven or eight houses in this area. The one I'm in she built in 1905.

My mother could speak French, but she wouldn't. My grandmother's house was in the next block, and in a matter of four minutes I would go from a different lan-

Mildred Fossier

guage, a different culture, and a different age. You see, they spoke French and lived in the past, but my mother was modern and lived in the present. And although she wasn't a suffragette, she and my father fully supported her sister, who embraced the cause.

I'm a Catholic, so on Sundays you went to church. In this section of the world most of the old French people were Catholic. My parents wanted to send me to [the elite Academy of the] Sacred Heart . . . but there was no one to take me, so I went to the [neighborhood] parochial school. My mother didn't drive, and my father's schedule as a doctor couldn't be predicted. They decided to wait until I was old enough to go on the streetcar by myself, and then I went to Sacred Heart on Saint Charles Avenue. In high school I took part in athletics, in swimming and basketball, and at the convent I was a cheerleader, but my main interest was acting. I started a dramatic club and was director.

After high school I went to Newcomb and graduated in 1936. I spent a lot of time at the theater. This was in the depth of the Depression, and the theater was really a godsend to young people at the time. There'd be young men graduating in law with no jobs, no office, and no clients. They'd go down to the theater, and those who didn't want to act would build scenery. Some of the leading legal minds in this community played at the theater. They had an outlet of some kind and it kept them off the streets. Nobody expected anything of me because I was a girl. In fact, when I first went to work my mother said, "What are you going to work for? You're not starving." And I said, "I want to find out what's going on in the world."

I went to work as a recruiting representative during World War II. I traveled all through Texas recruiting stenographers and typists for Washington. I got to be head of the Skilled Trades and Engineering Department. I was the only woman in the United States with such a job, and I did things exactly opposite from what they'd always done. The men with Civil Service had been trained so differently; they thought I was a genius. This gave me a very good grounding in administration. After the war, however, I had to leave because I had a war service appointment, and I didn't have a permanent status.

After the war, I returned to New Orleans and got a job as secretary of the real estate board. There was no other way to work. Nobody would take me because I was a female. At forty years old, I decided to learn a profession. I went to the school at Tulane and earned my master's in social work.

I went to work as the social director of the Milne Boys Home, which was run by the city. That's how I got into the city and became director of the Department of Welfare. I was at Welfare for ten years, and in the beginning, the mayor [Victor Schiro, 1961–1970] didn't want me.

My father had written a book, *New Orleans: The Glamour Period*, and so I asked him to autograph a copy for the mayor. Then I asked for an appointment to see the mayor, stating that the city was in the same transition as when my father had written the book and he wanted to present a copy to the mayor. That changed attitudes. Things began to turn around for me.

[In 1972, because of her success at the Welfare Department, Mayor Moon Landrieu recommended Mildred for the position of director of Parkways and Parks. Mildred quickly set about employing people who were not getting hired or promoted to better work positions.]

What happened was the city was in the doldrums and Mayor Moon really wanted to get things going, but there wasn't anybody at Parkway with a college degree. So when the director and his secretary quit, Moon decided to hire me because I had reorganized the Welfare Department. Well, you can imagine, in 1972, men [employees of the Parks Department] learning that they had a woman director—who had been a welfare director.

Well, one thing I noticed was that there was no black person, above laborer, in that whole department. There were white supervisors and black laborers. And there was no opportunity for a black man to work his way up. So when examinations were held and the registers would come in, I'd hire the first one on the register. So I began to get black people and women into better positions. I hired the first black secretary in city hall.

As superintendent of the Parkway and Parks Commission, I was concerned about what was happening to the trees on South Carrollton Avenue. I fought the widening of Carrolton several times. Workmen would run things as close to the trees as they could and cut off the roots, but there was no reason to do that because these oak trees have shallow roots. You know they are only eighteen inches under the soil, and all the men had to do was lift the roots and keep them moist. It didn't impede their work at all. I fought the city departments, particularly the Sewerage and Water Board, Streets, Entergy Corporation, and others. Mayor Moon Landrieu told me to "go out and protect every inch of city property and every tree." So I did it, and that was my job. The guy who was head of the Streets Department said, "You know, you're just like these little old ladies in white tennis shoes. You're just a birdbrain." And so I said, "There's song up there, there's birth, there's life, and there's love. And what have you got? Cement." So they called him "cement brain" and me "birdbrain."

The litter, when I first went to Parkway, was just awful. I'd have men work on Sunday afternoons to pick up litter so it wouldn't be seen on Monday. I explained to my men that the whole mood of the city depended on them. If they preserved the trees, that took carbon monoxide and turned it into oxygen; the health of the city was dependent on them. That's where I put the environmental focus. I always took positions for the environment. When Sidney Barthelemy became mayor, my efforts intensified. He had succeeded me as director of Welfare when I went to Parkway. I felt sorry for Sidney because the previous mayor had left $30 million of debt. So I wrote him a letter and said I would volunteer. He called me and replied, "Help in any way you can."

Well, in Dutch's [Dutch Morial, mayor of New Orleans from 1978 through 1986] day there had been a mayor's breakfast, which was an environmental breakfast meeting. It was a very small group of maybe twenty people at the most, and I used to go. So I suggested to Sidney that I be his environmental consultant. I would work between him and the environmental community. He was happy about that, and so I took over the breakfast, and we went from twenty to about a three hundred membership. It kept the environmental people together. Marietta Herr [also featured in this book] helped, and between us we did this.

At the time, the Bayou Sauvage National Wildlife Refuge was in limbo, and the federal government didn't want it, but Congresswoman Lindy Boggs, Congressman John Breaux, and [Mayor] Sidney Barthelemy did. The Levee Board wanted to put an airport there, so there was a great deal of opposition. We had a meeting and John Breaux and Lindy Boggs were there. I was there as Sidney's volunteer consultant. The whole thing ended in agreement.

Then I began getting calls from people in the environmental community saying the agreement had been badly written. There was a male employee on Sidney's staff who was assigned to write the report. He represented the city on the Levee Board and his sympathy was with them. The concerned environmentalists said that the way he'd written it up, if it goes through like this, we will never get Bayou Sauvage. So I told Sidney that the write-up was going to defeat Bayou Sauvage because the way it was written precluded our getting this preserve. Sidney called in the writer of the report, and after some loud words between this person and me, the mayor directed him to correct the report. Many believe that without this intervention Bayou Sauvage would have been lost.

The Nature Center is another example of intervention. The Junior League asked if I would be on a committee to establish a nature center—we had none in this area, although they existed throughout the United States. My department "did over" Joe Brown Park and reserved eighty acres. Kids needed a place to explore and learn about the woods. We put everything in the area where all the trees had already been cut as a space for games and buildings. But the Planning Commission was constantly pressuring to put a football stadium and roads in there. They'd say, "We're the Planning Commission." And I'd say, "I'm Parkway." We had battles like you've never known, and finally I said they couldn't do it—period. And I had my board behind me. We saved the eighty acres, and then I was very anxious to get the center there.

I got Moon interested in a nature center and he got the money and it went through the Parkway budget. I moved the nature center through all city departments, and finally they got a fifty-year lease. That's how the Louisiana Nature and Science Center came in this area. It never would have happened any other way because they had no location for it.

There was another nature park we obtained funding for just before I retired and the mayor retired. He made a deal with the Coast Guard to maintain a wilderness at the foot of the Algiers, where they had their station. They needed a guarantee that no noisy activity would be nearby. We obtained $1 million of federal money to buy adjacent land with the city matching funds. This park has never developed. I believe it's now rented to the Audubon Institute at one dollar a year for their species preservation [center].

The Police Department wanted to take Palmer Park and put a police station in there. It was free land and they decided they needed one up here and they wanted it there. I fought that. And I told them they couldn't do it. You know, I had jurisdiction. I developed the parks and redeveloped some of them. In Palmer Park, I planted, repaired sidewalks, and had benches put in. There is a plaque in the middle of the park with my name on it.

[In the mid-1980s, Freeport-McMoRan Corporation, headquartered in New Orleans, sought a permit to dump 12 million tons of gypsum into the Mississippi River each year.]

Marietta Herr called one day and said that someone with the Sewerage and Water Board, named Maureen O'Neill [also featured in this book], wanted to come to see me. So I invited her for dinner. I was listening to her talk about this dumping of gypsum into the Mississippi River—12 million tons a year. As I listened I remembered that I had gone to one of these breakfasts, and the head of water for the Department of Environmental Quality kept saying, "We should back this—gypsum won't hurt the river." And I had thought to myself, "I don't know a damn thing about this, but you're lying." So when Maureen came to me, I believed her.

I went to Sidney, and here he was with a $30 million shortfall, and Freeport-McMoRan was practically financing the libraries. Sidney couldn't take a stand against them. I told him, "I will follow Maureen everywhere she goes, and, Sidney, I will watch out for your behind." And that's what we did, and I am telling you—that girl—I've never seen anything like her. She was a whirlwind and all I did was follow. She's done fantastic things for this state. She defeated Freeport-McMoRan, in Washington, when they were going to latch on permission, for the dumping, onto another bill. She got that defeated. She defeated them in the state legislature when they were going to do the same thing. She defeated them in the city council.

So we went up and down the river talking to all the parishes that got water from the river. The word of mouth was so strong when she got started. She got labor interested in it. So when Edwards wanted to run again, for governor, he decided the issue was too hot. But Freeport-McMoRan had gotten two of the foremost environmentalists on their side. They'd called up city hall trying to get Maureen's job, and Sidney would call me sometimes at twelve o'clock at night and say, "You know what they are saying?" And I would say, "Sidney, I was there and this is not true." Just like I was able to point out to him about Bayou Sauvage—nobody could have gotten to him otherwise.

You see, it's just being at the right place at the right time. Knowing people helps. I do think that the Nature Center and the Bayou Sauvage have been very good for the city. I feel very good that I had some little role to play in getting that fixed for this area.

## *Afterword*

They had a meeting just before I left the city, of women talking about how to get up the ladder and what they should do. Some women talked about how men played games and we should know their games. And I listened to a lot of stuff, and I said just the opposite, that women had a certain way of looking at things. We had to be ourselves and we had to operate in a way women would. We had to do a lot of toe dancing, perhaps, but we had to be ourselves. Confrontation wasn't always the best way—but if nothing else was there, you had to have the guts to confront.

Also, you are not somebody pretending to be a man. It's not that you don't know their games and their rules. You know them, but your main idea is not to be a junior man. You don't give up your way of doing things because women have a different way. They're much more thorough than men and much more fundamental. I think the environment is a place for women because women can take flack without fisticuffs. They call women hysterical, but they have been doing that for years. After all, women scream when they are giving birth. They've got to deal with the fundamentals of life. They can't pretend.

# MARY McCASTLE

Mary McCastle, of Alsen, Louisiana, began her involvement with the environmental movement in 1980 when she founded and was the leader of the group Coalition for Community Activism. She became an activist because she and many other members of her rural African American community suffered from a variety of health problems, problems that they attributed to the Rollins Environmental Services, Inc.

One of the last interviews Mary gave was for this project in January 2000. She was very ill at the time, and her son Simms provided supporting information. The story Mary tells in this chapter is also supplemented by an interview with Willie Fontenot.

### Narrative from Mary McCastle (b. Alsen, Louisiana, 1920, d. 2000) with Simms McCastle and Willie Fontenot

I was raised up here in the rural area as a child.[5] My parents were born here. My parents worked on a farm, raised hogs, chickens, and cows. I went to school when I got big enough; you know, big enough to take care of myself while my parents worked in the fields. I finished high school. I picked cotton and helped raise corn, chickens, cows, all of that. And when I got to be a young lady, well, then I married. I married right here in Alsen. We had five children. I worked at Exxon for ten years. Then I left Exxon and went to LTI and I worked there for twenty years.

### *Simms McCastle*

My mother was one of the first ladies to walk in the LTI gates to be hired. She worked as a supervisor for twenty-two years, and when she retired she started working in the community. Several people came to her and they were telling her that this and this happened, and she said, "Why are these people bothering me? I just retired." So she took up [the cause] one day when they came and said they smelled something in the neighborhood. She started walking and going all over the community, smelling and going back there to Rollins at night, all hours of the night.

The smell was terrible, and sometimes it smelled like sulfur. She started calling different people. She called Pat Screen [the mayor of Baton Rouge], she called the governor, and she started calling everybody. Nobody was really interested in the environment. So she just went at it. My dad would say, "People going to kill you." But she started writing letters and getting us to write letters. People would call and say they smelled something and she would get up and go. She kept us up all night some nights because we'd sit up until she would get back.

Then my mother started having problems with her chest. She went to the doctor and they asked her if she had been around chemicals. And that's when she started calling meetings and asking different people, who were sick, what their symptoms were. That's when they started complaining about how they felt burning eyes and all of that.

I think Mother was calling a meeting every other day or so and different people would come to her and she'd tell them to go to the doctor. She filed a lawsuit and asked the community to come out, but just a few came and she said, "I'm going to get a lawyer." So she did. But the lawyer said that in order for him to take the case, he would have to have $500 to start. Well, nobody gave anything. So then she started calling her children for money. So, with her $100, my hundred, Royal's [brother's] hundred, and my sisters', she got the $500 dollars. My mother started having meetings with the lawyer, and then the people started coming in because now they were interested.

## *Willie Fontenot*

In 1975 or 1976, when I was working for the Louisiana Wildlife Federation, Dave Ewell [citizen who lived near Rollins and Alsen] had talked a lot about the pollution problems and had taken me into Devil's Swamp and some of the industries in the Alsen area to show me what they looked like and what some of the problems were. And then I went to work for the attorney general in 1978, and Dave showed me more of the swamp and his concern about how you could dig down in the ground and find contamination on his property.

In 1980 one of the new attorneys in the attorney general's office was Pat Norton, who later became secretary of the Department of Environmental Quality (DEQ). And Pat said, "Willie, you should have been here yesterday. There were three workers that came here. They worked at Allied Signal, which is next to something called Rollins, and they say it's really terrible; you've got to put on a gas mask the fumes are so bad." She asked, "What should we do with this?"

I called up Mary McCastle and I went to her house. It was in the evening, and when I walked into the living room there were maybe thirty people in the room, and I was the only white person. They talked about how bad the fumes were and how they would have to put a wet towel over their head to be able to breathe and it would wake them up at two or three in the morning. They had blotches on their skin, talked about aching joints, how they got tired all of the time, how flowers wouldn't bloom, and how pecan trees weren't producing.

I had worked enough with Dave Ewell to know something about the area and what some of the industries produced, and a little bit about how they operated. There were a couple of paper mills, and to the west of them there was a lead smelter. There was also a petroleum coke plant, and that plant has four stacks and would put out tons of black, dusty-looking stuff. Even people here in Baton Rouge would get black dust particles, and people wouldn't know where it was coming from. They were also getting light material on their homes and in their homes from Allied Signal Plant, south of Rollins, which was a high-density polyethylene plant.

So I asked the people in Alsen if they were having the same problem and they said, "Yeah, we get that white dust, and we get that black dust." And I said, "Do you ever smell anything that smells like a dead horse?" And they said, "Yeah." And I said, "Well, that's from Rollins." I told them every time they smelled an odor, or got any dust, that they should write down the time, the date, and the wind direction. And if they could take samples of the dust material and scotch tape it to a piece of paper, then it would be preserved. Mary McCastle and Mrs. Emma Johnson were the two people who did the best job of keeping diaries.

Doris Falkenheiner, an attorney, called me in March of 1980 and said, "Willie, did you know that Rollins is coming up on the agenda of the Environmental Control Commission (ECC)?" So I called Mary McCastle to see if she could come to the ECC the next day. And she was very sick; they'd just gotten some really bad fumes and they had made her very sick. She had become very sensitive to the environment, so she couldn't make that meeting.

The ECC staff came back with this report where they were going to investigate the Rollins facility, and this is the first time, to my knowledge, that an industrial facility in the state of Louisiana was ever scrutinized. They found thirteen places where there was waste leaving the site, other than their discharge pipe, and a whole lot of different problems. They didn't get so much into the fumes because there were barrels leaking and waste oozing off the site.

So when the April report came back and shows how bad Rollins was, Mary was able to show up at the ECC hearing and she got up and spoke. And that was like the breakthrough because now we had a person who was not intimidated. She had some struggle getting her position articulated in a way that would fit into whatever little mold the agencies and officials had, but nobody really hassled her.

It was a struggle for Mary McCastle to get to the ECC meetings because of her health, and she didn't drive, yet she made just about every meeting for at least the next three years. They would get a bus from one of the churches and bring ten, twenty, or thirty people to every one of the ECC meetings. This was the first time that black people showed up in any numbers at all. There might have been one or two people before that point, but from April on, black people were visible at the meetings at the ECC and the agencies didn't know what to do with this or how to act.

Mary had a group called the Coalition for Community Action, and it was mostly immediate family members that were on her board. And she was sort of the matron of the neighborhood. Not everyone was connected with her group, but she pretty much represented the interest of the community. She was always looking for ways to improve the neighborhood.

I would go to Mary's house at least once a week for six or seven years and talk to her about what was going on. I'd look at the latest complaints that they had documented and what other problems they were having in the community. When Mary and her neighbors first started, all they wanted was for those plants to operate correctly. All they wanted was to be able to live in their community and in their homes, raise a garden, and have a place where the children could play. They weren't interested in filing a lawsuit against Rollins.

But by 1982 or 1983, it was obvious they weren't getting what they wanted. Industry just blew them off. All they were interested in was getting their permits and operating and not worrying about anything around their plants. Not other plants, not the community, not the environment, and that was true for the largest corporations and businesses in Louisiana. It was like they were in a foreign land, didn't speak the language, and didn't worry about the local folks. And if you do that, you can get away with it for a certain amount of time, but people become resentful, particularly if they find out that things that you are doing are costing them.

The ECC set up something called the "nose patrol," where agency people come out and smell different operations to figure out if those were the odors that were bothering them. Mary would call me at one or two in the morning or four o'clock in the afternoon or on a Sunday, and if I could get up there, I'd pick her up and we'd drive around to see what we could find. Usually the fumes were coming from Rollins.

After I'd gone up there lots and lots of times, I got the idea of getting Mary and her neighbors to start calling their city councilman and the mayor. I said to Mary, "It doesn't matter what time it is; you call their homes. You are miserable; they need to be a little miserable." And so they were calling Pat Screen, the mayor of Baton Rouge, at two and three in the morning, and he was upset. He got a consultant that was working for the city to start responding to Mary's calls, and they would go up to Mary's and investigate the complaints. In 1982 or 1983, they did a report before the ECC that says that they had gotten about 150 calls from the residents of Alsen. And of those, something like 136 times, they were able to document that the fumes were coming from Rollins. And they rated them on a scale of one to ten, and sometimes they felt they were health threatening. This was one of the first things that turned the tide for the citizens.

Another turning point was when the Health Department went to see if people were having complaints. Dr. Raoult Ratard, the state epidemiologist, went to Alsen with a nurse. They met in the Alsen Community Center, and they thought there were going to be twenty or thirty people and eighty people showed up. Dr. Ratard reported that everyone he saw had some physical manifestation of the problems that they were talking about. They had splotches on their skin and they had other health problems, and he thought that they should do a full survey in the community. For the first time they were able to get some validation that these were real troubles they were having, and it was because Mary had her organization and she was well connected in the neighborhood. And because her group had done political endorsements, she knew how to talk to public officials.

In 1978, Bob Anderson had become the environmental writer with the [Baton Rouge] *Advocate*, and by January of 1980, when Mary got involved, Bob had already figured out where some of the soft spots were in our environmental programs and he would be quoting Mary McCastle every other week in the paper. By 1985, she was one of the best-known environmentalists in the country and certainly in Louisiana.

Another changing moment in the Rollins situation was in 1985, when Rollins wanted to burn PCBs in their incinerator, and Mary didn't want any of that. And by 1985, because of Mary's vocal activism, I don't think there was a person in east Baton Rouge Parish that hadn't heard of her, Alsen, and Rollins. And when Rollins proposed burning PCBs, Mayor Pat Screen held a meeting at the Baton Rouge Centraplex. He had a panel of four or five top officials with the EPA in Dallas, all the top people with the DEQ, because by then the ECC had been replaced by the DEQ, and the whole Baton Rouge City Council.

They were all on the stage at the Centraplex, all these officials, and in the audience were about 1,400 citizens with protest signs. It was a more white than black audience. Marylee Orr [also featured in this book], now the director of LEAN, had started a group called Mothers against Air Pollution, and my wife had connected with her and they had gotten 1,200 or 1,500 signatures of people on a petition opposed to the PCB burn. The Duhé-Datsun Law Firm, which is a big supporter of Pat Screen, was also opposed to it. And the lawyers in the firm and their wives had all done these signs opposing Rollins burning, and they started a group called Citizens for a Clean Environment.

And there was Mary McCastle, and she was in her glory because she had never expected that they would get that kind of support. They had gone from being this little beat-up community in 1980, to 1985, when they had the whole community with them. There were no public officials saying they were kooks. The mayor, the city council, and the state legislators supported them. It was a complete change in five years, but it was all of those meetings and hearings that Mary and her neighbors went to and it was her understanding of how to work the political system.

When Mary settled her court case, the settlement ended up being, I'm guessing, around $2.5 million, which is not much when it's divided up by 1,200 people or whatever the number was. I know Mary got enough out of the lawsuit to rebuild her house. There was a man that showed up and offered Mary a check for about $50,000 or $60,000 if she would settle the lawsuit with Rollins and she refused to do it. She didn't want to be accused of selling out for her friends and neighbors and family.

### *Afterword by Willie Fontenot*

Mary's lawsuit was part of what ended up causing Rollins to change the way they operated. They ended up closing all of their open pits, which contained liquids in them, and some of them were sources of air pollution. They used to have a wastewater treatment system called Rollins-Purle, which was a source of a lot of air pollution, but they ended up having to close that. They ended up having an enclosed facility, a big warehouse, basically, for opening up barrels and things. So, by 1990, it was a completely different facility. They tried to expand a few times. They applied, but were denied permits, for a new hazardous waste incinerator and an expansion into new pit-burying areas. And that was one of the struggles when Paul Templet became secretary of DEQ. The citizens got involved in stopping Rollins from expanding and pretty much put them out of business. But it took ten years. It's a slow process, but Mary hung in there until the very end.

# FLORENCE GOSSEN

Florence Gossen is the type of woman who found direct reasons for concern in two communities in which she lived. First, living in Destrehan, a suburb of New Orleans, her children began having respiratory problems due to the grain dust in this area. She, her husband, and their neighbors began work that would, many years later, grow into the first Air Control Commission in Louisiana. Other issues also concerned her when the family moved to Lafayette, only to find that the North Dugas Landfill soon presented many health problems.

### Narrative from Florence Gossen (b. New Iberia, Louisiana, 1935)

My mother and father were born and raised in Loreauville, Louisiana.[6] My father owned land in Iberia Parish. He was a farmer and operated two cattle auction barns.

Florence Gossen

He also operated grocery stores and a funeral home. My mother had a large fruit orchard, and Dad raised melons and sweet potatoes. We grew sugarcane and rice and would have syrup and brown sugar made from the mill where we harvested the cane. During the war, brown sugar was rationed, and I can remember my dad would bring back a bag of brown sugar, which we would divide. Everything was used. You did not waste any food. My parents were involved in church activities, but also in political interests and what was best for the community. We were taught a love for this Earth and that we should protect it and have respect for what God has given us.

I went to school at New Iberia Senior High School. One of the teachers, named Miss Gates, taught me a civics course, where I learned a lot about participating and being a part of the community. And my parents taught me to work with people. I went to the University of Louisiana here in Lafayette and married in September of 1955. My husband was in the Air Force. He was stationed in Tokyo and was then transferred to Okinawa, where we lived for three years. Our first son was born there. We have five children. We lived in New Iberia until my husband was employed at Norco with Shell Chemical and we moved to Destrehan.

We lived in Destrehan for seven years, and then we moved here in 1965. We lived in Lafayette two years, before we acquired these twenty-five acres and built this house. We wanted to be out in the country, where we could raise our children and have a lot of space. My husband always said, "When we retire we will have a nice comfortable place." We were here fifteen years before the landfill.

[On May 4, 1979, an eighty-five-acre property on North Dugas Road was purchased by the city of Lafayette in anticipation of expanding the landfill by hundreds more additional acres. On August 13, 1979, the Louisiana Department of Health and Hospitals (LADHH) granted approval to operate a solid waste disposal facility, and on Mother's Day, May 12, 1980, operations began.]

My husband was in Houston on the afternoon we found out that the sale for the landfill would be signed that day or the next morning. So I called him. He called Mayor Bowen and said, "Kenny, don't do anything until I get back. I'm leaving Houston and it will take me four hours." When my husband got back the mayor said, "It's too late. The sale has been signed." The same thing happened to Clara Baudoin [also featured in this book]. There were no meetings and no input whatsoever. The site was permitted by what we had in Louisiana as the Environmental Control Commission (ECC), known today as the Department of Environmental Quality.

I talked to Clara from time to time, and I would say, "Clara, we have got to do something." She would say, "I can't get involved because my husband works for the city of Lafayette." One day, however, her mama was so sick from the odors in her own house that Clara called and said, "Flo, what can we do?" At that time I think the only lawyer that could have done something was the one we had. You could not have hired another lawyer in Lafayette to represent us, so Clara said, "I will go out of town." And she did get somebody from Walker, Louisiana, to represent her. Her attorney joined in with ours and we took them on. When we first started we formed a group called Save Our Homes and Land.

Anywhere from nine months to a year later, we were having problems with drinking water already. This is when Clara's family began to lose sheep. I took one of them to the LSU Veterinary Center and had them do an autopsy. They had a whole herd of registered sheep there that died.

We had a number of cattle that we had vets come out and check because they had heart attacks or they died at the water trough. I even had kittens that died. We all started getting very sick. Actually, we all had giardia. We had a daughter that almost died. After her second hospitalization, the doctor said, "I don't want you to take your family back to that house. Get out now or we will not release your daughter."

We were at Lourdes Hospital, and I got a call from every councilman in the city, saying, "What is it you want us to do?" I said, "Do? We are very, very sick and we asked you for help." I said, "You had better run some water lines out there today. And do not stop at my house. Go as far back as the school," which was five miles from here. I said, "You have eight hundred children." The principal had been telling me how sick the children were. They didn't want to believe us.

I rented an apartment on Gloria Switch Road. The doctor said, "Take only paper plates, napkins, your clothes, and no pots and utensils." We did that, but we couldn't stay because we were a family of seven in a two-bedroom apartment. We ended up buying the house near Carencro High School. In fact, we had mortgages on two houses and on this property. [Since the landfill closed, Flo has moved back to the property where the family first lived in the country outside Lafayette.]

When the city started digging the landfill, we asked them not to go deep. And they shouldn't go deeper than what the specifications said—12 feet deep. That was what the plan said, but the contracted company came in and said, "You can go 50 feet deep, put in more garbage, and make more money." They had a dragline in the cells of this landfill, and you couldn't see the top of the boom. When Judge Sue Fontenot came out here, she saw that drag line sitting in the cell. Since the clay barrier is at 50 feet, they had penetrated the clay basin into the sands of the [Chicot] Aquifer. I had the EPA come out, and they likened the site to a "cesspool sitting in the aquifer." So we have eighty-five acres of a cesspool sitting in an aquifer, and the site is three miles from the city of Lafayette. And our water well is less than 125 feet from the mound.

They were dumping hospital waste also. I have pictures of hospital waste and, God only knows, body parts, and hypodermic needles. And there were dogs. At night you would have possums and raccoons. The mound of waste is bad enough, but in the buffer zone you have eight burrow pits and they are full of water. So what you have is a ring of water surrounding a mound of waste. In the first two pits in the front they were dumping leachate, which is the water from garbage. They were taking contaminated leachate with bacterial organisms in it and spraying it all over the area. They said they were doing that to cut the dust. Plus the garbage trucks were coming in and out. Then they set up pumps to pump the leachate over the levees. They pumped this onto Clara's property. And it was the horrible odors, the noise, the birds, and the flies. There were hundreds of these big black crows, which are very common in Lafayette and Carencro, feeding on exposed garbage and dropping waste on the roofs of homes and hypodermic needles on my driveway. I even picked up an aborted fetus on my driveway that the birds had dropped. It was also bad when the hydrogen sulfite gases were being emitted and would envelop the house. There were times when you would think that something would explode. I was told to be careful and not to cut on the light switches at certain times of the day. We ran the air conditioner summer and winter, day and night, to try to keep the odors from coming in. After all of that, Dale Givens, who was head of the Louisiana DEQ, came to the house and told me my water well was contaminated from crawfish, not from the landfill.

They originally wanted six hundred acres of garbage in this landfill location—six hundred acres. We held them down to eighty-five acres. We took them to the courts, and we won every case up to the Supreme Court of Louisiana. And we have set a precedent case with this landfill site. When landfills are improperly operated, the taxpayers have a right to expect that their elected officials will do the right thing when they are doing things with taxpayers' money.

### *Afterword*
Clara and I have been threatened and we have been followed. I have been called emotional. But I will tell you—you are going to be emotional. If a mother does not stand up for the health and welfare of her family, there is no hope for families. There is nothing hysterical about it. It was a challenge to take on the city the size of Lafayette. It was a real challenge, but somebody had to do it.

Over that period of time I saw that this thing was going to be far greater than anybody could have ever imagined. And by beginning to look out for our families indirectly, it became an overview of all of the community. It's wrong for anybody to take advantage of minority, uneducated, and poor people. And that has happened all across Louisiana. They have located facilities in low-income areas where people are defenseless. They thought they could come in and subject people in this area to this and not have anybody oppose them. They didn't realize that we were here and we were educated people and, by God, we were going to defend ourselves.

# CLARA BAUDOIN

The next narrative is with Florence's friend, this woman we have already met, Clara Baudoin, of Carencro, Louisiana. Like Florence Gossen, she was a founding member of Save Our Homes and Land (SOHL). She helped revise the solid waste regulations for the state of Louisiana, and she was appointed to the Louisiana Resource Recovery Development Board, which approved all landfills in the state. She has held local and state offices for the League of Women Voters as a spokesperson on solid waste, oilfield waste, and injection wells. Clara served three terms in the Louisiana House of Representatives (1996–2008).

### Narrative from Clara Baudoin (b. Carencro, Louisiana, 1941)

Daddy was a farmer.[7] Mama was a housewife, and she helped him on the farm also. When she went in the field, I stayed home and did the housework and prepared lunch. They didn't have a watch with them, so I would put a white rag on the clothesline so they knew it was 12 noon. In the summer, when we were not in school, I picked cotton in the afternoon. I dug sweet potatoes, but not a whole lot because that was heavy work. We raised our chickens, beef, and pork. Dad raised the corn and we would take it to the mill and make our cornmeal and grits for the

Clara Baudoin

year. We had vegetables, fruit, and other things that were all home grown, and that is what the family survived on. He raised sugarcane and we made syrup. You made use of everything. The clothes were hand-me-downs. Mom sewed most of our clothes when we did get new clothes. Few things were purchased at the store. Nothing was wasted.

We had a cistern in the back of this house. It was a big hole, and the meat would be put in glass jars, tied at the end of a rope, and let down into that cool water. You milked the cows in the morning and in the afternoon. It was hard work, but I wouldn't trade those days for anything.

Schools were not as available as they are now. So you were fortunate to go to school. We didn't have a school bus. My dad didn't have one day of schooling, so he wanted us to get an education. He spoke only French. My mom had gone to school until the third grade. Both my parents were twelve in the family, so they had rough times. My grandparents' families came from Nova Scotia. They were deported, originally. We didn't hear many stories about their deportation because my parents didn't share them with us, but I think they went through tough times. This room [currently her legislative office] where we are sitting today is where my grandmother was in bed for ten years. My mother took care of her, raised a family, worked the field, and did all of the work in this house, maintaining the clothes and food. I spent a lot of time in here with my grandmother.

[Clara graduated from Scott High School and attended some college classes. She was married in 1957. She and her husband raised three children. In 1979, she heard that a municipal solid waste landfill was planned for her community. The issues surrounding it would soon change the course of Clara's life.]

Adjacent to my daddy's farm, and where we all lived because daddy had given us each an acre of land, the city of Lafayette purchased property for a municipal solid waste landfill. This was going to be a "state-of-the-art" facility, so we were given reassurances that we would not even know it was there.

Until this kind of thing affects you, you don't realize how important it is for you to be involved. I got extremely concerned about the groundwater because our water well, which was 110 feet, was the maximum depth of wells in that area. And these people [city employees] were digging big holes and putting garbage and everything in them. Common sense will tell you that anything that goes into a landfill will decay and form a fluid. I have now learned that the liquid is called leachate, and I was concerned that it would enter our groundwater—the water we had to drink.

It was not long after that when we found out that we had more fears than just the water, and we were going to have to tolerate a lot more than we ever thought about because the odor soon became unbearable. We were faced with flies, rodents, and stray dogs. But the thing that hurt me the most was seeing my mother having to live the way she had to live. She was no longer able to sit on her front porch because the odor and the flies were so bad. You couldn't mow the yard without having to swat the flies away. On certain days she actually got sick from the odors. A lot of families were sick. Animals died. It was a nightmare! We lived several years in the conditions that you would think would exist in a Third World country, and they were calling the facility a sanitary landfill.

Florence Gossen [see narrative before this one] and I ended up working together. Her daughter and some neighbors were hospitalized. But after her second trip to the hospital, she was told not to bring her daughter back home [adjacent to the landfill]. The doctor said, "I don't want to be treating your family for kidney or bladder cancer because of the water situation."

Several years later, I lost my brother-in-law to kidney cancer. After he was diagnosed, his son was diagnosed with kidney cancer. He was later diagnosed with thyroid cancer. My brother had a kidney removed. He has kidney cancer.

Florence and I joined the Sierra Club and the League of Women Voters and got involved in the community. I found out that this was a wonderful way to educate myself about what was going on and how to go about doing things. People are not aware of where their garbage goes. It goes away, so you don't think about it. But when you dig a hole in the ground and you put all of the garbage in it and it's not watched or regulated—and this site wasn't because there were drums of chemicals and other toxic things found in there—then the contamination will eventually get into the groundwater. In our case, we were concerned because the Chicot Aquifer serves not only our parish, but fourteen other parishes in southwest Louisiana.

At night Flo and I would attend public meetings and tell people about the landfill. We would talk on the telephone at all hours of the night trying to get our plans together. We also shared concerns about our safety because of a particular night at a meeting when one of the waste company guys said, "I would be careful on the way home if I were you-all."

After several years we were not able to get relief from anywhere and we ended up attending one final city council meeting where I again asked for assistance. There I was told that they were doing the best they could. But by then the community and that whole area of people were sick and scared. We had to do something.

When I left the meeting that night I cried. My husband was with me and I cried all the way home. I cried from being hurt, from being mad, but mostly from knowing they were telling me they were doing the best they could and we were faced with living the rest of our lives under those conditions. It shouldn't be allowed and it certainly needed to be stopped. You just do not do that to people. That night I decided I was going to do what I had to do. I was on a mission and somebody, somewhere, was going to listen. I had never seen the inside of a courtroom. I had never had an attorney, but I knew I needed to do something. I thought about it for two or three days. And then I walked into my boss's office and told him, "I need an attorney. I'm going to sue the city of Lafayette."

My husband, Joe, had been employed by the city for eighteen years, and I had relatives employed by the city, so it wasn't an easy decision. I feared for my husband's job. We had insurance and benefits put on the line. I prayed for courage and guidance. Joe was amazing, and I am grateful for that because without his support, it would not have worked. He learned to become a good cook because I spent a lot of nights, a lot of hours, and some traveling to fight this issue. And he was willing to let me drain our savings account since we did not make much money. And to do that with the possibility of not being able to put it back was a scary thing.

[Clara filed the suit and began the litigation process. The district court, court of appeals, and the Supreme Court all ruled in her favor, but the case dragged on. After eight years of work and mounting expenses, her perspective on the lawsuit shifted.]

When I first sued, it was not the money, but the frustration. All I wanted was for them to operate the facility properly. I wanted to make conditions better for the people who lived around the site. It would not have cost them anything but a little work and a little effort. But now it was eight years down the road and things were different and I was not going to back off. It had become much more expensive and a lot of things had developed, after so much time, and I was no longer willing to negotiate. I did not want a nickel more or a nickel less than what the judicial system had ordered. I had incurred a lot of additional expenses that I had no idea I would need—like experts. I spent everything in our savings account trying to get what was needed. You don't just file a lawsuit and go to court right away. We had quite a bit of time to worry and wait to see if Joe would get fired. But they never bothered him.

I quickly found out that the judgments against the city of Lafayette didn't mean a lot because you can't seize public property. We could not force the city to pay these judgments. My attorney said, "We need to meet with Governor Edwin Edwards to try to get the funds that go to the city of Lafayette frozen and put into escrow until the judgments are paid," since there was no need to go before the legislature if the governor was going to veto the matter. He [attorney] called me at work one day and said, "Meet me at the governor's mansion at 1:30 this afternoon." I have this problem when I get nervous. My hands get ice cold and sweaty and my heart goes racing. I was like, "OK, I have got to drive to Baton Rouge to the governor's mansion by myself." I didn't travel much growing up. And after I got married I didn't travel a whole lot either, so going to Baton Rouge was not something I was used to doing. And I am just a country girl, but by that time I had done a lot of things that I didn't really know how to, so I got in the car and drove to the governor's mansion. I will never forget—the governor sat there and he had blue jeans on. I had never met a governor, so that was quite an experience for me. And he agreed that he would not veto the legislation if it got to his desk. The legislation passed. The city of Lafayette would pay the judgments. The lawsuit was a nightmare for us, yet it was a tremendous experience. I was doing things that look like a dream today when you stop to look where I started and where I was going.

[Clara was now being urged to run for local office, but after her great disappointment in many of her elected officials, she declined—at first. In 1995, however, after a bit of coaxing from her colleagues, Clara decided to run for state representative.]

I had an opportunity and decided to run for state representative, once again not knowing what I was going to encounter. I had no idea how to run a campaign. But the very last day of qualifying, at 3:30 in the afternoon, this gentleman came to my office and said, "Clara, I understand they are trying to get you to run for state representative." He looked at me and he said, "All those things you have been working for all these years will never change unless you are willing to take a chance by offering yourself to be a public servant." My boss's office was down the hall. He had heard the conversation and came to my door and said, "Clara, get your purse. You are going to go qualify and you are going to run. I will drop you off at the courthouse." I looked at him, picked up my purse, and went.

That weekend I started knocking on doors and handing out my homemade fliers. I didn't have many hours to campaign because I was working until five every day. The first contribution that I received was $5 from a lady that really couldn't afford it. And those kinds of contributions is what really said to me that I was doing the right thing. I ended up winning the election in 1995, spending under $10,000 dollars. People can't believe that.

### Afterword

A city council member once called me and Florence Gossen two country goats. But I felt like he had not yet seen the work that two goats could do—but he was fixing to experience it. It hurt me, but I think those kinds of comments give you the courage and ability to be more determined to make things happen. We used to have landfills everywhere, and now we have a limited number. I think the lawsuit directed the state of Louisiana toward shutting down a lot of landfills. The first city to recycle in Louisiana was the city of Lafayette, and that started because of this landfill issue. A lot of people would talk to me and tell me, "You can't beat city hall." But I said, "Well, maybe you can't, but I will find out." And I learned, of course, that not only can you fight the battle—you can win the war. You can beat city hall.

# LIZ AVANTS

Before someone like Clara Baudoin came to office, politicians often stood in the way of these women's efforts to fight environmental pollution. They saw a laissez-faire approach to regulating the activities of major industrial companies as good for the state. The next women to speak recall both a childhood and an adulthood influenced by this attitude. Liz Avants and cousin Les Ann Kirkland (next in this chapter) founded the environmental group Alliance against Waste and Action to Restore the Environment (AWARE).

### Narrative from Liz Avants (b. Brulie, Louisiana, 1950)

When I was an infant, we moved to [the city of] Plaquemine, where my relatives lived.[8] That is where I spent all of my growing-up years. I can remember going to my grandparents' on Sundays on a two-lane highway. There were big, beautiful oak trees on either side of the road and sugarcane fields beyond that.

Dow located here in 1956, when I was a child. When they came in, it prompted other industries to locate in our area. Industry was already in Baton Rouge with the Esso Standard Oil Refinery, and Dow got cranked up in 1958. The reason they came here was because they had access to the river, with barge transportation and rail transportation, and the other lagniappe that came with the state of Louisiana in the way of tax exemptions.

I graduated in 1968 from Saint John High School. In the years that I was going to school there, especially in middle school and upper elementary, there was a

Liz Avants

third floor to the school building, and from there we could see plumes and plumes of smoke coming from Dow Chemical every day. It was like burning waste, and not just plumes from the stacks. It was kind of like I never really thought about it [being harmful].

After I graduated, I went to Baton Rouge Vocational Technical School for a year. I took a secretarial course and then worked in the office for seven years. While I was at the trade school I married Rusty Avants. We had five children.

In the 1980s, the Community Alert Network, the CAN system, came on line, and they used to tell us to "cocoon," which was the thing then. If you heard the sirens, you needed to go into your home and shut off the heat and cooling system and close your windows. Sometimes it meant putting rags under the doors and in the windows because we have many people that have cracks in their floors and windowpanes missing. I mean that was a really scary thing. I guess if you really thought about it, nobody would live here, because at any second of any day we could have an accident like Bhopal, India. So I tell people that God has been really good to us. I mean, if you want to look at the reality of it—that is the reality.

I kind of got involved in the environmental movement but not by a conscious decision because I was really busy raising my family. My husband left when my youngest child was not quite two weeks old. It was all I could do to continue maintaining a full-time job and keeping up with my kids and just the regular routine of living every day.

In January 1986, it was in the newspaper that the EPA was conducting a public hearing and taking comments on a feasibility study as to how to clean up the CLAW site (Clean Land, Air, and Water). The site was located in Bayou Sorrel, which is about thirty miles from where I live. It was shut down and became a Superfund site because in 1978 an eighteen-year-old young man dropped dead at a waste [hazardous] pit. He was hauling waste and when he opened the valve on the truck to let the waste loose in this open pit, with the combination of the toxins, he just dropped dead right there.

I heard about this and I said, "Let me go see what is going on." I went to the meeting and I took two or three of my kids with me. I was amazed at the people from Bayou Sorrel who came and who had gone to so much effort to see about getting this site cleaned up.

At the hearing the engineering firm and the EPA were proposing a solution that the people really didn't like. They proposed to dig the waste up and install geothermal liners, which were plastic. They would then put the chemicals back in, cover it [pit] with an eighteen-inch clay cap, and monitor the site for thirty years. And that would be the end of it. But that was not a viable solution; at least that is what the people thought.

I met Willie Fontenot from the Attorney General's Office in Baton Rouge at this meeting, and Les Ann Kirkland [also in this book], a distant cousin of mine, was also there. The EPA meeting was in January 1986, and then in March of 1986 Dow proposed to do a commercial incineration at their site. So Les Ann drags me off to Willie's office one afternoon [to discuss the proposal] and he was saying, "You all really need to start a group and Louisiana Environmental Action Network (LEAN) is forming and you need to come to the conference." We went to the conference and started our own [environmental] group Alliance against Waste and Action to Restore the Environment (AWARE).

So anyway, we come back home and we were fighting DOW, who wanted a commercial incinerator. Dow had done what Dow wanted all along. From 1956 to 1986, thirty years, they had no opposition or negative publicity. If they had a little spill, a little fire, a little problem, it made a little news, but it was not a big deal. Some folks worked out there, so it was like everything was hunky dory. We knew a little bit about the Rollins incinerator, in North Baton Rouge, and that was not the way we wanted to go. We had had enough of the production of toxic chemicals. Then all of a sudden we said, "No! Commercial incineration is not the way to go. You already have two incinerators out there and that is not what we want for our community." And when we said that—they backed off.

In 1987 or 1988, they came out with the Toxic Release Inventory [TRI] program that forced industries to quantify all 313 chemicals. Well, actually it was 100 of the worst of the worst. Then it kind of expanded—since there is something like

80,000 chemicals out there. So this is what is required by the TRI. You have to say what your inventory is and how much you are releasing of these specific chemicals. However, there is no means to gather that data in accumulation—and how it mixes together like a toxic soup. It is measured chemical for chemical. And when you read those numbers from 1987, you'll see major, major reductions. But if you think back before the TRI, what Dow was spewing out all those years hadn't been monitored, and we were not even talking about Esso or Exxon, or Standard Oil in North Baton Rouge, in operation since the 1930s and 1940s. And so Dow was not monitored or required to report what they were releasing for a lot of years. This is where their minds were: "The people do not want to look at this, so we are going to build a levee around the site and they really will not see what is going on." God! How was that going to contain the poisons that might come out of these things? What is that going to do in a worst-case scenario?

I would go almost every Saturday and do a little bit of homework. Those records of emissions and other data related to Dow and others were in our local library. If there were a particular permit for a public comment period that I needed to be doing research on, I would do that. At other times I would be looking at what was there to see if I had missed anything and how I could pull future data. The information on the library shelves went back to the early 1980s.

Well, it was the end of July and I went to the library to look things up and they had moved the files. The assistant librarian told me the EPA took the data. But I said, "Most of the data was not EPA, it was DEQ data." And so he replied, "That's probably who it was then." I was so ticked because all they left was a tiny bit of data, which was up for public comments right then. I had used the public records for hearings related to a number of issues. Now we don't have any of those documents.

I tried calling Dale Givens at the DEQ, but there was no listing for him. I tried to call three other people because I was so infuriated, but I couldn't reach anyone. And the library's reasoning for them taking the material was to make space in the library. Finally, I was able to contact the DEQ, and a spokesperson said, "It just got disposed of." They did send me an inventory—four single-spaced pages identifying volumes of information that were gone.

## *Afterword*

I learned that the Freedom of Information Act, that the information is not really free. After one public comment period, I wrote for a copy of the transcript, and I will never forget that. They sent it and told me that I owed them twenty-five dollars. I was floored. I was fortunate that I could pay, but it really opened my eyes to the extremes you have to go to get information and how inaccessible it really is.

# LES ANN KIRKLAND

Les Ann Kirkland, of the city of Plaquemine, Louisiana, joined her friend and distant cousin Liz Avants to start the environmental group Alliance against Waste and Action to Restore the Environment (AWARE). The group was formed in 1986, when Dow Chemical applied for a permit to operate a commercial hazardous waste incinerator in their community. Les Ann was a founding officer of Louisiana Environmental Action Network (LEAN) and served as secretary for the organization's first two years. In the late 1980s Les Ann traveled extensively as an environmental ambassador.

### Narrative from Les Ann Kirkland (b. Baton Rouge, Louisiana, 1954)

My dad's first job was as a projectionist at a movie theater.[9] His skills and interests are varied. The majority of his work experience, twenty years, was spent at Dow. My mother was a legal secretary and a social worker. She makes bridal veils and is a wedding coordinator in her retirement. They raised four children.

I attended Saint John the Evangelist Catholic School in Plaquemine, Louisiana. I wanted an education with a little more diversity and something more connected to the real world than what I was learning. I didn't want to go to college. And it seemed like the things that I wanted to do weren't the things you could make a living at, like art and photography. In school I hated science and I hated debate and I hated chemistry. And when I landed in the environmental movement, what did I need? All of the things that I had avoided.

Paradichlorobenzene was the first chemical that I learned about. That's the chemical used in mothballs, which is an insecticide. I immediately looked it up after I started doing environmental work to see what it was.

I didn't do this alone. My friend and distant cousin Liz Avants—we did this together. We had lived next door to each other when we were little and our families were friends. She is as strong and as stubborn as I am. Faith is what motivated us. We somehow wound up at a hearing in Plaquemine, Louisiana, only the first or second hearing we had been to, and Linda King [also featured in this book] and Jerry Speir were there. They came over to talk about this permitting process and they were against it. They said, "We are going to have a big meeting and we want y'all to come." And I'm thinking—you mean there are others? So we went to this meeting, which was to become the organization LEAN. Liz and I were so excited. Here are all of these people interested in the environment. You think it's just you and then there you are in a room with all of these people and they feel the same way you do.

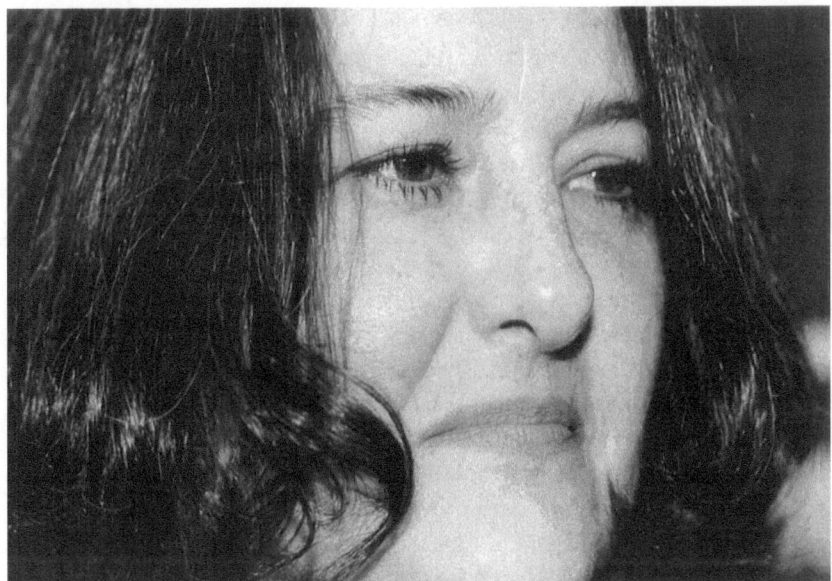

Les Ann Kirkland

Two days after the LEAN conference Elizabeth and I started an environmental group called AWARE, which means Alliance against Waste and Action to Restore the Environment. AWARE was LEAN's first baby. When we first started we had nine petrochemical plants on our side of the river and eighteen on the other side. Iberville Parish is split by the river, so that was one of our first decisions, whether we were going to cover both sides of the river. And we decided to do that, of course.

[In March 1986, DOW Chemical applied for a permit to incinerate commercial hazardous waste.]

At the time, Louisiana was making 25 percent of the nation's chemicals. Therefore, we were disposing of 25 percent of the waste, and they wanted to get a permit to commercially incinerate waste, which meant that it could also come in [from out of state] by ship, by rail, by barge, and by truck. And that was what made us come out of the closet, so to speak.

I'm not a hysterical housewife, a kook, or a wacko. But it's just all so basic for me. It's about common sense. If you are going to make a known carcinogen and you can't contain your process, then it's like taking a gun and shooting into a crowd—and that's how they operate every day. They can't keep the carcinogens inside the fence line—they are out in my air—and no, I don't accept that. But, I tell you what, when you stand up in front of a room the first time and you're on the record, your name, your address, and you're at the mike, and there's a bunch of industry guys in dark suits and with briefcases—it's like presenting yourself to take a bullet. To actually go on record and say this is what you believe and to know that you may be hurt is a very hard thing to do. I mean, my teeth were chattering. And that is so unlike me. But you have to risk it. The directives are very clear in any historical religious work. We are supposed to be stewards of the Earth. This is about stewardship and kindness—the opposite of greed. The commercial incinerator project was defeated. That was unbelievable. God gave us that victory early on to hook us into this, you know.

One of the first fights that we got into was in Saint Gabriel. Some guy wanted to take part of the Spanish Lake Bluff swamp and put a dump there. So we put fliers in everybody's mailboxes. We didn't know that was against the law. And so all kinds of people went to the meeting. I accidentally met Kay Gaudet [also featured in this book]. I went to her drugstore and told her who I was and that I wanted to put a sign on her door about the landfill in the swamp. She said OK because she already knew about the proposal and was against it. We forged a great alliance with Kay and her husband. It was very rewarding to beat that issue.

In the middle of this Kay's sister came up to me and said, "You know, I and ten of my friends were pregnant at the same time and eight of us miscarried, there was one stillbirth, and one live birth. Do you think that's important?" Well, I was about to cry. And so we got together and Richard Miller suggested that I look up the stats on miscarriages nationally. Well, the rate for Saint Gabriel was extremely high. And so we incorporated it into a press conference with the Sierra Club. We delivered it up at the capitol and brought these figures. Our part of it was very short, but it hit big. Immediately after that I was on my way to Germany [to testify for the Green Party]. And in New York a national TV crew asked me about it. At the same time, the attorney general's office was responding to Kay and it went from there. The next thing you know, Oprah Winfrey called Kay.

Initially, people in the community were very happy we were involved. We had five police jurors at our first meeting. However, when they found out that we were more than fluff and we were talking about making real changes, they didn't like us anymore. There's always a mixed reaction. We don't really have a whole lot of people who will come forward in public and support us. It's a little by little kind of thing. What this is about is giving people information other than the sole source programming they have been used to getting from industry. And you have to make them understand that they can understand. Industry is throwing all of this mumbo jumbo at them. Well, all of that can be distilled into something understandable.

Vinyl chloride is used to make plastic. We make a lot of vinyl chloride in Plaquemine, and it causes a rare liver disease called angiosarcoma. It targets the brain, liver, lungs, lymphatic systems, and causes mutations and reproductive problems. We make more of that in this part of the country than anywhere else. When we first started the group, Dow was making seven of the eleven carcinogens produced in the state.

It touches me when I see another picture of a child on a jar, sitting on a countertop in a convenience store, and he's got cancer and his parents can't afford it. I'm tired of that. They're everywhere. They're all over Plaquemine. And now people are trying to deal with that by trying to fund Saint Jude's. So what do you want to do? Do you want to get cancer and try to get over it, or do you want to not get cancer—period? The money needs to go to the source of the problem.

Our state representative had been sent to prison, for what I don't know, but a year of his term hadn't expired yet. So Willie Fontenot or Darryl Malek-Wiley pops up and says, "Why don't we run Les Ann?" And the next morning that campaign was rolling, and so I ran for state representative. It was an eye-opening experience, and I was realistic about the outcome. I was going to have to make speeches, and, therefore, people were going to become educated about our environmental situation. And for the seven other guys running, they had to get their own environmental platform, which was non-existent. It was a real eye-opener for the public. The guy who won eventually spent so much money. Somebody did some numbers and discovered he spent about sixty dollars per vote, not buying votes, but this was spent on his advertising and all of the other stuff. On the other hand, I spent three dollars.

When people are threatened, that's when they pull together and get to know one another, forging alliances that they never would have forged in the first place. The environmental movement does that. It pulls people together who wouldn't normally have been together, and it makes people see their similarities. There's sort of a distillation process that goes on when they reconsider what is really important.

When I first did environmental work it was every day, all day. It was into the night until they turned the lights off. There were phone calls from all over the country because the environment was hot then. I was on a circuit and I was doing conferences and speaking. We had pieces on National Public Radio and other national media. You think you're going to put one little toe in the water, but you're sucked into the swirling vortex. It takes everything out of you. It ruins you financially. It puts lines on your face. But it's worth it no matter what.

## *Afterword*

Those pictures you see of Earth from space are when it really hits you. What a wonderful creation this is. Earth is like a little blue pearl out there, and I think people are destroying it. I think there are untold mysteries and miracles that we have already destroyed without even knowing them. I love life. I don't care what it brings, how hard it is, how desperately poor I am, how bad I feel, how tired I am; I don't care. I love it. It's a gift and I want to hang out here as long as I can. And when I go, I will never be on my deathbed wondering if I could have made a difference. Sometimes a campaign is successful, sometimes not. For me, victory is in the effort.

## MARY TUTWILER

Calling herself a child of the 1960s for whom social issues were always important, Mary Tutwiler, of New Iberia, Louisiana, received a BA in classical studies, Greek and Roman civilization, from Barnard College. No one was likely to call Mary, the youngest woman featured in this chapter, a country goat, although people found other ways to demean her efforts. A young mother with an eighteen-month-old child on her hip, she was labeled a "meddlesome housewife" when she joined and eventually led the environmental group War on Waste (WOW). The group organized in 1987 to oppose a proposed residential and commercial solid waste landfill from being built in Cade, Louisiana. She now runs a restaurant and resides in Lafayette, Louisiana.

### Narrative from Mary Tutwiler (b. New Orleans, Louisiana, 1955)

My father's family was in the bakery supply business for generations.[10] He did that until he retired. Following that he opened a photography business. When I was growing up, my mother was a housewife and raised three children. Once we all left, she went to work as an archivist at the Historic New Orleans Collection, after that at Touro Infirmary, where she set up the hospital's archives. At eighty, she's New Orleans' authority on Jewish history. I learned to love nature at a very young age, and that's always been a driving influence in my life. I was the poetry editor of the high school magazine, and I liked to write. I liked English, history, art, and the humanities. I found, though, that the tools that I need most today are the things that I really didn't like in high school. I fell in love with my high school English teacher when I was a freshman in high school. Everybody teased me about it for years. I married him a week after I graduated from college in 1977. Our first child was born in 1980.

I went to Windham College in Vermont for two years before I ended up at Barnard. I have a BA from Barnard College in classical studies, Greek and Roman civilization. We moved to Sewanee, Tennessee, where my husband taught school at Saint Andrews [Episcopal School]. We loved living in the woods there. We loved all the aspects of nature. Every afternoon when he got off school, he'd go out hiking or camping with the kids from school and I'd go with him. After two years I realized that I could not live without crawfish, oysters, shrimp, and crabs any longer. So we had to come back to Louisiana.

I am a child of the 1960s, and so social issues were always really important to me, and there's never been a time when they weren't. In the 1970s I was marching

Mary Tutwiler

for anything that there was to march for. In the 1980s, I was raising children and working part time. It was kind of a peaceful time in this country, so I wasn't doing anything active in the 1980s until the landfill issue. I was home with my third baby on my hip. She was eighteen months old when it was announced that Waste Management had decided to site a landfill about a mile and a half from the school.

[Mary was a volunteer at the Episcopal School of Acadiana (ESA), where her husband also taught. The ESA faculty members founded the environmental group War on Waste in 1987. Mary quickly realized the full extent of the landfill problem, particularly given its proximity to the school.]

The head of the school was involved and most of the parents. People at the school were concerned about it mostly because of property values in the community. The more I listened, the more I realized that this was much bigger than real estate problems. This was about the community where the landfill was going to be located, which was Cade. It's a small town between Lafayette and New Iberia, Louisiana. And it was about drinking water. The Chicot Aquifer is the drinking water for all of southwest Louisiana, and that was going to impact the aquifer not only for the local community, but for everyone around it. The more I learned, the more horrified I became and the more involved I became—because I had the time. I was being a mom and I was home. I took on more and more responsibilities of the organization until all of a sudden I found myself in charge of it.

The site was for four hundred acres, and the roads around that area are all two-lane highways and the school buses run on those highways. People were concerned about a lot of garbage trucks on the road. And then we realized that the proposed facility was large enough to import garbage from other states. There's also a railway line that runs parallel to the highway, which would have been the main entrance to the garbage dump, and we realized that this wasn't just about Cade, and it wasn't just about New Iberia, Lafayette, and Saint Martinville. It was about Waste Management, a multinational corporation finding new sites for garbage.

I had to start learning science and hydrology. Basically, landfill technology, these days, is you dig a big hole and you line it with something, either clay or a plastic liner, and then you put garbage in it. And garbage, when it gets rained on, begins to produce a liquid called leachate. The basic design is like a big dish with a plastic liner down in the ground, but because the hole would have been thirty-one feet deep and the upper sands of the aquifer were twenty-eight feet deep, you had this bowl of garbage floating in the upper sands of the aquifer.

So there was an immediate concern for the neighbors and then for the water wells of the outlying communities. Their wells are deeper, but when you pump water it pulls; it pulls horizontally. This is part of the hydrology lesson. You get what is called a cone of influence, or how much is pulled into a certain well. We were concerned that the more the well was pumped, the quicker any leak from the landfill would begin to permeate the water tables. Also, the aquifer flows in a direction—it flows a little bit to the south and to the west—so communities that weren't that close might also have been affected. This is where our drinking water comes from. Our only other source of drinking water would be the bayou.

Wilma Subra [also featured in this book] was our technical advisor. She taught me how to read permits, and then the more we read the more flaws we found. The biggest one obviously was this ridiculous notion of putting the garbage into the aquifer. We couldn't believe that the DEQ would accept this kind of proposal.

We have the honor of having the largest and longest public hearing of DEQ's history. It started at six o'clock one night and went on until five o'clock the next morning. We stayed all night because there were so many people who wanted to tell DEQ how the landfill was going to affect them. We had at least five hundred people. Well, the permit was granted anyway under such political circumstances that not only were we angry and upset, we were very suspicious. We had requested that the permit not be granted. It was granted the day Governor Buddy Roemer handed over the governorship of the state of Louisiana to Edwin Edwards.

The first thing I did was burst into tears. The second thing I did was call up Wilma Subra, who patted me on the back and then said, "OK now, put on some lipstick, go call the television crew, and tell them what you're going to do." And so we did. We immediately announced it. Actually, as the news of the permit being granted was hitting the airwaves—we beat them to the punch, saying, "OK, we will sue the DEQ and the state of Louisiana." So we had to file a lawsuit, and meanwhile we were still working on our local politicians, who didn't quite know which way the wind was blowing yet, and some of them were [on our side] because Saint Martin Parish was always in favor of fighting the landfill. They understood, but we had to talk to a lot of political jurisdictions over the course of the next couple of years because people just didn't want to fight with the state and fight with DEQ and fight with the Edwards administration.

We had a wonderful attorney, Bob Boese, who took the case on pro bono partly because he lives in the area and he understood the impact of what would happen to his home. What was happening was the state was just issuing permits, and they had no real, and to this day don't have any real regulations for things like landfills. And so Bob, who loves law and also who loves policy, wanted to create a decision that would help influence policy for the future of Louisiana.

The first part of the lawsuit we won right after Thanksgiving. The First Circuit Court of Appeals overturned the permit on the grounds that the landfill was in the Chicot Aquifer and would harm our drinking water. The legal precedent was a case called the IT decision [*Save Ourselves v. Louisiana Environmental Control Commission*], which basically meant the DEQ needs to act as a protector of the environment rather than an empire.[11] Just seeing that a permit meets the regulations is not good enough.

We won and we all celebrated on the landfill site. We were trespassing just a little bit with a big bottle of champagne. It was a big win, and then Waste Management appealed and it went to the state supreme court, and we won at that level also.

Governor Buddy Roemer was my favorite governor because he put Paul Templet as the head of the DEQ, and Paul is an environmental scientist who cared about the state and worked in every way possible to get this state to be proactive environmentally. And I don't know what kind of hell that man went through. It must have been terrible for him to have so many other organizations, like the chemical organizations, and the oil and gas people fighting him every step of the way.

Edwin Edwards obviously would be on my list of least favorite governors because you couldn't work under him. You couldn't get a regulation in place; politically, he undermined all the regulations, all of the work we would do in the legislature. The DEQ couldn't do its job because of the cronyism that was going on. No matter what the DEQ wanted to do right, Edwards would pick up the telephone and undo a whole permitting process because that's the way he did business in Louisiana.

## *Afterword*

My husband—I cannot tell you how many nights I was in meetings being "meddlesome." The first thing I was called was a "meddlesome housewife," and he was home feeding babies and putting them to bed. They were well taken care of and loved by their father. No one could threaten us financially because my husband worked for the school and the school was the source of the fight. That took a huge amount of pressure off of me because it wasn't like I had people in the community saying you're going to get fired or your husband's going to get fired, which is a terrible threat that happens to lots of people that get involved in these fights.

When I hear what I've preached coming from the mouths of my children, I know they learned it. They understand and respect me for doing what I do. I've had all of them at times say, "I wish you were a regular mom. I wish you brought cookies to school and stuff like that." I'm not very good at doing that. But over the years they've gotten older and set foot out into the world a little bit, and they've come back to me and said, "Mom, I'm really glad that you are the person you are, that you do what you do, and I'm glad you're not a regular mom." And man, that will keep me going every day.

Chapter Six

# "WHEN SOMETHING IS NOT RIGHT, YOU HAVE TO DO SOMETHING ABOUT IT"
## *Career Activists Build Bridges*

*Perhaps unwittingly, some politicians also contributed to the cultural mindset that enabled industry to take advantage of workers and wreak havoc on the state's environment. Former Governor Edwin Edwards, for example, once dismissed environmental activists' concerns about the alarming number of health problems in the state by attributing them to Louisiana's famously well-seasoned cuisine.*

In this chapter, we hear from five women who made careers in environmental activism. Time and time again, these professionals energized a grassroots group's flagging efforts by providing technical information, guidance on strategy, and moral support. In so doing, each of the women made a unique contribution to Louisiana's environmental movement.

Perhaps more than any other state in the country, Louisiana needed the knowledge, insight, and conviction these five women had to offer. Torn apart by the false dichotomy of economics versus clean air, land, and water, Louisiana had become a place where industry could exploit the state's rich natural resources and its residents' need for jobs. Opportunistic companies eager to locate where they could maximize their profits with little interference from individuals and government often took advantage of Louisiana's high level of unemployment and lax environmental policies. In noticing such inequities or even in coming face to face with health problems around them, the women activists here describe using their expertise in science, social work, and community organization to build bridges among groups of people with seemingly disparate interests.

As they themselves note, however, success has depended on the efforts of many people whose names may never be known. Their narratives thus underscore another common theme to the whole of the book: people need to work together at all levels to sustain the environment. The bridges these women have built will remain standing only as long as we all honor our connections to each other and to the natural world.

# SISTER HELEN VINTON

In 1980, Sister Helen Vinton came to work in New Iberia for the Southern Mutual Help Association (founded in 1969, SMHA), a nonprofit organization dedicated to creating viable, healthy, rural communities through affordable home ownership for some of Louisiana's poorest families, as well as comprehensive sustainable economic development for farmers and fishers. She and her friend Lorna Bourg (also featured in this chapter) worked together for SMHA on pesticide safety issues in south Louisiana. In the late 1980s, Sister Helen served on commissioner Bob Odom's Department of Agriculture Environmental Pesticide Committee. She received the Mother Theodore Guerin Medallion from her alma mater, Saint Mary-of-the-Woods, and is president of the Rural Advancement Foundation International USA. Her comments also contribute to the consideration of gender in the environmental movement. SMHA has always had an interest in women workers, for example, publishing, in 1984, *Plantation Portraits: Women of the Louisiana Cane Fields.*

### Narrative from Sister Helen Vinton (b. Gordon, Nebraska, 1932)

My parents were cattle ranchers all their lives, on our ranch on the Snake River.[1] There are many kinds of fruits that grew there: plums, currants, blackberries, and grapes. I would pick those in the summer and help with the canning. We had horses to ride and to work in the field. We had tomatoes, radishes, onions, peppers, carrots, turnips, and cabbage. We would pick wild asparagus. My grandfather was a beekeeper, so we had our own honey, and we butchered our own meat. It was beef, and occasionally we'd grow one little pig to be our pork. I attribute my good health to the fact that I had such good food. We had good well water from the Ogallala Aquifer.

I was born right after the Depression. I was delivered by a midwife because my parents couldn't afford a hospital. We didn't have electricity for many years until the electric company came through. We were poor, but you wouldn't know we were because we had good food, clean water and air, and we worked hard and had fun. I think the most important thing that I learned from my family was to be generous of the heart, and that if anything is worthwhile, you will find it to be hard sometimes.

I went to a one-room country school. There were only about eight children and probably eight grades. I graduated from a Catholic high school and then went to Saint Mary-of-the-Woods College in Indiana. I had some remarkable teachers in Winona, Minnesota, where I got my master's degree in science and biology. It was a Catholic college and there was a Brother Severin, who immersed me in what I liked most—and that was environmental stuff. Not only the problems with the environ-

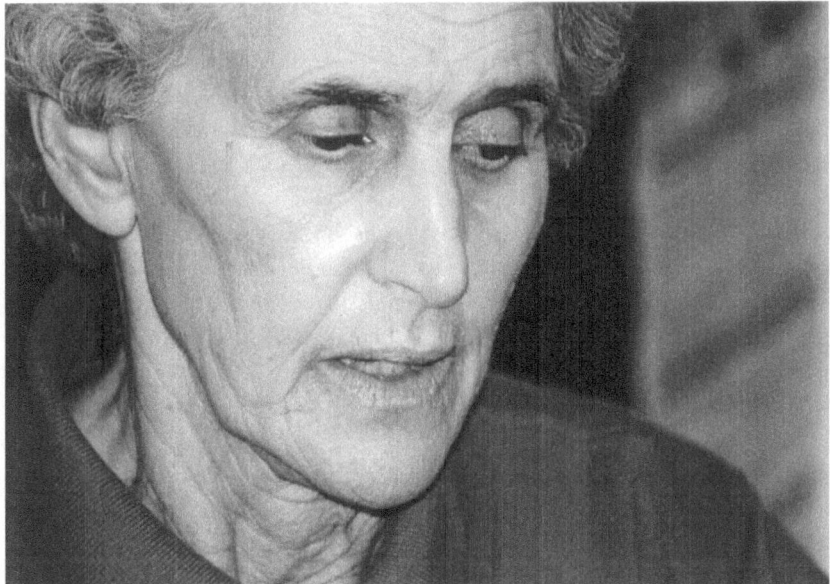

Sister Helen Vinton

ment, but what the relationships are in a good community: a plant community, an animal community, and a human community. That lesson has stayed with me because I see communities as how relationships are right among people, and people with the Earth and with those things that grow from the Earth, how we care for them and relate to them. It's more than just having grass and trees. It's how we are rooted in that Earth. I always think of the seven generations in Native American theology and culture. [Some Native American traditions hold that leaders must make their decisions with the welfare of seven future generations in mind.]

[Helen moved to Louisiana after meeting Sister Anne Bizalion of Southern Mutual Help Association at a gathering for the pope outside of Des Moines.]

Just before I came to SMHA in 1980, the *Sixty Minute* piece had aired with Morley Safer and it was a pretty tough piece about the sugarcane farmers. So when I came here, I realized that I would be with a group where they weren't afraid to take stands. And while I have never really been afraid of taking stands, you had to know which side you were on. Still, the more controversial issues of taking a stand on poverty, where you have class and racial and gender division, it shows up more in the South than it does in the North. So I realized that when I got here and stayed for three months. It was a great learning time and I'm still learning.

The purpose of Southern Mutual has always been the same: to help build healthy, strong communities that can become prosperous, especially with women and people of color. In fact, women's leadership is a priority. We have always had women as leaders of this organization. I think we see things with a perspective quite different from men's, especially in the way of business. As I have been here these twenty years, I've noticed that when things are not right it's the women that come forward. It's the women that come forward when there's illness and sickness in their families. So they'll come and put their hand to the hammer to do whatever it is that needs to be done.

But I think that sometimes we can upset people, so they won't listen to us because we don't have all the facts from where they're coming from. I have seen, for example, in farming, the environmental community separated from the so-called agriculture community because the environmental people saw the farmers as those guys that have a lot of money and who are polluting the bayous and fouling the air with their sprays, and indeed they have. But not to know where the farmers are coming from is a big mistake because the only way we have made any progress with farmers has been finding those with good hearts, as far as listening to concerns, and then working with them. And we have done that consistently, since about 1990, when the fish kills took place in Louisiana.

I was on the Pesticide Commission at the time of the fish kills and had been appointed, quite unwittingly, by our commissioner of agriculture, Bob Odom. He had not known that he appointed someone from Southern Mutual Help, known to be tough on issues. In fact, years before, we had stood up against Silvex or 2-4-5-T being sprayed on sugarcane. It has the worst dioxin in it that there is—the same dioxin that was in Agent Orange. And we had really done everything possible to get that stopped in this state. But he didn't know me from that. I was just Helen Vinton that worked at Southern Mutual Help, and, by the way, I was a nun—so I must be harmless.

[In the early 1990s, fifteen parishes were affected by aerial spraying of the pesticide azinphosmethyl, commonly known as nerve gas. The summer rains washed the chemical off the crops and into streams and rivers, causing massive fish kills.]

About 1990, all those fish kills occurred, and that really pulled the media and the environmental people out of the woodwork, and it was an opportunity to say that this is something that shouldn't be happening. And I knew that because I have an agricultural background, and I knew there had to be alternatives to the way farming was done here and still is, to a large extent. And I knew that there were ways not to be putting that much money into an acre of sugarcane and then having it all wash out. I mean, just looking at it in hard-core terms, it was a waste. Aerial spraying—where the spray drifts for fifty miles—that's foolish. So it was easy to say there are alternatives.

And then sports fishers came out and said stop, and commercial fishers came out and said stop. So that's how I got the attention of the farmers because I have an agriculture and biology background. So the TV stations and media kept picking me up, which was a great favor, of course, to the whole cause. And the message I kept giving was "There are alternatives."

Farmers started coming into our office and saying, "If you know these alternatives then tell us." Some of them were challenging, and others were sincerely saying we don't want to do this. We don't like spending this money. We don't like having plants and animals and people sprayed. By the way, there had been people seriously sprayed with azinphosmethyl. So just like it killed the fish—they go belly up and they are done—that's what it does to people. And as you drive around you will see homes all in among the cane fields.

So that was what brought us to build bridges with some of the farmers. There is a core of them trying to do something different, and they have influenced a lot of others. Not enough, however, because there are six hundred thousand acres of sugarcane in this state. I think a small crew of them has learned that these chemicals can be replaced organically. While not entirely organically, they can replace a lot of the spraying by rebuilding their soil, which since World War II has been steadily going chemically toxic. So some of them began detoxing their farmland, in a sense, and trying to rebuild organic matter in the soil. A lot of others are using some of the tips they've learned from more sustainable farmers. I don't know that any farm is yet—but they are moving towards sustainability, which means over the long term you will be able to have a profit and also be environmentally friendly in your community.

[To inform farmers about alternative options for pest control, Helen and SMHA held meetings to discuss sustainable agriculture. She invited environmentalists, organic food farmers, consumers of organic produce, and the chemically ill—people who were sick from exposure to pesticides and other toxins.]

We had our first Sustainable Agriculture Working Group conference in New Iberia [in 1990]. At that conference a lot of farmers came. Why? Because they were so defensive. They knew that sustainable agriculture was about chemical-free farming, keeping people from being contaminated, and keeping our food system healthy. They came to see what we were saying about them. But when they turn their faces and are simply not listening, I don't think you can spend the time to try to change them. There isn't enough time to get Louisiana's water clean and clean up toxic places where people's lives are at stake—where companies are not being responsible. Then I think there has to be confrontation and regulations that make them at least do minimal amounts so that people can live and have some quality of life.

[Southern Mutual Help Association advocated that buffer zones be established around area hospitals, schools, and homes to protect children and families from aerial pesticide application.]

It is necessary and was necessary because our fields, where spraying takes place in lots of cases and where fields are burned during harvest time, are right next to hospitals. They're right next to where people live. They're next to schools. A minimal buffer zone will enable children and people in hospitals and living in houses near the fields to have a chance to at least get away from those things that are shutting down their respiratory systems. I mean, some [people] are very allergic to all these things.

So we kept lobbying for it with the Louisiana Commission on Pesticides. I didn't do that single handedly nor did Southern Mutual. A lot of people did this. The initiation of all the regulations and their enforcement began in those early 1990s, when the fish kills took place, because at those commission meetings we had a lot of interest not only from aerial applicators and from farmers who were there to defend what they were doing, but also from citizens who were impacted. And so buffer zones came out of that. Regulations that were already on the state books, in the state law, began to have to be enforced. And the EPA in Dallas stood behind that [enforcement] because I think a team of us really influenced the EPA to get serious about these problems in Louisiana.

I see so much here in Louisiana that's rich and wonderful. And then we have intruders with chemicals coming here and dumping their garbage and toxins. I'm sure the political system has been at a great fault and that we've traded our resources for money. I see this in what's happening along the river parishes, and now it's a given that your water isn't good, and it's a given that your air isn't good.

Politics have not been about the business of an economy based on a good environment. It has been based on the profit that people can make from our resources. Certainly, the end result of trading off your resources is poverty—poverty in every way—poverty of spirit and poverty of money. It has been poverty of health, less quality of life, and no quality of life for a lot of people. Companies should pay royally to come and locate in a community. They should have to clean up as they go along. Instead we give away our most precious assets and let them come and extract from us something that can never be replaced.

## *Afterword*

I don't see myself as an environmental activist, but maybe that's the way it seems. I see a person who wants to build good communities, have right relationships, and who will stand up for whatever has to be done. And if that involves getting pesticide spraying stopped, I will do it. And maybe I don't see myself as an activist so much because I've always thought of us as belonging to the same family. And I know that sounds idealistic, but I believe that, and so there have to be a lot of bridges built to those people who are, through ignorance and greed, spoiling our place here in Louisiana. I don't want to compromise those things that made a good community, right relationships among people and all of life. I won't compromise that. I will do all I can to build bridges where possible and to find how we can influence them in the right way.

# LORNA BOURG

Like Helen Vinton, Lorna Bourg works for the Southern Mutual Help Association in New Iberia, Louisiana. Now the executive director of SMHA, Lorna became involved with the environmental movement because of her concern for the many impoverished Louisiana residents who were suffering from the effects of pesticides. But taking care of the environment means taking care of everyone, regardless of their economic situation. She pointed out, "The bottom line is the stuff that goes into the air and water doesn't know [economic] boundaries." Although she has faced much opposition in her fight to abolish the use of harmful chemicals, she strives to help people "come together to see what our common interests are." In 1992 she won the prestigious MacArthur Genius Award for her courageous and effective leadership. She also serves on the Louisiana Committee of the US Commission on Civil Rights, which addresses environmental justice and other civil rights issues.

### Narrative from Lorna Bourg (b. Baton Rouge, Louisiana, 1942)

My father sold fine wines and liqueurs from all over the world.[2] My mother had many gifts in art, culture, music, and design. Most of her life was spent developing the Estée Lauder cosmetics line at Godchaux's [department store] many years ago. And she worked awhile in the hospital, helping people.

I had an older brother flying for the National Security Agency during the Cold War who was lost over Soviet Armenia, and I have a younger brother and sister. My mom worked, and so when I'd come home in the evenings I would cook for us. We were working kids. I had to clean the baseboards, the Venetian blinds, dust, pull grass and weeds.

I lived with my grandmother while my father was at war. She owned a little grocery store in Crowley, Louisiana. When my grandfather would take a nap she'd go and get a Popsicle and we'd split that and then she'd tell stories. They were hard working. The most important thing I learned was to be honest and work hard. But I saw people, as I got out of high school, and it began to dawn on me that there were people that really did work hard and they didn't get anywhere. And that introduced me to the contradictions and the injustices that all people are not born equal.

I went to Saint Joseph's Academy High School on Broussard Street in Baton Rouge, Louisiana. Sister Jane Louise Arbour taught me English literature and enticed me into state rallies for extemporaneous speaking, interpretive readings, and radio. And so the preparing for that competition, I think, prepared me a lot for what I ended up doing later.

Lorna Bourg

I started out being a speech and drama major and then shifted after high school to being a philosophy major. But when I was in the eighth grade I wanted to go into law. And then I thought, no—lawyers are just sort of like clerks; it's not all Perry Mason. So that's when I switched to psychology. I used all of those interests, however, at this marvelous job at Southern Mutual Help.

When I left high school, with the choices that there were for women, you could be a nurse, a teacher, or a nun, it seems like, or you could get married and do none of the above. I knew I wasn't going to get married and have children because it didn't seem like you did anything else, and so I went to be a nun. That's when I majored in philosophy and theology in New Orleans at Saint Mary's Dominican. If you were going to go be a nun, you had to go to college, so it was never a question in my mind that I was going. I was the first one in my family to go [to college]. I have a bachelor's and a master's in clinical psychology. I [later] attended the University of Wisconsin for a very intense program on community development and planning. I went to Harvard University and the Kennedy School of Government. I also went to the University of Massachusetts' Center for Popular Economics.

Some of the most remarkable classes that put me in good stead for life when I was a nun were taught by Father Leo Shea, a Dominican priest in New Orleans. He was an extraordinary thinker. He taught me all the different kinds of thinking, you know, intuitive thinking, logical thinking, and cosmology, the study of existence and the universe. That has always pulled my mind to the edge of wonderment.

After I left the convent, I left New Orleans and Saint Mary's Dominican and came back to Baton Rouge and went to one class at LSU [Louisiana State University], but I didn't like it because it was too impersonal and too large. So I went to look at the University of Southwestern Louisiana (USL) campus in Lafayette and everything came together. It's such a beautiful campus. It has the rural flavor to it, and I got to meet the head of the Psychology Department, and there was a lot of green grass around and beautiful trees and archways. When I went to the Catholic Student Union on campus, Monsignor Alexander Sigur was giving a sermon, and he was so dynamic that I thought, "This is where I can make a community." And so I did my undergraduate and graduate work at USL, and then I met the Dominican Sisters. They were in Dr. Ben Kaplan's sociology class at USL, and these nuns came in these white habits, and they had these little accents, and I found that they were from France and that they lived in Abbeville. That's how I met Sister Anne Catherine. She was a professional social worker, having gotten her master's in social work from Tulane, the first nun ever to graduate from Tulane University.

[After graduating from the University of Southwestern Louisiana, Lorna was hired as a social worker aide by Sister Anne Catherine.]

I ended up living on Rabbit Hill in this little bitty dilapidated house. It had almost no floor in it. We began rebuilding it. There's a million stories connected with that whole thing, but it was a very, very poor African American section on the outside of Abbeville that didn't have appropriate running water. If someone ran the water, you couldn't get yours, and the streets were unpaved and there was no garbage collection. It was a picture of poverty if you ever saw it. And we began very seriously trying to integrate the Head Start Program, which had been 100 percent black kids and black teachers. We knew, however, that if you looked at the poverty statistics in Vermilion Parish, there were more poor white folks than there were black folks, but the white folks were not taking advantage of what was available to them and their children. So my role was [to] go out to the boondocks and find poor white people. And some of the poorest people I've ever seen in my life were in Vermilion Parish.

I remember walking into a house and there was one table, one chair, and nothing else in the house, no food, nothing—and I got to sit in the chair. And the guy was outdoors pulling his own plow trying to plant something. I was able to talk to that lady, listen for a while, and sit in her home, and visit. She was the first lady that made the breakthrough of sending her little white blonde kid to this all-black Head Start class. Pretty soon we had integrated the entire program and the staff. We began connecting what was happening to the children inside the Head Start classroom with what was happening to the children in their homes that were so impoverished and in a community that had been so segregated. And we began what was nationally recognized as one of the best parent-participation programs in the country, and it was on that reason, basically, that we got fired out of the program because we were bringing poor white folks and black folks together to question the policies that were being made and the resources that were being spent or not spent in various communities.

It seemed like the more affluent your community was, the more protection you had, the more you would have crossing guards for your children when they come off the bus. So the white parents and black parents [we worked with] formed a club, and they would invite their politicians in, and black and white together in the same room would begin asking their politicians, "How come in our neighborhoods we don't have this, and how come we don't have paved streets, and how come our children don't have crossing guards on the highway?"

And so they began to raise a little money by planting gardens together, and it became very clear that this was mobilizing a policy group of people. If you put all the poor black folks and white folks in the same common interest pool, they made up 52 percent of the population of Vermilion Parish. And so any public official who wanted to become a representative, like Edwin Edwards [future governor], saw that this was the largest amount of job patronage he'd get his hands on, and so he created a super board and appointed people to it. That super board clamped down on Sister Anne and myself, saying that we could no longer have these meetings without permission. We had to submit the agenda ahead of time, and any monies raised from their little garden had to be turned into the main office, and people had to write a proposal to them to get it back.

So we were dutifully insubordinate because we refused to tell people to do that, and so we were fired summarily. It was my best on-the-job training I could have ever received into politics and policy and poverty in the state of Louisiana. And it was out of that whole learning experience that we cofounded the Southern Mutual Help Association and went looking for the poorest of the poor in the sugarcane fields.

[In 1969 Southern Mutual Help Association started the first medical and dental clinic to help treat the poorest citizens of Vermilion Parish. In the first year that it was funded, the clinic served ten thousand clients.]

Medical people said it wasn't necessary and that we had a charity hospital and there wasn't a problem. But what I saw were people in this great state of Louisiana that had charity hospitals—supposedly to care for the poor—that had never seen a doctor. We did the first medical and health survey on two whole plantations, and out of approximately one hundred kids, you would find less than a dozen that would be medically normal. You know these are children. And you begin to listen and look. And, yes, it was the working conditions. Yes, it was the living conditions. Yes, it was the poverty. But you also began to see what was happening to people that were being sprayed and that were breathing stuff in. It was making them really quite ill. You could see it in their eyes. You could see it in their ears. You could see it in their skin, in their rashes.

I remember when we had our offices in Jeanerette on Main Street, and Sister Anne used to tell me this story. There was a guy, he was a white guy, and he stopped Sister Anne and he said, "I can't tell you who I am, but there's this man who has been exposed to some really terrible chemicals in a plant in the sugarcane mill. He was cleaning out the boilers and is suffocating to death as a result of his exposure to those chemicals." And I just began to see what was happening. If you listen and see, it changes your heart.

I guess Southern Mutual has always had this concern about what was happening to farm workers in the cane fields. And then Helen [Vinton] came and had this wonderful science background, and together we got Dr. Marian Moses here in 1986, and we began learning the science and the medical aspects of the exposure to dioxin, the worst kind of dioxin, and Silvex and 2-4-5-T. We realized, after I began reading, that this stuff was banned everywhere in the United States, except you could use it in forests, you could use it in rice, and you could use it in sugarcane. I thought, "That's what is being used here in Louisiana."

Sometime later I myself got sprayed. Helen was on the State Pesticide Commission, and we were just a little piece from our office and this guy was out spraying, in like twenty-five-mile-an-hour winds, all of that yellow stuff, and I had the window down. It was one of these wonderful days like this, and that stuff just came in. We called right away. I got all the documentation on the wind velocity. We were out there when they went to take samples, and they made us go away when they took them. They said they wouldn't take them as long as we stood there. We found out the samples later showed there was no spray. So the guy got off, but he still farms around here, and just the other day he was burning sugarcane and a fire marshal almost ran into the back of a school bus because he was burning it in higher than ten-mile-an-hour winds.

CNN came out to interview us. The camera people were supposed to meet us here at SMHA's property, but before they came here they went out to Lynn Minville's property. He called the sheriff and said I was trespassing on his property, and meanwhile I was out in a community being interviewed on some farm workers' housing deals. Helen was here at the office, and they arrested her and then came out to arrest me. I turned myself in to the sheriff. CNN was livid by this time and called our attorney and he came over and Sheriff Errol "Romo" Romero [1980–1996] was astonished that we had been arrested. CNN said the two of us had never been on the property. We hadn't been there at all. We hadn't trespassed. So all the charges were dismissed.

[The fish kills of the early 1990s in Louisiana brought the aerial-spraying issue to the forefront.]

Idiocy. Cowboys and planes, arrogance, greed—that is my take on it. They were putting azinphosmethyl into the fields and it was raining every single day. They would spray this stuff and then the rains would wash it all out. It makes people sick. It makes children have nerve dysfunction. It kills fish. You know it kills what is on the cane, but it does a lot more than that. I believe it is a nerve agent, and so the fish would die. So what's happening to the people? So what happens to fishers who earn their living? What happens to people who eat this fish? Aerial application looks efficient, but in the long run, you are probably spraying 90 percent, $150,000 a year, off target. It doesn't make sense. I mean, there are bugs, and you might need some, so we never advocated throwing everything in reverse, to use no pesticides or chemicals. But what you need to do is figure out a way to get it to where the bug is and to where the crop is—not on the houses, not on the equipment, not on the bayou, not on the fish, and not on the people.

How about interplanting and talking about healthy soil, because we know that bugs attack plants that don't have a healthy environment to grow in. There are lots of things you can do before you ever get to aerial spraying. I think it comes out of the whole war industrial complex, where after Word War II you didn't know what to do with all these industries and all these chemicals. And so you converted them to agricultural use, and our land grant colleges and our chemical corporations sold America and the farmers a bill of goods around this whole thing. And we're still picking up the bill.

When we first started working in the sugarcane fields, our lives were threatened and we were chased off roads and followed by helicopters. But Southern Mutual never wanted to have the position of being anti-agriculture or anti-farmer. That's just crazy. The point was not to drive people out of work or people out of business. The point was to make people not die as a result of being in the business or doing that kind work. Somehow or another, you have to, as a community, come together to see where our common interests are.

## *Afterword*

For a state that I love so much and am proud to be from, it's probably one of the most polluted places in the United States. And the people of Louisiana deserve better than that, and we need to get better than that. I haven't seen a lot of gated communities that have garbage dumps next to them or sewer treatment plants next to them or PPG or Conoco—they don't go there. You know they look for places where people are powerless and won't argue. So whether they are black or whether they are poor, I think they tend to choose those communities. But the bottom line is the stuff that goes into the air and water doesn't know boundaries. It goes beyond them and it gets us all sick, including the people in the factories, including the people behind the gated communities. So we've got to clean it up not just because it's right for poor folks and black folks, but because we're all connected.

# MARYLEE ORR

Marylee Orr, of Baton Rouge, Louisiana, began building bridges for environmental activism in 1983 after her second son was born with a lung disease. This prompted her to found the environmental organization Mothers Against Air Pollution, and in 1985 she became the co-chair of the newly formed statewide environmental organization, the Louisiana Environmental Action Network (LEAN). In 1987 LEAN made her its executive director. Since then, the organization has grown from representing six environmental groups to one hundred. In addition to organizing campaigns throughout the year, she conducts an annual statewide leadership conference to inspire and empower Louisiana's grassroots leaders. A 2001 issue of *Family Circle* magazine featured her for her environmental activism. In 2008 she was inducted into the OMB Watch Hall of Fame.[3] In 2010 she was the only American who was included as a runner-up for the Condé Nast International Environmentalist of the Year Award.

### Narrative from Marylee Orr (b. Milwaukee, Wisconsin, 1958)

All my remembering life is in New Orleans, where I was raised.[4] My father was Scottish and my mother was Irish. When they moved to New Orleans they thought they had come to another planet. My father was employed in business, and his employer wanted him in New Orleans to expand the territory. In Milwaukee it was freezing cold, and my mom was sick all the time. They said, "Send us to the sunny South." But, oh boy, it was a lot sunnier than they thought. The company took them to see the cemeteries and they ate raw oysters. And when my parents got back to the hotel, they said, "What kind of place have we come to live where they feed you raw oysters and show you cemeteries as a way to have a good time?"

My dad had a college degree and my mom had two years of college. Dad was the Indiana State tennis champion, and my mom was a dancer and taught dancing. She actually went on the road in an era when women didn't go on the road. They had four children. One child died and I have two older brothers. My oldest brother served in Vietnam. With the revolution to end the war and my brother a Tulane graduate and a decorated veteran—being treated so badly when he came back—was very hard. My other brother is an attorney in New Orleans.

I grew up in a traditional family and a military family, so it is interesting that I became an activist out there protesting. Faith was a very big part of my growing up. My family was pretty traditional and nothing that would have brought me to where

I am today. My parents taught me that service is the rent you pay for the space you take up. I had twelve years of Catholic education. It did give me a sense to give back and to think outward and not inward. I went to Saint Francis Xavier in Metairie through the eighth grade, and then I had the real pleasure of going to Sacred Heart Academy on Saint Charles Avenue. That was one of the influences in my life because it was a very progressive, all-girls school—very empowering of women.

I went to college at LSU and married my high school sweetheart, who was also attending college. My husband graduated with a master's in forestry, and he went to work for the Department of Agriculture and Forestry. When we moved to Lafayette, Louisiana, I got my realtor's license.

In the late 1970s, I had my first son, Paul, and became aware, when I talked to other mothers, that there was an epidemic of kids who had severe asthma, respiratory problems, and sinus infections. Moms would be at their wits' end, or their child would be on an antibiotic for months and then develop yeast infections. There was something terrible going on. That was the beginning of awareness to me.

In 1983, when my second son was born in East Baton Rouge Parish, it was a life-altering experience. That's what made me an activist. Michael was born with a lung disease, hyaline membrane disease, and he was susceptible to respiratory illnesses and pneumonia. I brought Michael home from the hospital, and the air was unhealthy to breathe seventeen times that year. I was like, "Somebody's got to do something." I learned the lesson we all learned: We are somebody. And I had to be that somebody or I couldn't complain, and that's how I became involved and formed the Mothers Against Air Pollution. I learned to become an advocate for my son before I became an advocate for myself.

I had a full life and I really didn't want to do anything like this. I was like most people. I thought I put up my window and I had clean air and that I had clean water and it was a basic civil right. And then I read an article by Bob Anderson in the *Morning Advocate*, where they were going to burn polychlorinated biphenyls (PCBs) in Alsen, in North Baton Rouge, a predominately African American community. I went out to Alsen and met my African American neighbors and heard all the stories about the people. They would throw up, couldn't breathe, had terrible respiratory problems, nosebleeds so severe they had to go to the hospital, air so bad their kids couldn't play outside, and the women talked about pigment changes to their skin and the high rates of cancer in their community.

When I realized people weren't coming forward in reference to Alsen, the newly formed group Mothers Against Air Pollution started a petition against the burning of PCBs at Alsen. We had probably five or six moms that in about six days got thirty-five hundred signatures and brought them to the mayor of Baton Rouge.

There was a public meeting to stop the company from burning the PCBs. It was one of the biggest meetings I think we've ever had in the history of the environ-

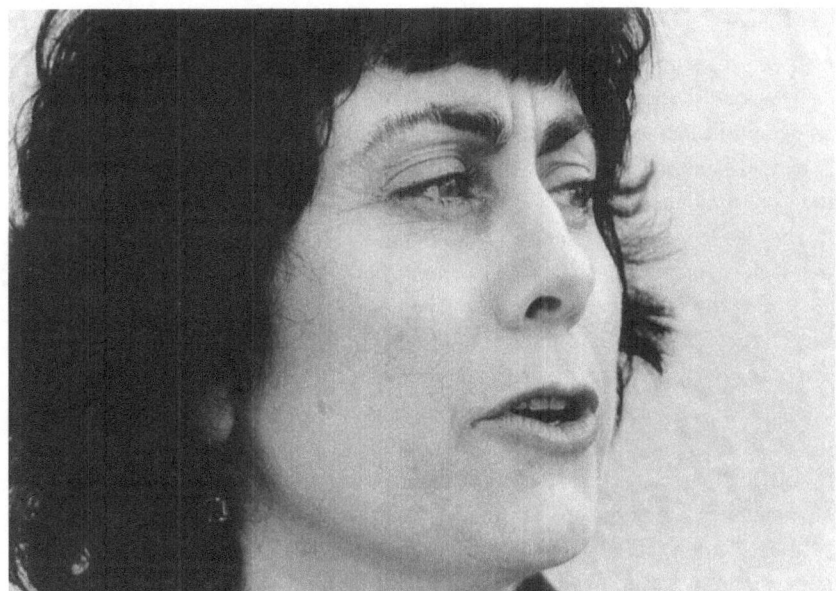

Marylee Orr

mental movement. Lots of people worked on that issue. Another group called the Citizens for a Clean Environment (CCE), which still exists today, decided to have this community meeting. We [MAAP] participated and gave people white ribbons when they came in. The company didn't get the permit to burn the PCBs. And I thought, "Well, that's good. That's it. I won't do this anymore." But then Louisiana Environmental Action Network (LEAN) was founded in 1985. First the environmental community had an anonymous donor give $2,000 so we could have our first meeting on campus at LSU. Lois Gibbs came and Will Collette, and Lois's husband, Steve. It was two and a half days long. And afterwards we didn't want that sense of unity in the community to end, so LEAN was born. It was a wonderful but difficult path to give birth to this organization.

Part of LEAN's purpose was not to duplicate efforts and to be more effective because folks in the communities felt like their foes were enormous. And industry was well organized, well orchestrated, and well funded, and we were not. So we needed to have a central body where we could, hopefully, all work together towards making a better community. I don't think we dreamt that we'd be where we are today.

We had vision meetings where we said what we wanted to see happen in the next five years. We didn't have an office, so LEAN leased an office and we hired a director, who stayed with us for a year and then resigned. I agreed to be the interim director until someone could be found. I was serving in that position when the office burned down to the ground. I said, "This is it. This is too much for me."

Will Collette [featured in this book] flew down and said, "Don't quit." I'm still here eighteen years later.

However, it has not been easy. When I started I had to work against the stigma of being anti-economic development. People called me a communist and a "pink-o." They said I was an ice princess, a witch with a "b," and that I was against jobs. They even put a picture of me in a plant [refinery] with a red circle and a slash through it. They are in your face yelling and screaming and telling people, behind your back, that if the company doesn't get this permit, they are going to lose their jobs.

I think the SLAP lawsuit against Miss Ann [Williams, also featured in this book] was certainly a tactic used to try to shut up activists. There are other tactics too—where they will embrace the most outspoken person and give them a job or offer them something. So it can be very intimidating, on many levels. It also causes a tremendous strain on the marriage and their place in the community because they [women activists] become the catalyst for change, which can be very stressful. My neighbors were not very supportive. When I walked the neighborhood with my petition, I think they thought I was cuckoo. My family might have a little bit too; however, not my boys. My boys are my biggest motivators.

At the beginning I was called an "environmentalist," but I was not a traditional one. Now I am proud to say, "Yes, I am an environmentalist." But I am the most conservative person. I can remember Liz Avants and Les Ann Kirkland and all the other ladies saying the same thing. We just want clean air, clean land, and clean water. We want to have something to give to our kids.

Chernobyl and Bhopal and other catastrophic environmental events, I am sorry to say, have awakened people. So environmentalists have gone from the 1980s, where people saw us as outside agitators, to the mainstream. Today, one of the number one concerns, along with crime, is the environment. People want a healthy place for their children. Conservation and environmental issues have come together in a better marriage. It used to be that conservationists saw the environmental community as a threat with different goals. But through the women's work and the community's work of building bridges, they see that we really want the same thing. We have a lot of natural resources, and we haven't been smart about what we've done with them, but I think people are now more willing to stand up about it.

[Many women helped support and inspire Marylee, including the nationally famous Lois Gibbs and fellow activist Ramona Stevens, who devoted herself to research on the Louisiana environment before an early death at thirty-nine.]

Ramona was a really tough woman, and it was a privilege to work with her. Nothing intimidated her, and that was great. She was also a little more cynical than I was, and I think I balanced that out in her. We were an unlikely pair to do this, but we were unified by the fact that we were moms. She was also good at doing research and getting data, and I think I was a little bit better sometimes at getting it out there. It was a division of duties.

When I first started, Lois Gibbs was a big role model for me. She was very inspiring because she came out of a community, she was a mother, and she was very vocal and aggressive about her issue. Then she moved into a leadership and staff role, where she actually had an organization. It was very inspiring to me. I looked to her, you know; she's making it, so I guess we can.

I have learned that people are very threatened by women in authority. People don't like to see women in leadership positions and they want to knock us out of it, not only in the local level, but also at the state and national levels. As someone who has been in a staff position, I have had to work three times harder than if I were a man. But we are the government, and these women [activists] are making choices, in their houses, in a meeting hall, or wherever they are, and they are going to change history.

There is also a catch-22 for women. You are trying to make a good environment for your kids, like being a room mother and taking them on field trips, being involved with their friends, and doing all of these things, when all of a sudden you are doing something that pulls you away from them. You are out there in the meetings at night while your son or daughter is at home. We're out there to save our kids, literally, and to make a better future for them, and that takes us away from the very thing we are trying to protect. To me that is very painful, and I certainly have seen it in other women as the thing that causes the most pain. But once your eyes are opened to this issue, you are not the same; your priorities and what you want to do with your life change. And, to me, life became ever more fragile and ever more precious. And sometimes your partner doesn't grow that way, or it's not a priority for them.

The most painful thing for me, however, and the biggest learning lesson, is the animosity between the people in the movement. You don't expect that to happen—to come from your friends or colleagues. Jealousy, ego, and envy are alive and well in this movement, like they are any place else. Everybody is motivated differently, and that's not always bad, but when it's negative and destructive, which sometimes it can be, it's devastating.

You have to renew by nurturing yourself in whatever way that helps because if you don't, you will burn out. I pray every day. In my faith you pray the rosary, which is a form of mediation. We pray a lot at LEAN. Before we went to the DEQ we held hands and had prayer. It's a spiritual journey.

## *Afterword*

The environmental community is alive and well and even more diverse and powerful than it ever was. The family I have made is incredible. Our paths would not have crossed if I had not done this, and that has made my life and, I think, my family's life much richer.

# LINDA KING

Linda King began her career as an environmental activist by following a trajectory similar to the one Marylee Orr took. She got involved with the environmental movement as a grassroots volunteer in Nitro, West Virginia, because she and her children developed serious health problems that she believed were caused by environmental pollution. Starting at the grassroots level taught her vital lessons about empowering people, lessons she realized she could share with the people of Louisiana.

Linda organized the first citizen's conference on health issues related to the environment in New Orleans, Louisiana, in the 1980s. In 1989 she founded the Environmental Health Network, Incorporated (EHN), to assist communities, injured workers, and individuals with exposures to toxins. Linda King is a certified mediator for EHN, helping groups learn negotiation and conflict resolution skills. She is the author of *Chemical Injuries in the Courts: A Litigation Guide for Clients and Their Attorneys* and helped publish a report to Congress called "Inconclusive by Design: Waste, Fraud, and Abuse in Federal Health Research."[5]

### Narrative from Linda King (b. Millington, Tennessee, 1952)

My paternal great-grandmother was a Creek.[6] My paternal great-grandfather was a Cherokee and a well-known dowser. Some of my relatives were on the Trail of Tears. My paternal grandmother is one of the few heroes in my life. She raised thirteen children during the Depression and literally walked from Tennessee to Little Rock, Arkansas, with one baby on the breast and three kids under the age of five—to get to my grandfather. When he died, my grandmother published a book of poetry, wrote a song and had it recorded, and learned how to drive and fly an airplane. She was a remarkable woman.

My father was in the navy for twenty-two years, and my mother was a housewife. She grew up in an orphanage. My father was actually born on Davy Crockett's old property. My parents were caretakers, and they lived off the land and got their water out of the river. They had two children. Since my dad was in the navy, I went to kindergarten in Hawaii, first and second grade in Newfoundland, Canada, third through seventh grade in Norfolk, Virginia. I went to junior high and high school in Aniack, Alaska, and finished high school in Virginia and then started college there.

In 1981 or 1982, after I married my husband, we moved to Nitro, West Virginia. The real-estate agent in Nitro took us to this beautiful house. We'd never owned a home and I fell in love with this place. It had five lots with cherry and walnut trees on top of a hill. Out of the front windows I could see a mountain. I felt like I could stay there for the rest of my life. So we bought the house and sunk every penny we had into it. But when we moved in the odors were horrible. We didn't realize that during the summer you can't see what's down the hill because there are leaves on the trees. But below the hill were six specialty chemical companies, a hazardous waste incinerator, a guy who made experimental pesticides, and a chemical tank-cleaning company. Back then they didn't know what hazardous waste was. Today, the area is called "chemical valley."

I'd never smelled chemicals before, but I started getting very sick and I had always been extremely healthy. The only time I'd ever been in the hospital was to have a baby. I started swelling to the point that you couldn't recognize who I was. I had rashes. My joints would swell and I couldn't move my fingers, my wrists, or my arms. My lips would start swelling around three in the morning. I started not being able to digest my food. Then I wasn't functioning as a mother or wife.

My three kids were getting sick. My oldest son was unable to digest proteins properly and he was very thin. My middle son's ear started bleeding, and he had a hearing loss as a result. He was reading at the age of two, doing math, and had an IQ of 146, but by the time we left that community he was hyperactive, had dyslexic symptoms, and couldn't function in school. My daughter has had some problems, but I'm hoping she's going to be okay.

My kids were affected, and I was affected, and so I started trying to figure out what to do, and that launched my twenty-year environmental career. I started having meetings in my house. I started going out into my community and trying to organize people. What I found was people were really sick. I helped to design the first health survey in my community, and the things I found out were really scary. On my street alone six people had died of cancer, three more people had cancer, two had lupus, and one had MS, and this was only twenty houses. As I questioned more people, it got worse and worse.

I started getting my name in the newspaper, and my husband actually worked in the chemical companies that I was protesting against [indirectly, through other contractors], which didn't make for a good marriage. I would get my name in the newspaper and he would come home and say, "If you get your name in the newspaper one more time, you're going to get me fired."

When I started organizing in West Virginia I really didn't know what I was doing. I was getting anonymous phone calls saying, "Why don't you go home and bake brownies and be a nice housewife?" And then I'd get anonymous calls that said, "If you're going to do it right, look up this particular lawsuit and read carefully." I didn't know where the information was coming from, but I would look it up and would find it. I was so green and had never been in such a scary political fight.

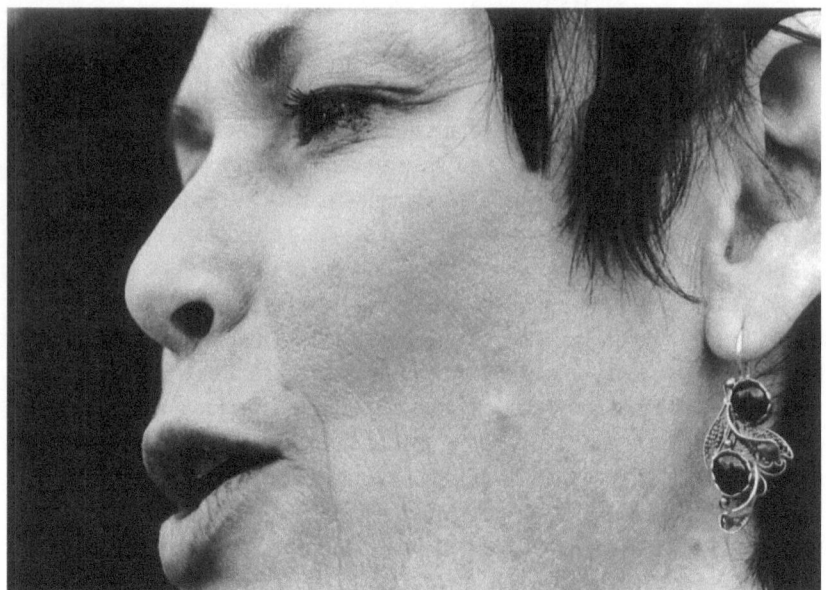

Linda King

Poor people can't fight back. There was a report out from industry a long time ago, and it laid out for chemical industries the kinds of places they could go and get in with the least amount of resistance. And there were, I think, seven criteria. It was poor, low education, low employment, Catholic, minority, rural, and South. They graded communities to find the most vulnerable. I thought it was real interesting that they said Catholic. The Catholic religion tells you to obey those people who you think are superior.

During this time I met the people with [the national] Citizens' Clearinghouse for Hazardous Wastes (CCHW). And then I moved to Ohio and met Will Collette, who also worked for CCHW. I helped organize environmental groups in Ohio. When we moved to Louisiana I was hired by CCHW to be their southern regional organizer. My territory was Florida, Georgia, Alabama, Mississippi, Louisiana, Texas, Oklahoma, and Arkansas. As I started getting more involved with the groups politically, I was threatened, and it was scary at times. In one incident when Will and I were attending a landfill hearing in Alexandria, Louisiana, the employees of a waste company blocked the back doors and wouldn't let us out.

Another time I spoke at a pesticide conference with farmers and pesticide companies. I basically told them that they wouldn't be using pesticides in another twenty years. I said, "You can either quit now and do the right thing or we will drag you kicking and screaming later on." And the farmers had to protect me going out of the room, but they came up to me quietly after the meeting and said, "I have this cancer. I have that cancer, or I'm dying." They knew—the farmers of Louisiana knew that what they did for a living was killing them. And it really touched me because of the way the whole system is set up. If the farmers don't buy the chemicals, they don't get the loans, and if they don't get the loans, they can't farm. The system has been stacked against them for a long time and they don't have workers' compensation.

After working for CCHW for nearly three years, I decided to start my own organization. In May 1989 I started the Environmental Health Network (EHN). It was the first environmental health organization in the United States and it started in Harvey, Louisiana. I started it because nobody at that time was solely concentrating on health issues, and that's really where I came from. When I was ill, it took me six years to find a doctor and ten years to get better. And everywhere I went as an organizer, I would say, "OK, we're going to work on the incinerator; we're going to work on the landfill," and the people would say, "OK, but what about our health?" And doctors were saying, "I have all these patients that are having these weird symptoms." So I started hooking up doctors with experts, the communities with experts, and going in and talking about how to organize on health issues. Then I started having health conferences to bring lawyers, doctors, social workers, and community people together to discuss the issues and the latest science on environmental health because that was one thing where we were lacking scientific proof that we were being poisoned.

I held five health conferences in the United States, and they were very successful. And what was so successful about them was that I had an attorney track and I brought in experts to discuss attorney issues, toxins, and health issues. I also had a social track and a medical track. And the community people could go to any of the tracks they wanted to and hear any of the issues that they wanted to.

[Linda heard about an international conference being held by the federal Agency for Toxic Substances and Disease Registry (ATSDR). The agency was releasing health studies to scientists but would not release them to the communities that had been examined. When ATSDR refused to drop its $700 per-person fee so that citizens could attend the conference, Linda organized a protest.]

I started fund-raising to get money to organize a complete crash of ATSDR's international conference. We got the money and we brought people who really represented their communities. I was determined that every community that wanted to participate was going to be there. When ATSDR realized we were there, they started putting armed guards at the doors. We hid our protest signs near one entrance, then as a group we went inside and stood in front of the speaker with our signs. They didn't dare drag us off, and they even allowed us to speak. We talked about all the communities and why we were there, how ATSDR was charging these extraordinary fees and how the study results by ATSDR were being withheld from the communities actually affected. After we spoke, every scientist in the room was on our side. After that protest, ATSDR stopped releasing the results of the studies until they notified the communities.

### *Afterword*

The word *community*, for me, has different levels. There's a personal community of my dear friends—people that mean a lot to me, outside of my biological family. They have become my community, and most of these people are social justice activists in some way. Then I have a much broader view of community because I've traveled internationally with my work in Eastern Europe, Japan, Canada, Mexico, and Europe. Community for me, on this level, is this idea that we are all one on this planet. Wherever I have gone, I have looked into the eyes of another person, and even though they spoke a different language or grew up differently from me, I have always felt a common link. And it's usually been over a social justice issue, specifically, the environment. And once we sit down, we aren't very different. In every state and every country, it's the same political battles—powerful people dictating to people who don't have as much power as they do.

Sometimes I think I haven't made a difference in the world at all, and then I will get a phone call and somebody says, "I read your book and I want to thank you." And then I think to myself, "Well maybe I have made a contribution," and am proud that I brought environmental health issues to the forefront.

# WILMA SUBRA

Wilma Subra, of New Iberia, Louisiana, scientist and owner of Subra Company, has worked with all of the women included in this book, as well as with hundreds of individuals and over four hundred grassroots community groups throughout the United States, Mexico, Canada, Japan, England, and the Middle East. Widely viewed as a hero in many Louisiana communities, Wilma has shown countless citizens how to use technical data to navigate state and federal regulatory systems. She is also an expert in oil and gas waste disposal and has testified extensively regarding those issues. She serves on many regional, state, and national advisory committees. In June 1999 Wilma Subra was the recipient of the prestigious MacArthur Foundation Genius Award for her efforts on behalf of the environment. In 2003 Wilma received a Volvo for Life Award for her activism. In 2011, at the ninth annual Human Rights Award ceremony, she was named the "Domestic Honoree" for fighting for the rights of local communities following the Gulf oil spill. A follow-up narrative from 2011 by Wilma appears at the end of this book.

## Narrative from Wilma Subra (b. Morgan City, Louisiana, 1943)

I was raised in Morgan City, the eldest of six sisters.[7] When I was eleven we moved to Bayou Vista, a few miles outside of Morgan City. I always liked the sciences. That was my major emphasis in elementary school and high school. It was a natural fit. Every summer I worked for my dad [a chemist] in his office and in his [chemistry] lab.

At the time, people weren't aware of environmental damage. That was even before they were talking about the eroding coastline. But my dad always took us out—we were his girls—and we'd go to work with him. When we were small he'd take us down the river, where my grandfather was an oyster fisherman. We were always doing things with nature, and then when you started to see things, over time, that were impacting people, it was time to do something.

I was valedictorian of my high school, but I couldn't receive any scholarships because my dad made too much money. So it wasn't possible to go to some of the big universities where the tuition was real high because I was the first one of six girls and there was five coming up behind me. I went to college at the University of Southwestern Louisiana (USL) in Lafayette, Louisiana, which is now ULL, and finished with a masters in microbiology and chemistry.

[Wilma met her husband while attending classes at USL. He opened his own medical lab in 1979. They have three children and four grandchildren.]

When I went to USL, they had a grant for a project determining whether or not organisms responded to chemicals that they thought were causing cancer. So that very first summer I was doing cancer research on microbiological and chemical levels. And from that point on, it was always focused on what are the biological aspects? What are the chemical aspects that cause impacts to humans, impacts to animals, and impacts to microbiology?

When I worked for the Gulf South Research Institute from 1967 to 1981, a lot of things we were doing were about the impact on health and the environment. That is when they started requiring that chemicals be tested to see if they were causing cancer, birth defects, and developmental problems.

Part of the work we did was quick response projects for the EPA. They had a number of different organizations under contract, and whenever an issue would come up, they'd call and you would do whatever they needed. A lot of that was when Love Canal was first coming into light, and we were doing a lot of analysis. We'd get a call to be at Love Canal one week, and the next week we would start sampling. The interesting thing was when we went up there for a meeting and went to the office; it was actually in one of the homes that they [EPA] had bought out. When we were just getting in to get started, someone said, "Quick, move out the backdoor. The homeowners are coming." They didn't want us interacting with them. We were there to sample everything, but we couldn't interact with them.

Wilma Subra

We were doing these quick response projects for the EPA all over the country. But we were also getting lots of knocks on the doors. People wanted us to help them understand this pit that overflowed, and what is it doing to croplands; what is it doing to us as we're breathing it? We were actually going out a lot at night and having small group meetings—living-room meetings, meetings in churches—trying to help people comprehend that it wasn't against the rules for these things to happen. And through that kind of work these people then started going to Baton Rouge and saying, "We want the rules changed." But they had to have the information. Just going to Baton Rouge and saying, "We want the rules changed," isn't going to do any good if you don't have a basis, and we were providing the basis.

People would come to us and want their water well sampled or want their soil sampled. We were doing that through something like a petty cash system because we could do a $50,000 project, but we couldn't do a $50 project. So it was in that time period where people were constantly needing information, and it was difficult to be able to work it in within the system that we had.

My first structured environmental issue in Louisiana was in Vermilion Parish, working with the environmental group Vermilion Association to Protect the Environment [Gay Hanks, also featured in this book, was the president]. In the late 1970s in Vermilion they had fifty-five waste sites. A lot of the waste came in from Texas and Louisiana. And the parish was divided up into wards and each ward would have a chief deputy sheriff. Under the Edwards administration, he sent the word out that each deputy sheriff could dig a fishpond on a piece of property that they had, and he would ensure that waste would come in from Texas and that these truckers would pay them up to five dollars a load to dump in their fishpond. So throughout Vermilion Parish you had a fishpond being constructed in someone's backyard. As soon as it was constructed, the next thing you know, these trucks were rolling in with this waste and dumping it in the ponds. A lot of the ponds were merely a rice field with a rice levee around it. There was nothing like the impermeable liners that we talk about today. When the ponds would get too full or it would rain too much, they'd cut the rice levee just like you'd be draining a rice field and discharge it into the ditches and coulees. And in Vermilion Parish, down from these coulees, you had rice pumps, crawfish ponds, and grazing cattle. So suddenly it started having an impact. You'd have fish kills, rice fields destroyed, and cattle dying. I think Edwards thought he was sharing his wealth. He was providing the people in Vermilion, which in those days was very poor and very rural, with a means of livelihood and then telling the companies that Louisiana is a good place to come dump your waste.

In May of 1981, I left the Gulf South Research Institute to open my own company to provide technical assistance to citizens and victims of environmental issues. There was a huge need for this because there weren't many people working for citizens, providing the technical knowledge and the interpretation. The idea is to empower these citizens with enough information that they can convey it to whomever they have to. They can go to their parish meetings, city council meetings, and the state agencies, but they have to be able to represent their issues. They have to show up and give reasons based on the issues in their community, based on the rules and regulations that the company has to comply with.

[The Toxics Release Inventory (TRI) Program, begun in 1987, provided an invaluable tool for citizens who wanted to learn more about the discharge levels in their communities.]

The TRI was a process at the federal level, implemented as a result of the Bhopal incident in India, where isocyanate was leaked into the air and killed thousands and injured hundreds of thousands of people. After that incident, Congress asked if a similar thing could happen here because we had a number of the [same] facilities in the United States. The first response was that no way could it ever happen here. Then they really started looking, and, yes, the same chemicals were manufactured here, used at Weeks Island by Martin Chemical (in Iberia Parish) and used in Baton Rouge at a lot of facilities there. It's used all over the United States. So Congress enacted the TRI, where each of these facilities were required to report on a yearly basis how much they emitted into the air, land, and water, out of the three hundred most toxic chemicals.

Before 1987, the first reporting year, when we asked what was coming out of the stacks from these industrial facilities, the response was, "Just steam." But when the data came out, suddenly what was coming out of those smokestacks wasn't steam. It was chemicals known to cause cancer in animals, suspected [cancer] in humans, birth defects, neurological impacts, respiratory problems, skin rashes, eye irritation, and a whole host of things. And these were only the most toxic of the chemicals. Louisiana was number one in the nation in quantity of these chemicals emitted into air, land, and water.

Suddenly you had people in these communities reading in the newspaper about these facilities in their community. A lot of what I had been doing was fighting permit applications, doing cleanup orders, and trying to investigate. Now I had an opportunity to go into these communities and educate them about what was coming out of the stacks. I started doing a lot of education, and then from year to year we started looking at the trends in the data.

My children grew up coming with me to meetings at night and sitting on the back table with their juice and cookies and coloring books. I'd take them with me. They thought everybody takes vacations to start a new project because whenever we'd go somewhere during the summer it was to start a new project.

[Wilma has worked on a many issues throughout Louisiana (and many other states) from Superfund sites to landfarms and waste pits. One of her best-known cases involved the Marine Shale facility in Morgan City.]

I became involved with Marine Shale when it started impacting Sally Herman [also featured in this book] and her husband's business. Their business was across Highway 90 from Marine Shale, and the emissions would fill their warehouse with vapors. Frequently, they had to send workers home. She, as a working mom, often brought her children to work and didn't want them or their workers impacted. She called and said, "We need help to understand the issues and what can be done."

Many a day I stood outside Sally's business and saw colored smoke coming out of the stack. I called DEQ and watched long enough for them to have called someone [at the facility] and the smoke would stop. So clearly at first the agency was very supportive [of the company]. This was in Edwin Edwards' time frame.

[After five children in the Morgan City area were diagnosed with neuroblastoma, a form of cancer, concern about the safety of the Marine Shale facility mounted.]

When Marine Shale was burning a lot of creosote waste, there was a facility in Illinois with the same type of waste. It wasn't creosote, but it was the same chemical constituents. It was an old gasification plant, and I received a call from a guy who said, "We have a cluster of neuroblastoma and I understand you have one in Morgan City." They actually won in court, proving that it was those chemicals that caused the neuroblastoma clusters in Illinois. In addition to the neuroblastoma, you had high rates of cancer and lots of other weird diseases. A pediatrician specialist came to town saying that he was treating diseases and conditions he never saw in any other location in the country.

Once we had children with neuroblastoma, a lot of the community joined Sally in the fight, realizing that it was impacting the health of the people in Morgan City. However, a lot of the community members had financial considerations. The company actually went into the community and hired a lot of people when the oil industry went bust. They did business with all the businesses in town and strung out the payments, so every time there was a threat that the agency may shut the facility down these companies wouldn't support it because they were owed money. This was one issue that divided the community—economics versus health.

The DEQ was divided, so you never knew, when you submitted a complaint, whether or not you were going to get a response. One Friday night I received calls that air emissions were really bad, and so I called the DEQ hotline and nobody would deal with me. I called her [Martha Madden, DEQ secretary] at home and woke her up. I told her what the issue was, and I said, "The citizens are going to call you in just a moment." She turned off her phone and turned it on to the answering service. And we had just met with her the week before with the grandmothers [Helen Solar and Miriam Price, also featured in this book] of the neuroblastoma babies, and at that time she sent us to the Health Department, saying, "This is a health issue, not an environmental issue." So it was that kind of stuff that citizens had to deal with.

No one wanted to deal with the issue. No one wanted to go down there and have the company jump on their case, have the citizens be against them, and be expected to do the right thing. The air agency had no monitoring equipment, so even if they went, they didn't have the ability to take a sample. It was just unbelievable, and the citizens kept up the pressure and kept up the fight. Every time we had a public meeting it was always jobs versus the environment.

At one EPA hearing they [EPA] decided to have it in two segments, one in the afternoon and one at night. Marine Shale was operating around the clock, so the night shift [workers] had to attend the afternoon hearing and bring their wives and children, and they had to sign in at the Marine Shale table to verify their attendance. They were told if they didn't attend that they wouldn't have a job the next day.

Every time Marine Shale proposed a new permit, we'd get the information and the permit would be denied. However, they [Marine Shale] would appeal everything. And they were making so much money that Jack Kent [the owner of Marine Shale] made the decision to throw the money to the legal fights. He had lawyers from everywhere. He had the best money could buy. He was able to keep the issue in court, and by keeping it in court he was allowed to continue operating. And people who were supporting him said, "If it was that bad—they'd shut him down."

They had a stack, which was the stack from the incinerator, and then they had large mixing vessels in a hopper barge with a backhoe. And they frequently had explosions and fires, and when you passed by, the emissions were horrendous. They also had blow downs from their bag houses, and you'd pass by and it would just coat your car. This was before the new Highway 90 was open, so that the road in front of Marine Shale was the only way to go between Morgan City and New Orleans. So people were impacted as they traveled by the facility. People at adjacent businesses, like Sally Herman and ones next to her, were awfully impacted as far as health was concerned. Most of them closed up and moved away.

There was enough data to clearly prove there was a problem. From the analysis of fish in the bayou, when they were dumping a lot of the hazardous waste in the bayou, we found high levels of heavy metals and mercury. They were polluting the water, and we had a lot of data that showed the air was really getting bad.

The women there have been the strongest I have ever worked for because, in their case, the community was often against them and they were always willing to look up the issues, investigate it, get up at the public hearings, and attend the court cases. They were always there working the issue no matter how much criticism was brought against them.

[Between 1988 and 1992, during Governor Buddy Roemer's administration, the case against Marine Shale gained ground. Progress made during this time set the stage for the facility's court-ordered closure in 1996.]

When Roemer was governor he pulled together people in various disciplines to look at the issues, within the state agencies, and look at what needed to be done. He was the best environmental governor as far as getting rules and regulations in place and actually enforcing them. Even though there are regulations on the books, without enforcement, industries know they can operate however they choose. Under the Edwards administration, little to none were followed through on. The regulations that were in place under Roemer, Edwards immediately got rid of, so we lost the regulatory authority that we had been able to implement.

When Roemer ran for re-election, Jack Kent spent a huge amount of money—some people estimated $1 million—on TV ads opposed to Roemer, which allowed Mike Foster [gubernatorial candidate] to get the upper hand. We've heard that he [Jack Kent] also sponsored a lot of newspaper ads. Foster was for the most part an unknown, and then, all of a sudden, he was visible in every newspaper in the state. Jack Kent takes great pleasure in saying he defeated Roemer and got Foster elected.

## *Afterword*

So you just keep moving forward because if you give up, that's what they want. Then they've won and they don't have to deal with the issue. I see that at the national level. I serve on a number of advisory committees of the EPA, representing the grassroots community. And when I start a new committee, the industry people always try to dismiss you like they dismiss a grassroots person. However, after you work through the process with them, they realize that what you are bringing to the table is correct and needs to be dealt with.

Chapter Seven

# "WE AS A PEOPLE ARE BETTER THAN OUR POLITICS"
## Allies, Experts, and Adversaries

*Many political analysts, not to mention Roemer himself, say his insistence on holding industry to higher environmental standards than previous gubernatorial administrations led to his losing bid for reelection. Among the changes made under Roemer that industry particularly disliked was the creation of an environmental scorecard giving industries tax credits based on how they had impacted the environment. This innovative method of penalizing or rewarding industries for the way they handled natural resources led the Sierra Club to name Louisiana "State of the Year" in 1989. Other states subsequently followed Louisiana's model.*

*"Women understand that being a human being is being a part of a network of relationships. And I think that women also understood that pairs are a very efficient way of getting through the day, having your partner who gives you the strength and the backup you need." (Will Collette)*

To accomplish the goal of protecting the people of Louisiana, the women whose stories we have heard here regularly interacted with government and industry leaders and organizing and legal experts. Sometimes these people proved themselves a mixture of both allies and adversaries, and just as often, they proved one way or another. This chapter presents interviews with some of these people. Their perspectives offer insight into the complex issues that had to be considered before a law could be changed, a policy created, a permit granted, or a regulation enforced.

The voices here do not, of course, represent an all-inclusive list. There were many other decision makers whom we were not able to interview, especially those who did not support regulation in the state. There were also people who could both help and hinder, such as former Governor Edwin Edwards and former Department of Environmental Quality (DEQ) secretaries Pat Norton, Martha Madden, and Dale Givens. Finally, there are those who helped in infinite ways, still help, and that we did not have the time to interview. In this last camp should be noted Oliver Houck of Tulane Law School. For almost forty years, Oliver's teaching has consistently emphasized the relationships between ecology and law in our state. His students, in turn, have come to support our coastal ecosystems, the Pearl River, Atchafalaya swamps, and other natural areas.

In addition, another word should be said about the Tulane University Environmental Law Clinic, which Oliver started with the active support of John Kramer (dean of the Law School, 1986–1996). All through the 1990s, Law Clinic staff Bob Kuehn and Audrey Evans provided legal help and outreach directly to the citizen groups they represented. Their narratives appear here. What is not heard is how that assistance has increased under Adam Babich and several supervising attorneys and outreach coordinators. Indeed, it is important to say that such work continues. The Law Clinic's work has garnered numerous awards, but, more importantly, it has lent credibility and enforcement power to the movement and its women leaders.

Finally, of course, there are the nameless people who have helped. If you are one such person, know here of the gratitude of others. Change is never made even by hundreds of people, but rather by thousands, from the simple impulses of those who contribute a word of support to those others who can give more.

## CHARLES ELSON "BUDDY" ROEMER

Throughout this book, the women interviewed have praised former Governor Buddy Roemer for his proactive stand on environmental issues. Roemer certainly would recognize all who have contributed. In 2012, he made an early bid for the Americans Elect and Reform Party's nomination for president of the United States. He previously ran for the Republican Party presidential nomination but withdrew in the fall of 2011. He is also involved in community banking. In other words, he thinks big. He is a rare person, beloved by many in his home state and beyond.

Roemer spent his first sixteen years on the family's four-thousand-acre cotton farm. He grew up with a strict work ethic, working in the cotton fields during weekends and summer vacations.

**Narrative from Charles Elson "Buddy" Roemer (b. Shreveport, Louisiana, 1943)**

It was a wonderful time to grow up in the '40s and '50s.[1] America was generally at peace. It was a Dwight Eisenhower kind of time, where the cotton farm was a haven.

It was a place to learn lessons, like hard work and teamwork. I walked the fields. I had horses. I fished in streams. I came to appreciate the Earth and the people who appreciated it. To this day, I love and admire farmers. They are the most courageous business people I know. They risk their fortune every year, hoping it will rain in July.

I was very close to my grandparents. Granddaddy Ross McDade, my mother's father, was the most persistent storyteller. He was a politician, and like me, sometimes he was a failed politician. He ran for sheriff and he lost. And he carried a gun when he was running for sheriff. He said he lost so badly that he bought another gun, and from then on he wore two guns. My family members were known as Civil Libertarians. We believed in integration. We believed in one nation, one community. That came from my grandparents. My granddaddy told the stories of how African Americans had been treated in Bossier Parish and how many tears it had brought them and how it is changing over time but very slowly. Our family was a member of the NAACP, perhaps the first white people to join in Bossier Parish.

[When Buddy was fourteen his father suggested he might want to do something other than farming. At fifteen, Buddy applied and was accepted to Harvard University. He was the youngest student in his class, having just turned sixteen. At Harvard, Roemer received an undergraduate degree in economics and a master's degree in business administration. After graduating, Roemer began his political career and was eventually elected to the US Congress.]

The job I enjoyed the best was being a member of the United States Congress. It satisfied the needs on my mother's side—caring. I was paid good money to get involved in solving problems of the state, of the country, and of the world. It was a great job. You got cussed sometimes and discussed sometimes. You couldn't make everybody happy, but every now and then there would be an issue where you would make a difference. And it was such a good feeling.

I was an average supporter of environmental issues, and that's about all that I was. I'm a realist. I was considered the most environmentally conscious of the Louisiana delegation, and that put me in the mainstream of congressional values. I can't think of a single issue where I distinguished myself, but I was always involved in issues of land use, water conservation, and balance with industry.

[In a surprise upset, Roemer defeated populist incumbent Edwin Edwards and was elected governor of Louisiana in 1987. He served one term, from 1988 to 1992.]

Governor Dave Treen started the Department of Environmental Quality [in 1984]. We were the last state in America to do it. And this Republican, this conservative, Dave Treen, said there ought to be a place where we overlook [supervise] the activities of the polluters. And he was right. But when I became governor, some eight years later, that department had never been funded. It lived on federal grants and on fines—and it didn't have many fines. So what I did was fund it. And I said, "Let's go find the polluters; let's don't wait for the consumer to call; let's see if there's a smokestack. . . . Let's go check it out. Let's measure the bacterial content in our waters and streams." That's when we started doing it. Treen gets credit though; he gave us a platform and we just built an environmental system on it.

I didn't think industry should be given tax credits and then not be held accountable for how they impacted the environment. When I became governor, one of the first things that I did was have an environmental scorecard for the industrial tax credit, the only state in America to do it. Now most every state has copied that, but we were the first, and the Sierra Club and all the groups gave us the State of the Year award because of that. I think it is good business to have clean air and bright water.

Paul Templet [secretary of the Department of Environmental Quality under Roemer] was one of my great appointments. Probably cost me re-election. But, you know, Paul Templet did more good than any person I appointed. And I appointed some really great people! His focus was air and water and how we were not going to be measured by how peaceful the department runs. We were going to be measured by how much we clean up the air and water and what kind of public attention we draw to this issue.

Economic development, ethics in government, educational excellence, an environmental friendly state, those were my four Es, and Paul Templet accomplished one of them for me. He had the whole department focus on their mission to clean up the air and water, and he didn't really give a darn what toes were stepped on. I was the reasonable one of the marriage. And I would say that eight and a half out of ten environmental ideas that Paul brought to me, I endorsed and we passed: environmental scorecard for tax credits, shutting down the Calcasieu basin because you couldn't eat the fish and putting up signs to say that. I thought they [opponents] were going to die, but it was the right thing to do. That water is much cleaner now. Flying out on a Sunday morning by helicopter to look at Marine Shale and closing that plant down. Wow! That's Paul Templet, and I give him total credit and honor for doing it.

[As new environmental regulations were beginning to be enforced, pressure mounted between industry and the Roemer administration.]

Industry is brutal. They are their own worst enemies. I'm a graduate of Harvard Business School. I'm an industrialist, OK. I'm a job governor. I believe in jobs. But I do think balance is the way to go in life. You can't be clean air and pristine water and no jobs. And you can't be no air and no water and full jobs. We have to be wise in our decisions.

My phone rang off the wall [with industry protests about DEQ's actions under Templet's leadership]. But you know, I would try to be fair with them, and I'd say, "If what you say happened, it's not fair. Let me get to the bottom of it." Well, it never was like the phone call, OK? There were clear measurements for water and air. There were fines that had not been paid. There were reports that were expected. There were cleanup efforts that had to be made for water—and water is critical for life. I would call the industrial spokesman back and say, "I want you to know I have checked it out, and I support our department. Could I meet with your leaders and tell you what happened?"

Maureen [O'Neill, assistant secretary for Water Resources at DEQ under Roemer] and others have had to leave the state. And there are others who fought the good fight here and left us in better shape than we started out, but who took so much personal grief that to get a decent job they had to go somewhere else.

When I ran for re-election [four years later], I went before the Chemical Association. They are important to Louisiana as they create a lot of jobs—not as much now as then, but a lot of jobs. I said, as governor, that I thought we paid a price for those jobs, and we should know what that price was. That's all I said. I went before them and asked them to support me for re-election, and it was quiet. There were like two hundred or three hundred people in this room. I will never forget—one guy got up and said, "Who are you going to appoint as head of DEQ?" And I said, "I already have a director. That will change only when he steps down." You could have heard a pin drop. You could have heard it. And I said, "Ladies and Gentlemen, it's in Louisiana's best interest, and it's in yours, to have a knowledgeable man of integrity at the top. And not one of you can say that Paul's ever been unfair, uncaring, or unwilling to listen." I said, "If you feel that way, I want you to stand and tell me." No one stood up. It was a political, nonsensical moment from the leadership of that industry. It didn't reflect the groundswell of things.

Industry went against me. They voted. They had rallies and meetings. They were for anybody but Roemer. Millions of dollars were spent to run ads about how I was "ruining" the state. I lost by a half a percentage point, a few thousand votes.

If you've got to lose, why not lose on principle? I wish we hadn't lost, and that I had been healthier physically and less worn out mentally. We almost won. But we could have pulled this thing over the line and we'd be telling a different story now. The citizens wrote me by the hundreds. A mom and dad who lived on the bayou, people who lived in small towns, people who lived near a big plant could know that at night they didn't see strange gases being emitted. I got heat from the big boys, but I got love from the little ones. I wouldn't make that trade for anything in the world. It was a good trade.

[The women activists in Louisiana] never asked for anything unreasonable. Dredging of Lake Pontchartrain—that was us—we stopped it! Oh, they said it couldn't be done. All the nah, nah, nah, but we did it! Boom! And I thought the world was going to come to an end for a while. But it didn't; it was the right thing to do. You know, we can improve the world in which we live, sometimes just by doing the little things.

I find when I speak to national groups on the environment there is always a Louisiana contingency there. Louisiana is well thought of in the fight for environmental balance in spite of our tragic record of one hundred years. We used to clear-cut [cut all the trees in a given area, without consideration of growing patterns and needs]. We used to do everything imaginable to put a strain on the environment. Even in these times, the citizens of Louisiana have been so strong that we have developed a reputation as caring about the environment. Our politicians don't have the word yet. Our congressional record is not even average. There is almost no leadership in the last eight years of the governor on that. I don't like to criticize, but let me put it this way—we have a long way to go. Our politicians do not reflect our people, in part, because our politicians don't do their jobs on economic development. If we had a jobs program where we could see that it means more jobs to have clean air and clean water, we'd all be better off. So that's kind of what I work on now, an economic end to environmental balance, that is, clean air and bright water means more jobs—not fewer.

### *Afterword*

I was proud to work with the environmental groups. I was proud to do my mother proud, for caring about that, but this work is not done. We spent four good years at it, but it takes years to turn a state around. We had our chance, but it wasn't just me alone. I stood with others. There were some on whose shoulders I stood who came long before the Roemer revolution, but we put our own twist on it. I had a simple message from which I never deviated. And the message was, "We as a people are better than our politics, and it's something we can do something about." This was the message, and I said it enough times, under enough pressure, and under enough temptation to back up from it, but I would not back up from it, even if I finished dead last. I wanted somebody to represent my values in the governor's office, and the value is "politics last, not first."

## CARROLL WASCOM

Carroll Wascom, of Baton Rouge, Louisiana, was employed by the Office of Conservation from 1980 to 2003. From 2000 to 2003, he was director of the Injection and Mining Division. He is currently employed by the Environmental Treatment Team (ETT) in Baton Rouge. During the years he spent working for the Office of Conservation, industry and environmental activists alike regarded him as both an ally and an adversary. His narrative, more than others, shows the flexibility of the philosophy of stewardship of the Earth, as well as the various interpretations of care that residents bring to the conservatism of the state.

## Narrative from Carroll Wascom (b. Baton Rouge, Louisiana, 1950)

I was raised primarily in Baton Rouge and Pineville, but for the majority of my life, I lived in Covington, Louisiana.[2] From 1971 to the present, I've lived in the Baton Rouge area. I remember my grandmother. I didn't know my grandfather. And the best thing I remember about them is the week I would spend each summer at their home, feeding the chickens and cows. Just enjoying a good time away from home.

I graduated from Louisiana State University (LSU) in 1972 with a major in geology. I was always interested in the Earth and what composed it. As a child I would take different colored soil and make things with it in a jar of water and see the layers. I was encouraged to pursue a degree in geology. And I did so.

When I got out of school, there were not many jobs available, so I applied for a job with the Department of Transportation and Development (DOTD) in their soil mechanics lab as a geologist, doing environmental engineering, building bridges, roads, and highways in the state. After eight years of working there, rumors were flying that the engineers were going to cut back the geologists. So I saw an ad in the paper for a geologist in the Department of Natural Resources and then was offered that job.

In the Office of Conservation they needed someone to help get the Underground Injection Control (UIC) program started. We took the federal requirements and drew up a program description, which basically told the Environmental Protection Agency (EPA) what we were going to do to administer and implement a federally improved underground injection control program. We had to prove to them that we had the staff, the money, inspectors, equipment, and whatever it took to get the program going. Of course, the object of the UIC program was to protect groundwater from injection well practices, from oil and gas practices, hazardous waste, industrial waste, and disposal wells. All those mechanisms were in place through the federal government. But the state government had to implement those to make sure that the program was at least as stringent as the federal one.

I remember vividly receiving phone call after phone call from oil and gas operators and concerned citizens wanting to know, "What's this all about?" And, of course, it was new to me too. Some of it I knew; some of it I didn't. And, I think, that period of my life was probably the most learning time that I've ever gone through.

During that period, I realized that there were a lot of people who felt that injection of waste was not a good idea. Because how do you know it's not polluting the groundwater? And I could understand those feelings. But as a professional and as a geologist, understanding the regulations and how companies were supposed to implement those regulations, there were safeguards in place to make sure that that would not happen. Of course, things do happen, and some companies don't comply, or do things exactly right. We all know that nothing's perfect. The world's not perfect, regulations are not perfect, industry's not perfect, and regulators are not perfect. But we did feel that if the program was implemented properly, we would protect, better protect, the groundwater than what was being done prior to that time.

James H. Welsh, now the commissioner of conservation, was the director of the injection and mining division. We went through a lot of public hearings, and we were the targets of a lot of criticism because of the UIC program, because of the commercial facility program. We often talked about how we're just trying to do our jobs and protect the groundwater and protect the environment of the state. But we were getting a lot of criticism and a lot of flack. And as a regulator, you have to learn to balance both sides. You had the regulations, which told the companies this is what you have to do. And we had to make them do that, and then we had citizens saying, "You need to do more. You need to tighten regulations." And it's really hard sometimes to find a good median. Jim used to say we were damned if we did and damned if we didn't. He helped me realize that one way to know if you're doing your job is if you have no friends in industry and no friends in the citizens. The oil companies may be mad at us because we're making them do something, and the citizens may be mad at us because we didn't do something. It was a very difficult situation to be in.

We wanted to make sure that the companies wanting permits were going to comply with the rules. And as long as they were going to do that, then we were okay with issuing permits. One of the arguments we had at the public hearings is that the citizens thought, "This man asking for the permit is no good. He's a crook. He steals money. He's not good to work with." But I couldn't find anywhere in the regulations where it said, "We can't issue a permit to a crook." We may have believed it and thought it to be true, but we couldn't take that into consideration. We had to just make sure that the letter of the law was being met.

One thing I've tried to teach members of the organization, in injection and mining, is that the people that need this information, the people who want these permits, are the people that we serve. We must provide them whatever they need to the best of our ability—whether it be Wilma Subra fussing at us because of a permit we've issued and wanting to look at information to use to argue against a permit, or whether it's an oil company asking for a permit and trying to find out how do I do it. We wouldn't just be the big regulator who comes down on people.

I guess we could have had more meetings with community leaders, which we did have. We had many of those prior to public hearings, where we would try our best to explain what the rule required, what the applicant wanted to do, and how we were going to protect the environment. But many times, people didn't want to hear that. I guess, just like I didn't want to hear that they were going to put a subdivision right behind my house. I didn't care how nice the houses were. I just didn't want it here. And I guess, in that regard, a lot of people just didn't want it [an industrial facility in their neighborhood]. They were afraid, I think, of the unknown. And, I think, if they knew how our regulatory framework worked, they would have felt more comfortable.

[Many citizens did not trust the Office of Conservation to effectively protect the environment and oversee industry.]

For a lot of the time that I worked, there was a governor in the state who's now in jail. And so, over a period of time, people realized that they can't trust the government. Can't trust the governor. Can't trust anybody. So, you know, when a regulator goes into a public hearing with citizens, we're at a disadvantage already. They don't trust us. They don't want to hear what we have to say. They don't want to know what we're going to do to prevent the environment from being polluted. They just want to gripe. Now saying all that, I will say that many, many times, citizens, I think primarily the ladies, would touch on subjects that were very new to us. And [they] would make us, as regulators, think that we needed to take a second look at that application. Because they know the community better, and they may know of a problem there that we did not know about. So we would take those into consideration as we would respond to comments or amend the permit, to make sure that the company did what they needed to do.

But, the citizens—I don't think they realize that by saying, "I don't want it here," concerning an application, is[n't] good enough. They've got to know those rules. They've got to know what the applicant wants to do. And we did deny applications. We did not permit every facility that came to us. And there were several occasions when the comments were very helpful in making decisions on an application. But in many cases, it was very emotional, and I can't tell you how many times I was called a baby killer. And to drive home after a public hearing was rough. Jim Welsh and I had some of our deepest conversations on our way back from Cameron or Plaquemine. But it was all part of the distrust for government. And we realized that. They didn't know us, and they didn't know what we were doing with our job. They just knew we worked for the government.

But, you know, one person with pertinent information could help me decide, as a regulator, to either grant or not grant that permit, more than a hundred people screaming. I don't blame citizens for thinking that if they get the numbers out there, then maybe we'll be convinced. But you can't do that as a regulator. You have to go with what you're provided in the rules. 'Cause if you don't, you'll get sued by the applicant. Now if they didn't do everything they were supposed to do and were granted the permit, then the citizens could sue us and say, "Well, you granted them a permit." And, you know, Wilma [Subra] would be right down my throat, saying, "You didn't do what you were supposed to do." So we were kind of stuck between a rock and a hard spot.

I think the reason a lot of people had that opinion and took that direction, of course, is they see companies or facilities that have no regard for the rules after they get a permit. They will tell you they are doing everything, but then they get the permit and forget it. And that happens. That's why people get upset.

But there's one thing that I always said and that is that if the company is not going to comply with the rules, and they're going to use political pressure to skirt the rules, sooner or later they're going to hang themselves. Every one that did that is now gone. Big Diamond's gone. Mar Services is gone. Marine Shale is gone. The ones that are doing it right, they're going to stick around.

[One public hearing Carroll attended was the Willow Springs hearing at LaGrange High School in Lake Charles, January 23, 1985. There were over seven hundred concerned citizens in attendance.]

I was up on the stage and thought, "Oh my gosh! We're going to be here all night." I'd never seen anything like that before. What amazed us was that it was our public hearing, but the politicians were up there too. They just took residence up there on the stage. Normally at a public hearing, everybody's in the audience. And when somebody wants to speak, they come forward and they speak, and they go sit back down. But it was a shock. I have to say, I think that's probably the biggest hearing that I ever went to. I don't remember a whole lot about the comments that night; it's just a blur. But I do remember the Girl Scouts being there. That was, I think, probably the first time anything like that has ever happened to [the Office of] Conservation.

We had public hearings that lasted from six o'clock to 1:30, 2:00 a.m. in the morning. There was an interesting hearing [May 15, 1986] in Grand Lake, where the lights went out about 9:30 p.m. It was a scary moment because it was a pretty emotional hearing. It ended up with everybody taking their chairs next door to the fire station. And they backed the truck out of the fire station and we finished our public hearing there. There was a mob of people there that night.

I can't remember the lady's name. She was relentless and sometimes a little disrespectful toward the regulators. The man, Odell Vinson, lived next to the site in a big house with a motor home. And the lady asked me where I'd been the week before because she'd noticed that Mr. Vinson's bus had been gone. She wanted to know if I'd borrowed it to go on vacation. And that indicated to me that the citizens think that the regulators are in the pockets of the people with facilities. And that is not the case. We, in the injection and mining division, did what we were supposed to do. And the regulators were doing a good thing in getting that facility [Big Diamond] out of the pits and into land treatment. The pits were leaking. We realized it. And we told them you had to get out of it and go to something else. So they were attempting to go to a better treatment mechanism and [the owner] ended up going bankrupt and leaving the state after having to clean up the problem. The trouble is, we didn't have any money. So the oil companies had to pitch in. That facility, right now, is being cleaned up by several of the oil companies that took the waste into that site.

Of all the people that have ever testified in public hearings, Wilma Subra does the most homework and has the most knowledge of the industry, the problems, and the environment. Her comments, more so than not, are focused on the problems and the applications and the things that a company did or didn't do as far as the regulations required. I think she's probably the champion of that effort. I admire her because of her persistence and her ability to gain knowledge of the industry so that the comments provided were legitimate and to the point and helped the agencies make a decision. That's really what we were all about. It was not a popularity contest. It was not who yells the loudest. It's not who wants it the least. It was whether or not a company can meet the regulations. And that's what it boiled down to, and I think she realized that.

Clara Baudoin and all her efforts in the Mar Services case helped her to understand the politics of it all. Even today we're friends. And if she needs information, she asks. I remember Miss [Gay] Hanks as being a very nice lady, very intense and involved in what she felt was important in her community. I remember her as one of my favorite speakers at public hearings.

I think, generally, these women were concerned about their families, their communities, and their children. And I think that's probably where all the signs and the "baby killer" comments came from. But, you know, without the signs, without the input, we probably would not have been as conscious of what was going on. They made us look closer at what we were doing. 'Cause you know—and we always said this, Jim Welsh and I—that if it was our community, we'd be saying some of the same things. And that was one of the most popular comments at the public hearing, "Would you have this in your backyard?" Now, personally, in most cases, I wouldn't mind having it in my backyard, knowing the regulations and how they're being implemented by most of the companies. But would I want a Big Diamond in my backyard or a Mar Services in my backyard or a Marine Shale Processors in my backyard? Probably not, because they were operated by people who did not particularly care to comply with the rules. I'd just have to say, except maybe in the Big Diamond instance, they did at least attempt to comply with the rules.

I think we need to be good stewards of what God gave us. And that's why we have regulations. It started with the Ten Commandments. If we don't have rules and regulations, it would be chaos. But in light of eternity, some of the things that we deal with are not going to matter at all. And I wish that people would focus on the things that are really important. And I'll be real serious about this. In the effort put forth to protect the environment, which to me in many ways is worship of the Earth, we substitute a worship of the Earth for a worship of the God that created it. I think that's misguided. If we would put more effort into protecting the unborn child, and the many thousands being aborted every day, to me that's a lot more important than whether or not a waste disposal facility goes next to my house.

## *Afterword*

I retired from the state April 11, 2003, and I had an opportunity early last year to go to work for one of the companies that I regulated. I was offered a position as vice president of the health, safety, and environmental treatment team with one of the three companies in the state that receives and treats solid exploration and production waste. Now, you have to go through the Ethics Commission to get approval to take a job like that. You have to find out what the guidelines are for what you can and cannot do—and for two years I can't interact. Since I've taken the job and transferred to ETT, I've been very careful to follow those rules. In fact, it's kind of hard to not have a rapport with the people that I spent twenty-two years working with at Conservation.

# MAUREEN O'NEILL

During the years she spent working in local and state governments offices, Maureen O'Neill, like Carroll Wascom, had to consider all sides of an issue. But her forthright stance on the need to empower the public often made her unpopular with industry. As Mildred Fossier exclaimed in her narrative, "That girl!" And, indeed, Maureen made a very big impression and many lasting changes. A former resident of New Orleans, she served as director of planning for the New Orleans Sewerage and Water Board from 1982 through 1988. In 1986 she helped stop plans to dump radioactive gypsum into the Mississippi River—the sole source of drinking water for New Orleans. In 1988 Governor Buddy Roemer appointed Maureen assistant secretary for water resources for the Louisiana Department of Environmental Quality (DEQ), where she set standards for public participation at the agency. She was also responsible for establishing new water regulations, increasing enforcement, and passing some of the most comprehensive water quality standards in the state's history. She developed an online constant-monitoring program for major industrial discharges and expanded the Lower Mississippi River Warning System to protect the drinking water of 1.5 million people.

Now residing in New York City, Maureen works for the US Environmental Protection Agency as a senior policy advisor. [Legal note: Maureen's comments represent her views and do not represent a statement of the US Environmental Protection Agency.]

## Narrative from Maureen O'Neill (b. Chicago, Illinois, 1946)

I started out in Chicago, where my father had a car dealership and my mother was a housewife.[3] I was an only child, so I was expected to keep out of trouble, work hard, and do my best to succeed. I went to Waukegan, Illinois, Township High School, where I was, in those pre-Internet days, a bookworm. I loved studying and reading, which gave me perspective and insight into other people's lives. It taught me about other cultures and communities and not just one way of doing things.

While my father had been supportive of my receiving as much education as I wanted, my mother disagreed. She thought going to college was a waste of time. From her perspective, my goal should be to get married and have kids. This had been her life, and she thought it was a model for how mine should be.

But I could not change my overriding thought: "I want to see what's out there. I want to look at life." At eighteen I went away to the University of Illinois at Champaign–Urbana. I was three hundred miles away from home in an enormous school packed to capacity with baby boomers. I couldn't believe my eyes—so many kids my own age, as well as more opportunities to party than I had ever seen!

My father died that first year I was away at college, which changed my life drastically. I dropped out of college and had numerous jobs. The one that stands out most in my mind was working in a factory packing typewriters on the night shift. I quickly figured out that this was not what I wanted to do with my life.

I had been fortunate enough to grow up in a middle-class family with older parents that resulted in my needs being more than adequately met. However, once my father died and my mother relocated to Florida and was in ill health, I went from a carefree life to having nothing. It was a very sobering experience for an eighteen year old.

As with all challenging things that face one in a lifetime, there were some positive aspects. I am grateful I had to learn about money and responsibility at an early age. Years later, when I was able to eventually return to college, I worked much harder to get the most out of my education. If I had stayed at the University of Illinois, I don't know that I would have learned as much. Sometimes, when things are too easy, you don't try as hard, nor do you understand the hardships that other people have to go through.

I eventually found my way to New Orleans when I went to see Mardi Gras. I fell instantly in love with the city and the people and decided to stay. It was clear I needed to finish school, and I did so, receiving my undergraduate degree from Loyola University in New Orleans. I then was fortunate enough to get a fellowship to graduate school at the University of New Orleans.

[Maureen's first job after graduate school was with the New Orleans City Planning Commission.]

Maureen O'Neill

At that time people were talking about recycling, which was considered very avant-garde! But I was concerned about chemical exposure. There was so little knowledge [on the subject].

I felt as though I needed to look deeper, but it wasn't clear where to start. The incident that triggered [my interest] involved railroad tank cars leaking in the French Quarter. Many times when the City Council of New Orleans gets an issue that isn't routine, it is sent to the Planning Commission to take under advisement and conduct a study. So the council asked us for a study, but no one wanted to do it. I thought it was a great opportunity to look at some of the chemical issues that had been puzzling me, so I quickly volunteered, which must have been a relief to the rest of the office.

Well, that is what started it off because I really started digging. It turned out that this was the first study ever done in the United States on the issue. When I finished it, the National Transportation and Safety Board sent it out to other cities in the country and suggested that they use it as a model. But I wasn't interested in just studying it. I was interested in fixing every aspect of it, which may have been a little grandiose because one doesn't necessarily solve every problem. However, some substantive positive actions occurred. We got railroad tracks repaired, as well as additional safety inspections.

In 1982 I went to new challenges at the New Orleans Sewerage and Water Board. That was a wonderful opportunity because the drinking water for the city passes through 40 percent of the continental United States before it gets to us at the end of the river. As we used to always say, "It passes through some of the finest people and plants along the Mississippi River before getting to New Orleans." That was an eye opener for me. In a perfect world you could fix everything in the city of New Orleans and still have numerous issues because of external factors. To truly fix the Mississippi, you needed to start at the headwaters in Minnesota! Before this, I had not given interstate issues much consideration since my world was totally New Orleans.

I was deeply concerned about the quality of the drinking water [in the city]. If you recall, the Safe Drinking Water Act for the United States was passed because of the numerous cancer-causing contaminants that had been found in our water. To improve water taken from the Mississippi River, there are two things that one needs to do. Cleaning up the river would result in a better water source. But you also need to have good laboratories and treatments. We were able to do that, so that we would know that the quality was being monitored to give the public the best protection.

While I was director of planning at the New Orleans Sewerage and Water Board, Freeport-McMoRan, the only Fortune 500 Company in New Orleans, as well as a few other companies, wanted to get an exemption from the Clean Water Act pending before Congress. What that would have done was allow them to dump a low-level radioactive waste product—gypsum—that wasn't allowed to be dumped anywhere else in the United States. It would have set a nightmarish precedent to allow radioactive waste into the Mississippi River, which could enter our drinking water. Freeport acted as if they were beyond the rules and that they could just change things to fit their needs. That's why I felt so strongly about the issue.

I thought if we had rational conversations and presented data and went through things properly, then we could reasonably work things out—but it was not like that. It was a brutal battle. And the more brutal it got, the more I was convinced that if we didn't do what needed to be done on this, then we were going to have even worse water quality coming into New Orleans and possibly getting people sick. It is impossible to know the exact impact this would have had, but no doctor or public health person that I ever talked to thought that drinking this waste was a good idea.

The Freeport-McMoRan issue was an interesting, albeit scandalous, battle. Edwin Edwards was governor during this time, and his brother Marion was on the payroll of Freeport-McMoRan as a "messenger." Freeport also hired Tommy Boggs (son of Hale and Lindy Boggs, former US congressman and congresswoman) to be their lobbyist to change the Clean Water Act in Washington so that they could do their dumping. I am grateful that it ended on the side of the public. It was a happy ending. But I would have to say that nothing would have happened without Mildred Fossier [also featured in this book], who I had never laid eyes on before the gypsum battle. She was there to guide me with her wisdom and skills.

[In 1988 Governor Buddy Roemer appointed Maureen assistant secretary of the Office of Water Resources for the Department of Environmental Quality.]

I had never met Governor Roemer, never applied for the job, and I wasn't lobbying for it. So when I was offered the job, I was shocked. Paul Templet, who the governor had appointed as secretary of the DEQ, called me. Paul was aware of my work because we had both been active in the environment [gypsum and coastal issues]. At the DEQ I was the chief regulatory authority for water resources, which meant oversight over enforcement, surveillance, permitting, and engineering. It was my signature that would have to go on any major issue dealing with water resources for the state of Louisiana.

It was the most challenging thing I ever did. I had a very good understanding of New Orleans, and I knew things about the state with the railroad transportation issues and the Mississippi River drinking water issues. I definitely had looked outside of the city limits. But I would be the first to say how much I didn't know about many of the other issues facing Louisiana. I had to get up to speed very quickly. There were many communities that I barely knew. It was a huge learning curve. I did nothing for four years but work, work, work. I knew I owed it to the public to work as hard as I could to increase their protection.

Everything I did was for the public; it was vital to me that they be involved. In the past, many decisions and meetings that impacted public health and the environment had been done behind closed doors, excluding those most at risk. For people to make reasonable decisions, whether it's the regulated community, the public, or the regulatory agency, they need to collectively discuss and understand the diversity of views. They do not necessarily have to agree with each other, but being in that room hearing things and having access to public information is absolutely critical.

I wanted it to be empowering, so people could go on to do what they needed to do. There is no piece of information that the public cannot understand. And if somebody can't explain it to them, there is something wrong. It means they are trying to hide something or that they don't understand it themselves.

[Maureen was revolutionizing the treatment of water resources at DEQ, and much of Louisiana's oil and gas industry did not approve of her approach.]

There was quite a push to get me fired at one particular point in time by the chemical industry. The head of [the chemical company operating a plant in Geismar, Louisiana] BASF in Germany actually flew to Louisiana to meet with the governor to complain about my cleanup plan for their chemical waste as being too strict. Governor Roemer stood by me. Paul Templet stood by me. And I was never told, "You do this, or you do that."

Some of the things that were so important were to seriously tighten up the water quality standards in general, pass regulations on the permitting of the oil and gas industry, and look at their waste issues. I passed a number of regulations. What I tried to do was to go for what I perceived to have the widest impact affecting the most people significantly.

One of those issues was oilfield waste, which has a certain amount of radioactivity to it. What happens, when you pull up oil and gas from a low-producing well where there is not much product left, is that you start pulling up more and more wastewater [produced water]. It's very toxic. It was being discharged right back into the water as garbage. When you have both commercial and recreational fishermen, as well as others in Louisiana, dependent upon these resources—we consume so much fish and seafood—it was critical we not throw radioactive and toxic chemicals and metal wastes into our food source.

I did pass regulations on produced water. Interestingly, what worked was requiring industry to collect data on their own discharges. We used their data so that we would not be questioned on our science or our approaches. It was urgent that this happen to protect our seafood sources.

I would get industry arguments about what regulations would cost the oil and gas industry. But the other part of the picture I had to keep repeating was, "What does it cost the fisheries industry, which is also a big industry in Louisiana?" "What does it cost the public?" There is not just one business or industry, so how do we live together? How do we accept the fact that we have the oil and gas industry, the fisheries, and the people? How do we do this together so that we can all win? That is the question and that is the key. It isn't that one group has to lose, but many people did not view it that way. It was a win–lose sort of situation to them.

There were a number of people that wanted Governor Roemer out of office. I do know that the environment played a role in it [Roemer's defeat for re-election]. There were people that wanted to return to the good old days—they didn't want good government. They didn't want an open door policy because it interfered with the taking of Louisiana's natural resources and sending it out of the state and then leaving the state with its waste and its problems.

I left Louisiana because I felt like I had to [after Edwin Edwards was elected governor in 1992]. I did not want to go to Washington, but I think it was the right decision. I had done as much as I could in Louisiana with enforcement, permitting, and surveillance. There were some special interest groups [in Louisiana] that really didn't want me to continue cleaning up the environment. I knew how to get things done, and that was threatening to them.

I have worked for local government, state government, and now for the federal government. I have done a substantial amount of international work both from Washington, D.C., and later while on loan from the United States to the United Nations in New York. I have worked all over the Middle East, in Africa, the Americas, and parts of Asia. I was used to working with many good women in Louisiana, so it was particularly evident to me how few women were involved in the international work. I think it's important that women be at the table because women usually examine issues and solutions peacefully. They don't want to see people harmed. They seem to know we can focus on what we have in common and build on those commonalities. Fortunately, there are men who also are willing to take this approach, but they are far fewer in numbers than women.

### *Afterword*

Rachel Carson was a government scientist who worked in Washington. I read her biography and her book, *Silent Spring*. I was struck by the battles she went through and how lonely it was. It is lonely. It gave me strength to realize she believed in what she was doing and she did it, even though there were special interests that did not want her to and who tried to minimize her.

In Louisiana, for me, it wasn't always lonely and it wasn't always scary, but there were moments. Harassment comes to mind. I insisted on keeping my phone number public. If somebody wanted to call me, I wanted them to be able to. And practically every night the phone would start ringing in the middle of the night. When I would go to answer it, there was just silence on the other end. But I learned how to deal with it.

I had my home broken into a number of times. I never knew who did it, but I always thought it was strange that just my papers were missing. One weekend after a break-in, I mentioned it at a staff meeting, and two of my colleagues [other assistant secretaries at DEQ] said their houses had also been broken into the same weekend! A few times I was scared, but then I got absolutely mad and thought, "Nobody is going to intimidate me." And they didn't. What it did was make me work harder. It made me reach out even more to the community in Louisiana. It was absolutely worth doing, and I will be forever grateful that I had the chance to make a difference.

# KAI DAVID MIDBOE

Like Maureen O'Neill, Kai David Midboe, of Baton Rouge, Louisiana, made an effort to reach out to the citizens of Louisiana during his tenure as secretary of the Department of Environmental Quality. Kai started his environmental career in the 1970s at the Louisiana State University (LSU) Sea Grant Program. When Governor David Treen was elected governor of Louisiana in 1980, Kai served as executive assistant for Federal and Environmental Affairs, where he worked to develop a plan to save the Atchafalaya Basin. In 1992 Governor Edwin Edwards appointed Kai secretary of the DEQ. In 2005 he was head of the Environmental and Toxic Tort Department at the Milling Benson Woodward LLP Law Firm, defending companies that are accused of environmental violations and helping them remediate those sites. He currently works for the law firm of McGlinchey, Stafford.

### Narrative from Kai David Midboe (b. New Orleans, Louisiana, 1944)

I grew up in a seafaring world.[4] My mother was second generation from Norway. My father was also from Norway, and all of my relatives on his side. He was from a small fishing village. It's very typical Norwegian, white houses with red slate roofs on an inlet from the ocean.

We were raised in the Norwegian community in New Orleans, around the Norwegian Seaman's Church. I lived there until I was ten years old, and then my father was transferred to New York. I actually grew up in Port Washington on a peninsula on Long Island Sound. I could literally walk to water in any direction from our house. All of my uncles were captains onboard ships. My father was with Norwegian Verities, which is a ship classification society. So just about every two years we went back to Norway.

My first real employment after law school was with the Coast Guard. I went in as council for the Coast Guard and was in their Maritime and International Law Division, responsible for enforcing environmental laws. I left the Coast Guard to go get my LLM at the University of Miami. I got my LLM, and while I was in Miami I went with a law firm and spent about a year with them. Then I was interviewed for the position at the Sea Grant Program at LSU.

At Sea Grant, working with Coastal Zone Management was interesting because the group working with them was Paul Templet [also featured in this book and DEQ secretary under the Roemer administration]. I was there, Paul was over at the State Planning office at the time, and Joel Lindsey [assistant DEQ secretary under the Roemer administration], who ended up at Southern University, was involved in it.

I was brought in to help develop the state's Coastal Zone Management program and also to help develop a course on maritime transportation. I got involved in it from the point of view of developing a mechanism to try and deal with the problems. We were, at that time, working within a Coastal Management Act that had just been enacted, and it allowed states to develop their own programs. This was my first involvement in really trying to resolve an issue. We set a program up, and it's still the law, although it's not funded anymore. I would testify before Congressman David Treen, and when he became the ranking Republican on the House Merchant Marine and Fisheries Committee, he asked me to come up and be his council. When he was elected governor, I came back as his executive assistant for Federal and Environmental Affairs in 1980.

At that time people were literally ready to shoot at each other over the future of the Atchafalaya Basin, and that's what I spent a good portion of my first two years with Treen working on. Treen and I were heavily involved in two things, the Atchafalaya Basin and setting aside wildlife areas. We set aside the Tensas Wildlife Area and managed to get, from Dow Chemical, fifty-four thousand acres in the Atchafalaya Basin. I received an award from the Louisiana Wildlife Federation for developing the governor's plan.

Back in those days, environmentalism was viewed as an enemy of development. They [committees such as ECC] were good sounding boxes. People could come in and make their positions known. All too often, however, you had dominant groups behind it—that controlled it. You had development interests that made sure that they captured control of these types of commissions. For instance, on the Coastal Zone Commission, the Landowners Association was very powerful. Where you started to see a change in the way citizens could get involved was when you had the IT decision (*Save Ourselves v. Louisiana Environmental Control Commission*). It made a big impact. It required agencies, particularly DEQ, to document why they make a decision. The Supreme Court of Louisiana said, in the IT case, "Here are the things that we want considered in ANY environmental decision. If they are not considered we will automatically reject the decision of the agency." So now the agency had to answer: "What are the benefits, what are the costs, and are there alternative locations?" That, to me, was a big opportunity for citizens to raise their concerns to the agency, who now had to answer those questions.

One of the things that [Governor] Treen did was set up the Department of Environmental Quality. I was one of four people assigned to implement the new department. We worked on it the entire time we were there, and in 1983 it was created. I think it was an important thing to do. The DEQ focused everyone. Before that, you had an office of Environmental Control Commission and that office was in the Department of Natural Resources (DNR). The DNR had a lot of inherent conflicts. They regulated the oil and gas industry, but they also promoted it. The state of Louisiana owned a percentage of the wetlands where oil and gas production was occurring. They had an ownership interest in a lot of decisions. So I thought it was very important, and so did Governor Treen, to create an independent office of environmental quality. That was a catalyst for then focusing on environmental issues and having one department with a constitutional mandate as the "trustee" of the state's environment. That's in the state constitution.

I'm a Republican and I have been a very strong activist in throwing David Duke out of the Republican Party. I have a Jewish wife and wasn't thrilled with having him in the party, so I formally endorsed Governor Edwards [a Democrat] to keep him from being elected. I joke around that I've always been opposed to Edwin Edwards and after he got elected he retaliated by making me secretary of DEQ.

I was very impressed with the way he treated me. He never interfered with the agency.

Environmental justice is also a very important issue. There are two different elements. The first is the environmental health issue from the chemical plants, and are they impacting the people based on race? And my answer to that is, "No, they are not," because the standards are set at the fence line not to exceed a certain level of chemicals outside that fence line. The standard that they have to meet is based on various levels of conservancy and on the cumulative impact of all of the industry in the area. So there is no way that the standard that a chemical has to meet outside of the fence line could be negatively impacting somebody based on race. If it's impacting people negatively, it's impacting everybody. If it's not impacting people, it's not impacting people.

That isn't the same as saying, "There's not a problem." There are problems in these neighborhoods: poor schools, no jobs, and the people who live around these plants aren't getting jobs inside the plants. And what they [EPA] basically have done, because of these social issues, is to look to the chemical industry, which is powerful, to try and help them. I think that is a legitimate thing, and they [industry] are a part of that community.

There's a legitimate reason for those plant managers to be concerned about these people and use their power to try and help them. The question that I raise is, Is the DEQ permitting process the legitimate place to be raising these issues? Or should they be directed at state and local government and what they are doing to protect those communities by providing proper health care and all the other things that should be provided?

If I'm the secretary looking at spending money, environmental justice issues are real, they are legitimate, but they are social issues and aren't really related to the permitting and the level of chemicals outside the fence line. So I'm an agency that doesn't have power in the social area. I can't set land-use restrictions. Where do I spend my money? I was interviewed by CBS when the environmental justice issues were getting started. and I was on national TV, saying, "Yeah, it's a legitimate issue, but really is up to local government to figure out how to improve their schools and how to locate facilities." I can't tell Dow Chemical, "You can't locate here because that isn't the appropriate industry for this location." I can tell them, "You cannot locate here because you don't meet the environmental standards necessary to locate here." That's a different decision.

One of the best programs ever is the Toxic Release Inventory [TRI] program, where companies are required to make public the amount of chemicals being dispersed into the air, land, and water. And that way the public can actually see how much is being produced and distributed into the environment. I think that has had more impact on industry reducing pollution than anything. All of a sudden they had to explain this to the local citizens. My only concern with the TRI program is that they keep changing how they do the accounting, so it's hard to follow from one year to the next whether you are actually getting a reduction or not. I think it should be more consistent reporting on issues.

[As citizens learned to use the new TRI program, their involvement in environmental permitting decisions increased.]

Citizen pressure. Absolutely, the public is simply saying, "We want jobs, but we want a safe environment also." And there is no reason that the two can't be compatible. It's hard to start from ground zero to get to where you want to get, so the public becomes impatient. But you've got to slowly move yourself toward that. There are things going on that could potentially set us backwards, and we don't want that; we want to keep moving forward on these issues and do it over time so the companies can adjust.

They [citizens] upset the status quo and politicians didn't like that. They had to recognize that a new player had come to the table, and this new player didn't necessarily agree with the way they were doing things. I went to Norway, for instance, while I was secretary of DEQ and took the opportunity to meet with environmentalists over there, and they had just discovered the offshore oil and gas industry and they wanted to know how Louisiana had dealt with it. And I said, "Well, come to Louisiana, study how we've dealt with it, and then do it another way." We didn't deal with it properly because that counterbalance wasn't there when all the canals were being dredged and the oil and gas was being developed. You couldn't do today 90 percent of what was done back in the '30s, '40s, '50s, and even into the '60s. Times have changed and people now understand that was wrong. Unfortunately, we paid a horrible price for it.

We have had dramatic improvements, however. Almost any scale you look at, pollution has been sharply reduced. The Baton Rouge area is still ozone non-attainment (federal standard indicating acute air pollution). But a good portion of the entire state used to be ozone non-attainment—now it's just this narrow area, and we only fail once a year or whatever it takes to trigger the sanctions. We no longer have Superfund sites being created; they are being discovered and cleaned up.

Most of your major environmentalists were women and were very active in the Governor's Task Force and had access to me. I had an open door policy; you didn't need to set an appointment to meet with me on an issue. They were very strong advocates, and several of them really made an effort to understand the issues. Wilma Subra is a good example of somebody who really knows their subject. A lot of people in industry don't like her, and the reason is that she is so sharp and she knows what she is talking about. She has been the technical arm of the environmental movement. She looks across the spectrum and gets involved, helping different organizations understand the chemical problems they are dealing with. She is not afraid to ask hard questions and demand answers.

I remember when I was with Treen, this is about 1980, and I went down to New Orleans to give a talk. There's a breakfast, an environmental group, with about thirty or forty people at the breakfast, and I was the speaker. I got up and I thought I'd give good advice, and so I said, "One of the things you need to understand is that when you come to us in government with a problem, you really can benefit yourself by coming with a recommended solution to the problem. And I still remember this little old lady got up in the back and she said, "Well, excuse me, young man, but isn't that what we pay you for?" She's right, I mean, the buck stops here, as they say, and you do have a responsibility to try and come up with solutions, but if you are an environmentalist and you understand the issues and you come up with proposed solutions, bring them to the agency. You'll be so much farther ahead. Then the agency is stuck in a position of having to say either, "It won't work and here's the reason why" or "Yes, we're going to adopt it." So it's better than coming to the agency and yelling at them and having them step back and try to figure out what to do about it. Become a member of an organization. Make your voice known. Appear at public hearings. If you don't raise the issue in the administrative process, it won't be considered by the agency and it cannot be appealed.

Put pressure at every level, from the governor on down. I was deeply disappointed in both [Kathleen] Blanco and [Bobby] Jindal [gubernatorial candidates in 2003 election] for not meeting the LEAN group when they set up a forum for them. LEAN, whether I agree with all the things they say or not, LEAN is still the consortium representing the environmental community, and they had a right to be heard and ask questions.

We have to have industry here, and we had to deal with those issues. We have 25 percent of the nation's wetlands in Louisiana, 25 percent of the nation's fisheries come out of those resources, and there is concern over hurricane surges that had to be addressed, and that's a critical issue for this state. Louisiana's a farming state. You've got pesticides; those are important issues; pesticides don't just disappear—they end up in drinking water and so forth. So every one of them is important, and every one of them has to be dealt with.

I've spent most of my life in government because I wanted to try to leave things better. Government gave me the opportunity to do that. Where else would a young kid like me get an opportunity to negotiate the Atchafalaya Basin compromise or preserve the Tensas Wildlife Area [Refuge] or to be involved in setting up the Department of Environmental Quality?

## Afterword

We hold the environment in trust for future generations, and we have to use it wisely. You can't separate man from the environment. We are a part of it. When we start leaving us out—we are in trouble. Until you have been out on a ship at night, seeing the billions of stars, seeing porpoises gliding through phosphorescent water, it's something hard to explain to people. It's just a supernatural wonder.

# DAN BORNE

Kai David Midboe recognized the importance of environmental justice issues, but he saw them as social issues and therefore separate from the regulatory issues the DEQ regulates. Dan Borne, president of the Louisiana Chemical Association since 1988, would agree with this position. He graduated from Nicholls State University in 1968 and worked briefly at Channel 9 WAFB TV in Baton Rouge, Louisiana. He taught at Nicholls State and then left for Washington, D.C., where he worked for three US senators. In 1974 he served as chief executive assistant and director of the Office of Federal Projects for Governor Edwin Edwards and then worked for Kaiser Aluminum. Dan also teaches a course at LSU on politics and the media and is known throughout the region as the voice of the LSU Tigers for his play-by-play sports broadcasting.

### Narrative from Dan Borne (b. Thibodaux, Louisiana, 1946)

I can recall the fact that my mother's parents were rich.[5] They had it all. They had a home in New Orleans and a home on north shore on Lake Pontchartrain. And when the Depression came, all that went south, and my mother came to Bayou Lafourche. She went to the bayou to grow up during the Depression and ended up meeting my father there.

My father's parents and five boys grew up in a three-room shotgun house in Schriever, Louisiana, between Thibodaux and Houma. They had no toilet their entire lives, (but they) had running water in the kitchen. My grandmother was christened in the Catholic Church but became a member of the Pentecostal Church. She could barely read and write, but she could play the piano by ear. And in the first room of the shotgun house there was a piano, and she could make it sing.

I was raised in Thibodaux until I was twenty-two years old. I can remember our house being built when I was in first grade. The rest of the land next to our house was sugarcane land, and there was a small building with a shack behind it that eventually grew into Nicholls State University. I have fond memories of growing up there in the '50s. We were a middle-class family. My father worked and my mother cooked three meals a day. During the summer, the entire town of Thibodaux took Wednesday afternoons off.

It was a racially divided community. It had a railroad track, and they had the white folks that lived on one side of the track and the African American folk on the other side. In the black community, the black businessmen were very important. The fellow who ran the dry cleaners was highly respected. And there was the fellow who ran a nightclub that was also a restaurant for African Americans, and he was influential and respected by the community. On the white side of the tracks, it was your traditional power structure: bankers, doctors, and lawyers.

We crossed the tracks on Sunday to go to church because my mother loved the preaching at a Catholic Church that served the black community, called Saint Luke's, and she loved the priests who were sent down to minister that church. The priests were white, but the altar boys, the choir, and the organists were black. As my own spirituality grew, it gave me a great appreciation for the depth of the African American faith because many were born into families that had been down so long that getting up never crossed their minds, and the poverty was so evident and the struggle so dire that they literally put their faith in God—and that's how they got along.

After I graduated from Nicholls in 1968, I came to Baton Rouge to go to graduate school. While attending classes, I anchored sports and news at WAFB. I started with a major in history and then began studying journalism. I went back to Thibodaux and I taught for a year at Nicholls.

[Dan moved to Washington, D.C., where he worked for a succession of three US senators: Allen J. Ellender, Elaine Edwards, and Russell Long. He then returned to Baton Rouge to work for Governor Edwin Edwards.]

Senator Ellender died in the middle of a campaign. Edwin Edwards appointed his wife to hold the seat until Bennett Johnston was elected. I worked for her and for Russell Long for about three years. I came back down here to work for Edwin Edwards as chief executive assistant and director of the Office of Federal Projects. I worked for Edwards the last year of his first term and the first couple of years of his second and became his executive secretary during that time.

I worked for Kaiser Aluminum from 1978 to 1988 as vice president and then came to work as president of the Louisiana Chemical Association (LCA), a petrochemical trade association for seventy companies that operate one hundred locations within the state. We also have a second group called the Louisiana Chemical Industry Alliance, which is those seventy companies and five or six hundred suppliers and vendors who provide services and goods. The third group is called the Louisiana Foundation of Excellence and Science Technology and Education. We use that to get money and funnel it into educational programs. I have a role in each of those. We also have the political action committee called Louisiana Manufacturer's Political Action Committee, which makes contributions to candidates for political office. I'm a registered lobbyist, but I rarely lobby.

What we [chemical industry] make here becomes the plastic that goes into intraocular lenses of people who have cataract surgery. We give sight to the blind. We give hearing to the deaf. We have a plant in North Baton Rouge which makes a chemical that goes into an AIDS inhibitor. The very carpet on which we walk, the very cars which we drive, the very medicines that are dispensed to us by the physicians that we go to see are all products of chemistry. Everything comes from the periodic table in some form or another. Down here, we tend to be more of the bakery shop of the industry. We are to the chemical industry what wheat and flour are to a baker. We make things that go into many other products, like the baker turns flour not only into large loaves of bread but into king cakes, sweet rolls, bagels, and the like. Without the primary chemistry that goes on along the Mississippi River and in Calcasieu Parish, the consumer products that we use every single day, medicines that we take would not exist, and we would be dying sooner. When we're depicted as merchants of death, we are actually purveyors of life. There are more people living longer because of chemistry than ever.

The restrictions on what we put into water and in the air are infinitely stricter than they were thirty years ago. They're stricter than they were ten years ago. Our position on environmental regulation is this: Make the regulations as tough as you have to, but give us some predictability in terms of when we can get permits because permitting is extraordinarily important to expansions and to modernization. Many times, you need new permits to add jobs, and those types of investments are made in order to get the economic window. If that economic window is not hit, then that investment does not come to Louisiana.

Since the 1980s, there has been a much more open process in terms of public input. I feel that the public should be involved because it affects their lives. You should have public hearings. You should have notices of public hearings. However, these public hearings should be in the areas where the facilities are being put. You don't have a public hearing in Baton Rouge about a facility in Oakdale. I think it has to be taken into context of public input and legitimate local concerns versus a pep rally for folks who don't want to see industry expand any time, anywhere, and that's what many public hearings become. They become soapboxes of people who travel from hearing to hearing, screaming about the great Satan that is the petrochemical industry. We know these things happen and we understand that, and we participate at public hearings ourselves because our companies are involved, but public hearings can get out of control very easily and become shouting matches unless they are well planned and well moderated by the DEQ. But public input is absolutely critical to the process. When the public is disenfranchised, they lose trust in the process and it causes lawsuits. It causes interminable delays, and it eventually hurts the person who's trying to get the permit rather than helps them.

I think they [women] had a very positive impact. Theresa Robert from Ascension Parish is an extraordinarily bright, articulate spokesman, and when Theresa speaks people listen because she researches her information. She presents it in a very organized, articulate way and she's a huge player.

Eloise Wall [see "Supplemental List of Women Environmental Activists"] was the wife of a very wealthy cardiologist, and she did not have to be interested in the environment, but she got interested in it. She rallied a whole group of women and formed Friends of the Environment here in Baton Rouge. And so she was a very positive factor.

Maureen O'Neill, as a regulator, not as a citizen activist, but as a regulator, helped crystallize some of the water issue problems that we have here in the state. She was a tremendously tough regulator but overall a very positive influence in the movement.

An umbrella organization for so many of the environmental groups here in Louisiana is called LEAN. And they have a good spokesman in Marylee [Orr], who does a great job for them. She works hard for her group. The Tulane Environmental Law Clinic provides free legal services for LEAN during the testifying. And what I'm seeing is fewer of the Eloise Walls, fewer of the Theresa Roberts, fewer of those women who were taking off their own time and money to do these things and more and more of a quarterbacked, scripted type of presentation in front of the legislative panels. That's not a good and not a bad. I think it's a reality that they're a very strong lobbying organization and LEAN carries a lot of the weight. There are certain folks who lobby environmental causes that are now recognized by the legislature as the "go to" people. Marylee is one. So they're better organized than they have been in terms of the legislative process.

The strongest [label] I've ever used—and it was in a flippant way—was calling a group of protesters "wing nuts." And the thing that interested me about the "wing nut" was that you could just spin it around and it would just keep going around, and it would finally lock down on something and you had it. But, no, those are derogatory terms, and I would certainly apologize for any time that I would use them. The reason is that people who are not paid to do this should never be assailed for either their integrity, their intelligence, or their motives because they are sincere. And we, from the industry side, have just got to understand that, that they believe that the position they're taking is an informed position, be it on fact, fiction, faith, or fantasy. We have to deal with it as their accurate perception, the way they see things.

Now, that being said, to me, a woman has more credibility than a man because women have an intrinsic ability to show concern and empathy because they are the wombs of the next generation and their concern is for their kids. And if a mother's concern is for her child, there's no amount of science that's going to change her mind. None. You can simply forget it. She may understand why a certain decision was made but, in many cases, will never buy into the rationale that supports the decision. It's a motherly issue, and men cannot transmit that kind of empathy because we do not carry babies.

[One of Dan's most memorable cases involving a woman activist was his encounter with Kay Gaudet, of Saint Gabriel, Louisiana.]

Oh, by far, the most memorable one was the miscarriage (rate) in Saint Gabriel, Louisiana. Back in the '80s there was a pharmacist in Iberville who ran a pharmacy in Saint Gabriel. Both she and her husband ran a pharmacy, and she asserted that there was a high rate of miscarriages in Saint Gabriel because of the women who were coming to her and talking about miscarriages. Well, first it got local attention, then it got national attention, and then it got international attention. It got to be such a big deal that Oprah Winfrey came to Plaquemine, Louisiana, and taped a show.

And I was asked to be on the show by Oprah's producer. Now, in advance of the Oprah Show, I called my wife's ob-gyn, who was also a woman, and I said, "What is the miscarriage rate in America?" She said, "The people I treat are people that understand when you get pregnant, you quit drinking and you quit smoking. I lose 30 percent to miscarriages, and there's a study that says the miscarriage rate in American is 31 percent.[6]

So Oprah does her show and months later the results come in. The miscarriage rate in Saint Gabriel is, I think, 12.5 percent versus the national average of 31 percent. So what that means is that you're twice as likely to have a healthy baby in Saint Gabriel as you are anywhere in the United States. And years later, the study finally being completed by four terminally degreed, board-certified women determined that there is no miscarriage problem in Saint Gabriel.[7]

[In regard to] this concept that we have a miscarriage problem in Saint Gabriel, I think it is extraordinarily important what the LSU [Louisiana State University] studies have told us. The Louisiana tumor registry at the LSU medical school in New Orleans is a world-class tumor registry.[8] The United Nations uses LSU's tumor registry, and what it shows us is that Louisiana is not "cancer alley." We do not have a cancer incidence problem here. We have a cancer mortality problem. You stand no greater chance of getting cancer in Louisiana than you do anywhere else in the United States. There is a much greater chance of dying here when you have cancer. And so that research screams, screams out for preventive care and care after screening. How many women [who] don't get pap smears are dying of cervical cancer? That's an atrocity when preventive medicine could have caught it and fixed it.

The way to dispel it [concept of cancer alley] is to continually point to the research every time there's this allegation. There are folks out there who will continue to use the appellations simply because it works to their political agenda and their social agenda. These are the true religious zealots in the religion of radical environmentalism because nothing you can tell them will change their mind. You can't reason with them. It's impossible. And many of the fervent, spirit-filled, radical environmentalists are also some of the most vocal anti-industry people who have the ear of the media because they make hyperbolic charges, and the media reports it because, hey, it sounds great.

[The environmental movement was gaining strength when Governor Buddy Roemer took office in 1988.]

Roemer was a very tough environmental governor. He appointed a tough DEQ secretary. He appointed some tough regulators. Maureen O'Neill headed up the water section. Dr. McDaniel, who is the 2004 DEQ secretary, ran the air division and was a regulator. That's the first time that we had a DEQ that climbed into the difficult position of regulating big time because all of the federal laws were then coming in. You have the Clean Water Act, the Clean Air Act, and the state had to adapt to those regulations. So we had a period of intense regulatory scrutiny on our industry. Those were tough times because some folks used this as an opportunity to be anti-industry rather than pro-environment.

The legislature enacted one of the first air toxic laws in the country. It was very contentious at first, and then the parties got together and said, "OK, let's figure out what we can pass here and improve on as we go along." And we have an air toxic bill here that covers more toxins than even the federal Clean Air Act. That's an example of that type of legislation that was contentious at first but eventually became something that all the sides can embrace all over the state.

Buddy Roemer is about the smartest person I know, but as governor he had a lot of problems. He had Edwards, who was always a factor, and he didn't have any support from industry. It wasn't so much the environment as something called the environmental scorecard, which put companies in double jeopardy when it came to getting tax exemptions. That delayed several $100 million of investment that would have been made in Buddy's term had the company not had to deal with the environmental scorecard. That's what really ticked them off. With Roemer we saw eye to eye on everything except the environmental scorecard and environmental regulatory issues.

## *Afterword*

I can remember burning cane fields and watching cane burn in Thibodaux, Louisiana. And as I flash back to that, I can project my mother in today's world saying, "Golly, why is that stuff coming in our house?" My mother would have been concerned too. She wasn't back then because it's just the way we grew up. That's just the way life was back then. But, yes, a sincere concern for children has prompted many, many, many women to become very strong and forceful spokesmen for the environmental movement.

# ROBERT KUEHN

By the time Robert Kuehn became the director of the Tulane Environmental Clinic in 1989, the conversation linking social justice and environmental issues was beginning to change. The dominance of industry leaders in making their experts the only voice heard was being challenged. Bob was part of this new conversation.

Bob earned his BA from Duke University, his JD from George Washington University School of Law, his LLM from Columbia University School of Law, and his MPH from the Harvard University School of Public Health. He served as the director of the Tulane Environmental Law Clinic in New Orleans from 1989 to 1999. Currently, Bob is associate dean for Clinical Education, professor of law, and co-director of the Interdisciplinary Environmental Clinic at Washington University.

### Narrative from Robert Kuehn (b. South Bend, Indiana, 1952)

We lived in South Bend for three or four years after I was born, and then we moved to Ft. Myers, Florida.[9] My dad was always a contractor. He built everything from single-family houses to hospitals and shopping malls. My mother never really worked for much of her life, but then my parents got divorced, and my mother went to work at the phone company.

I was always very, very good in math and got all sorts of awards for it. I think there was a sense somewhat early in high school where I saw myself as doing some sort of engineering. But as I grew older and more political, those sort of cold, detached numbers bored me. By the time I went to college, I wasn't really interested in that [math].

In 1969, the summer between my junior and senior year in high school, it was the summer of Woodstock and a lot [was] going on in Vietnam. That summer I got tired of the high school sports that I was doing and all of the nonsense that went along with it. So I started growing my hair long and becoming interested in music and politics. When I got back to school that year I quit the basketball team, and a friend and I started an alternative newspaper. What's more democratic than deciding to start your own newspaper and talk about things? Even though it seemed to me a fairly harmless thing that we were doing, I was described by some letter to the local newspaper, myself and my friend who jointly published this thing, as the most dangerous students in the county.

And because we were threatened quite a bit when we were publishing our paper and thought that these threats were infringing on our First Amendment rights, we talked to some local lawyers about helping us. That was probably when I got interested in the law as something to protect and support people when they want to speak out.

[Bob graduated from Duke in 1974. After completing travels in Asia and studies in law, he spent four years working in Washington, D.C., for the Justice Department's environmental enforcement section.]

I'd been working at the Justice Department for about four years, and one of the cases that I filed was this massive case against Bethlehem Steel. I was looking at this case and I knew I was going to be bogged down for a couple of years in it and was really feeling like I was ready to get out of Washington. Then I heard about this job at Tulane. It sounded like what I wanted to do. It offered me the chance to teach and also still do cases because [clinics] are about taking students and pairing them up with needy citizen groups that otherwise can't afford lawyers. This provides opportunities for students to get the hands-on learning that they just can't get out of the classroom.

I had six students that showed up for that first class, and we had some cases and some clients and we just ran with it. The criteria that the clinic always had, which we thought was consistent with both what the Internal Revenue Code expected of nonprofits as well as the student practice rule, was that someone had to show that they couldn't afford a lawyer and without the assistance of the clinic would otherwise go unrepresented.

The first environmental justice case I can recall was helping the community of Paulina in Saint James Parish. They were being inundated by grain transfer stations along the Mississippi River, all of this grain dust showering them from this facility. The Urban League in New Orleans was trying to help these folks, and we represented them and pushed the DEQ to do something. [The DEQ] ultimately had them [transfer stations] moved.

When I arrived here in January 1989, Buddy Roemer had been in office a year. He'd appointed Paul Templet to head the DEQ. And he had appointed Maureen O'Neill, who ran the water division of DEQ. DEQ was working hard to do its job, working hard to clean up a lot of mismanagement that [Governor] Edwards had caused over his terms. It was not the case where, as I think some industry people would like to portray, that the Templet people were basically giving citizens what they wanted. But the Templet DEQ was listening to citizens and at least taking their position into account, and seriously, before they made a decision. When Governor Roemer was there, it was my perception that if you participated in some meeting or hearing with the DEQ, you at least felt like they were going to listen to what you said and would seriously think about the merits of accepting it.

I saw my students come to the depressing realization after Roemer left that under [Governors] Edwards and Foster, they [at DEQ] just didn't give a damn what people said. They would accept the comments from citizens, but they had zero interest in adopting them.

[Still, the concept of environmental justice was beginning to affect discussions about how state and federal permitting decisions were made.]

I don't recall, prior to coming to Louisiana, giving much thought to the concept that minorities and poor people were being disproportionably harmed by pollution. It just wasn't something that I had thought much about when I was at the Justice Department. It surely wasn't something that was discussed in law school. It's very obvious to me, having been here for ten years and what I've seen and heard, that it does go on. Those certain persons, because of the color of their skin or their lack of financial influence, are left out of the process and are, in a sense, dumped on. Pat Bryant, who was the head of the Gulf Coast Tenant's organization, started talking a whole lot about this concept of environmental justice or environmental racism. And he came and talked to Tulane about it and began to raise that as an issue, which led to things like the Toxic March [1988].

People had been talking about this concept but struggling for some sort of legal handle. Finally, some legal scholar suggested the idea of using the Civil Rights Act of 1964 and a provision called Title VI, which says if you get money from the federal government, you can't discriminate. In fact, EPA's rules say that if you get money from the federal government, you can't discriminate even if you didn't intend to; if it's only the effect of your action, that's enough. And African Americans, lower-income community people started using Title VI and filing complaints with EPA, alleging that the state's action in approving [permits] would have the effect of subjecting people to disproportionate amounts of pollution. If you go into many of these communities today, at the fence line to these plants, and you talk to people, as opposed to ten years ago, they are very much aware of environmental justice, and they are much more aware of their situation and what is behind it.

The real question is what's going to be done about it. And I think that's an open question, both at the national level with EPA and at the state level, where the DEQ and the governor's office are enormously hostile to the efforts of these communities to turn things around. Even though the forces on the other side are very big and very politically and economically connected, I think that when people put their collective energies together and join hands and forces, and are persistent and creative, they can do a lot. They beat the biggest corporations in the country. You need a lot of energy, but I think you can do a lot. I think that's the whole premise of what Lois Gibbs and others teach, and I think you surely see it in Louisiana.

After the Tulane Environmental Law Clinic helped stop the proposed Shintech facility in Saint James Parish [1998], then Governor Mike Foster publicly labeled the clinic's students and staff "a bunch of vigilantes." The governor then attempted to restrict client access to the clinic by requiring that 51 percent of the citizens requesting help demonstrate proof that they lived below the poverty level. The case went all the way to the state supreme court, which upheld the governor's request.

I think what the Louisiana Supreme Court did was outrageous. It was so contrary to everything that lawyers are supposed to do. It is just really a shameful act by the court and a really poor example of what justice is about in Louisiana. I think that what I learned was that the supreme court is no better than the other politicians in Louisiana.

The pernicious thing about the rule is that it forces the people who are most susceptible to pressure to have to be the ones that have to bear the brunt of the environmental fight in the future. There's a reason why people join groups to fight these things—because of the nastiness of Louisiana and how resource intensive it is. Students will no longer be able to represent groups because no group will come forward with 51 percent of its members revealing their income, much less revealing it to be that low. So you're basically down to students representing individuals, and it's a tough, tough individual at the poverty level who is willing to say, "OK, I'm taking on Mike Foster." That's asking a lot, and that's what industry and the government knew. They knew that if they could get rid of groups, they could get rid of the individuals.

It was a strategy I think none of us thought in a zillion years would work. When we got the word of this at Tulane, our belief was, "Ah, come on. What court in the world would ever agree to deny people who cannot afford lawyers?" We were just naive.

There continues to be a certain level of blacklisting or boycotting of Tulane Environmental Law Clinic graduates by lawyers in Louisiana, which I think is unprofessional and contrary to what the practice of law is supposed to be all about. Nationally, I think the Tulane Environmental Law Clinic is held by lawyers with astounding esteem. It's gotten all sorts of awards, including the highest award that the ABA [American Bar Association] gives out for environmental law.

I think that, as was shown under Governor Roemer, the DEQ can be a very effective agency on enforcement and other matters, if that is what the agency and the governor want it to be. I think that DEQ is always going to need some strong federal presence like EPA when the Jack Kents [Kent, as owner of Marine Shale] of the world and other big players want to spend all of their resources fighting state regulations. I think that [under Foster] the DEQ is captured by the very industry that it regulates. I think the agency really needs citizens involved to stay honest. If you run the citizens off, then basically the agency just exposes itself to even more capture.

I resigned from Tulane in June 1999, not, as some people would like to think, because of all of the pressure that had been put on Tulane or threats against Tulane. I had decided that I was ready to get out because I had gotten married and had a son and was thinking that maybe there was another part of the country that I would prefer to raise him in.

### Afterword

I don't think that people ought to give me too much credit or too much blame for what's going on in Louisiana or what has happened at the Tulane Environmental Law Clinic. I may have started it, I may well have been the dominant personality that framed the direction of it, but, ultimately, it's about two hundred or three hundred students that have been in that clinic and represented all of these community groups. And the two dozen or so other supervising lawyers and community outreach staff that have worked there and put in a lot of time and effort also deserve the credit. All I did, when people came, was try to figure out a way to take what people wanted and make it happen, which is what lawyers do every day with every client.

# AUDREY EVANS

Audrey Evans was a strong advocate for the environment, especially so through her work as community outreach coordinator with the Tulane Environmental Law Clinic. Her warnings here about the danger of hurricanes and the erosion of barrier islands make this work all the more meaningful. Audrey is now a residential energy-efficiency consultant based in New Orleans.

### Interview with Audrey Evans (b. Baton Rouge, Louisiana, 1962)

My father was from north Louisiana and my mother was from southwest Louisiana.[10] Her people were Cajun and French. My father was an accountant for the Boyce Machinery Company, originally in Baton Rouge, and then he was transferred to Reserve, which is the town next to LaPlace, where we lived. My mother was an IBM professional in the keypunch days. When she had three small children she stopped and went into real estate. My mother's brothers were farmers who grew up on an expansive stretch of land in southwest Louisiana. That's one of the reasons why, I think, I was always concerned about the land. Environmental concerns have been very close to home in our family.

In my elementary years, in the 1960s, there was integration. I was bussed from middle school to Reserve, Louisiana, which had a larger black population. I wasn't brought up in a separate, isolated way, so I became conscious of people who were poor early on. And more so when I was working at the Tulane Environmental Law Clinic, when I went into communities, into people's homes along the River Road, which was even at that point somewhat shocking. I think even today it's amazing how people live in the open air, with no air conditioning, often without mosquito screens, and with an oil refinery right at the property line, day and night with noise and big intrusions into their peace and quiet.

I was the salutatorian in a class of 350 at East Saint John High School, which happens to be, I'm told, in the path of the air pollution from Dupont, which has a hazardous waste incinerator. That was on the River Road, which was the main drag between plantations and the original settlement in this area. I went on to finish my bachelor's degree from LSU at Baton Rouge in political science. I also have a master's degree from the University of Virginia in foreign affairs, international political economy, with a specialty in the politics of developing areas.

Environmental issues came to me little by little in lots of different ways. The first time I was in Washington I worked for Office of Management and Budget Watch [OMB], a watchdog group over the budget agency of the federal government. I got the health and environmental beat to watch the regulations that were going through the Reagan White House. I saw how the rules were being changed. I saw how less information was being collected by the federal government—because they were not concerned. In some cases they didn't want to know and didn't want the public to have more information.

While working for OMB Watch, I heard through a conversation with Richard Miller, who was in Baton Rouge working with the Oil Chemical and Atomic Worker's Union at that time, that there was going to be a march in Louisiana to raise environmental and toxic issues. I knew immediately that I needed to come home for that. And that's where I met the leaders who were in small communities up and down the river [Mississippi]. In some ways the march kicked off the environmental movement here in Louisiana.

[The Tulane Environmental Law Clinic was founded in 1989 to provide free legal advice on environmental issues to community groups and Louisiana residents who did not have access to that kind of assistance. Audrey's role was community outreach coordinator.]

It was very rare for that kind of clinic to be established. There were no clinics like ours that explicitly had a community outreach office. Certainly, in Louisiana, there was nothing of the sort. There was no free legal assistance, except for pro

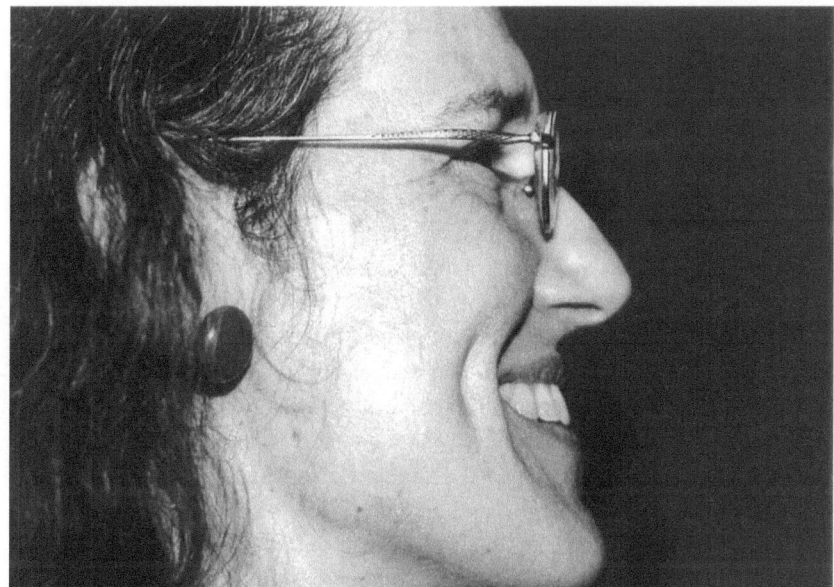

Audrey Evans

bono private lawyer assistance, but those lawyers were by no means able to fill all the needs around the state.

When I came in 1989 I hit the ground running. My work was to help find out what the concerns were and who needed help. That brought me all around the state, working with people of all types. I worked with housewives, upper-income people, as well as lower income, and all different races, including Vietnamese fighting landfills near New Orleans. The Tulane Environmental Law Clinic could then connect the source of the assistance, the law students able to take on the legal issues, and actually represent those community groups.

When I started at the clinic there was very little happening in the river parishes. But there were some very major threats, as we perceived it, to those parishes. Formosa Plastic was proposed soon after I came here, and Aristech Chemical was proposed in Saint John Parish, just up river from LaPlace. We fought medical waste incinerators and we fought Formosa and various other problems. We were very successful at writing letters to the editor and doing things to get the word out broadly, while trying to boil down the issues to the ones that people would understand. We had help from the existing organizations in Louisiana and from people who would come to council meetings with signs and get coverage from the media, who, amazingly, were supportive.

I was the communication nexus for so many people and groups and the connection point for scientific and technical and legal information and resources. It was an extremely strategic place to be. And I knew from the beginning that this was a very unique and special moment in time that should be taken advantage of, and so, personally, my effort was to max it out. It was, in a logistic sense, stressful, and emotionally one can't help but be affected by such strong issues and strong forces to deal with. So for me in this special position, I learned what my limits were. After about a decade of that kind of work, there came a time when I knew I couldn't do it anymore. The toll was becoming too great. For what I was giving of myself, I couldn't sustain it; and, yes, that's on every level. I just had to stop, and I realized that.

There was intimidation, and certain corporations were more skillful at subtle means of intimidation than others, and certain politicians were very effective at that. I could see it happening in different ways. To a great degree, I felt somewhat insulated from that raw edge because I was a professional and I had backing. And I don't think I was ever directly threatened, but certainly there was the air of confrontation, and that led to understanding that if you go a little too far there might be a problem. I saw again and again how a phone call from the parish president would silence certain people who otherwise were willing to write letters to the newspaper or go on television even just to say that they really are having health problems with their kids living next to this grain elevator or whatever their problem was.

In any number of circumstances, that kind of perceived or real intimidation also led to the breakup of marriages. Pressures would grow over time because women would take new roles in the household or the community and that would lead to a change in the dynamics of relationships. And the important thing in dealing with that kind of situation was flexibility, having in a small group, which most of these groups were, one spokesperson at one time and another spokesperson at another time or just being able to change depending on what seemed doable with limited resources.

What I saw, working at the Environmental Law Clinic, were problems at every level of the political world: community leaders, various different boards and commissions, the state legislature, and all the way to the federal had some aspect of corruption, and one can define that in different ways. It doesn't always get connected to money flow under the table or illegal activity, but there was certainly influence by the polluting industries or the destructive forces that have been a problem for the environment in Louisiana. I think that's why, eventually, there was such a political reaction to the kind of work that we were doing, which was exposing that kind of corruption. And it could be corruption in the sense of simply ideas and propaganda. Name-calling is what these things boil down to sometimes. But I think that the people that have the strength to go on, despite that kind of personal attack, are the ones that are really making the most difference in this work. I'm very proud to be a zealot. One should be zealous about the preservation of our resources.

Pollution follows the path of least resistance; if people oppose it, why should a company seek a conflict? It's easier to go where there's not going to be opposition. I think the resource base is the bottom line. We've got what it takes to have industry be successful. We've got the land. We've got the water. We've got the major access to the ocean and airports. We have poor communities that just didn't have enough protection from their elected representatives or within their own community.

There is no question that Louisiana has bountiful resources. To help people to realize that they have this treasure, to begin with, has been one of the challenges of the environmental movement. The coast is disappearing, and, no, it's not just an environmental problem; it's a hurricane threat and a global warming threat, and these issues are beginning to be accepted by the mainstream. Certainly, insurance and homeowners' issues are affected. And so a greater number of people understand that these labels we've used have another side to them. That this Sportsman's Paradise also includes a lot of fish with so much mercury that the Health Department advises us to take the fat out before we cook the fish because the toxins are stored there.

The environmental movement is a movement for justice, generally, and the racial component of that movement has never been insignificant. I've worked with African Americans, with Asians, with students, with, as you say, housewives, all sorts of different people, but it's been most interesting to work with the people that were least like me.

### *Afterword*
I think Louisiana's been a key in history. The timing was right. The development of the environmental movement focused here. The concentration of industry here, the extent of the problems, and the fact that we're worst on so many pollution lists have really made the situation so severe that people have had to react. The time that women have put into the movement, my own included, is enormous. I think it's been a very important element in the development of the national environmental movement. I believe we have even made a major contribution to the global situation in fighting injustices associated with multinational corporations.

## PAUL TEMPLET

When people talk about why Louisiana's grassroots environmental movement has become such a formidable force, most mention Paul Templet, a retired professor at the Institute for Environmental Studies, Louisiana State University (LSU), Baton Rouge, Louisiana. Paul served as secretary of the Department of Environmental Quality during Governor Buddy Roemer's administration from 1988 to 1992. Under Paul's leadership, the DEQ made great strides toward reducing industrial pollution while at the same time maintaining jobs in the manufacturing sector. During the years Paul served as secretary to the DEQ, industry increased its pollution-control spending by about $1 billion.

Paul now works as a consultant. His current research focuses on documenting the link between a clean environment and a strong economy, an issue that has often proven divisive in the state.

### Narrative from Paul Templet (b. Port Allen, Louisiana, 1940)

The first Templet came to Louisiana after being kicked out of Nova Scotia in 1755.[11] He went back to France and found a wife and came back to Louisiana and settled in Saint Gabriel. The Templets have been here for 250 years. The Templets are Cajun.

My mother's family also came from Nova Scotia but settled in Saint Martinville 250 years ago. They didn't speak much English. In the little town of Saint Martinville, I would spend the summers there, and I couldn't go shopping at the grocery store because I didn't speak French. I thought every kid's grandparents spoke a different language than they did.

My maternal grandfather had a garden and milked cows. He had chickens. My memory of grandmother was washing clothes on a washboard. My mother learned English at the age of eight, when they passed a law saying you couldn't speak French on the school grounds. English became her first language, although she was very fluent in French. When the family would get together they would talk French, but they wouldn't teach it to the kids. So I can't speak French, and we lost it in two generations.

My parents were big on education. My father had a two-year college degree. My mother had two degrees. I have three, and both of my sisters have degrees. My father was the business manager for the school board in West Baton Rouge at the time of his death. He died in 1953, when I was twelve years old.

Mother was a substitute teacher until my father died, and she went back to school and got a BS, a master's, and thirty hours toward a PhD. We had no money and my mother sacrificed quite a lot to get us through college. We went to LSU because it was convenient and cheap in those days.

I went to work when I was twelve in a drug store, working as a soda jerk. I worked there for four years and contributed some money to the family. As a teenager I worked construction at Dow Chemical, unloading sandbags from railroad cars. We didn't have much money. We didn't know we were poor; my mother kind of kept it from us by various means. She sewed all night long sometimes for my sisters, so they would have clothes. Everybody in Port Allen in those days was kind of on the same level. There wasn't any money to go around.

[Paul became a scientist and worked at Shell Chemical until the late 1960s. With the effects of pollution becoming more and more evident in Louisiana, he changed his focus and returned to LSU for graduate school. Paul began encouraging other students to become involved in environmental issues. His interest in organizing an Earth Day celebration made some of the school's administrators uneasy.]

I began to get phone calls from higher ups in the administration. Chancellor Cecil Taylor called me in and said, "Can I take you to lunch?" I was real surprised at the invitation. He took me to the Camelot Club, very fancy and very high up. We were eating lunch and he leaned over and said, "Are you going to shut down the university?" I said, "What?" He said, "Are you trying to shut down the university with this environmental stuff?" I said, "No, I'm not going to shut down the university. All we've talked about is a teach-in where we give professors materials if they want to use it in class that day. It is materials about the environment." He was noticeably relieved and he actually helped me after that, but it taught me a lesson—that what's important to people in high office is whether or not you can cause them some problems. It is not so much that you are a good student, but they really pay attention if they think you can cause some disruption. So Earth Day came off without a hitch and the chancellor actually helped. I had never done anything like that before and I was scared to death. I hadn't made public speeches. I mean, scientists don't, typically. I wasn't very good at it, but I would get up before five hundred people on Earth Day and speak.

I guess I got political when I realized that you really can't change anything unless the political structure goes along with it—the power structure. So government becomes important and I learned how government works.

[Paul completed his PhD and served as head of Louisiana's Coastal Management program, which was responsible for drafting regulations governing how the state's wetlands would be protected.]

We did a set of regulations and presented them to my boss, who was the DOT [Department of Transportation] secretary. He apparently had made some deal with the oil industry that he would give them the regulations first before the public got to see them. I said, "No that's wrong." I mailed copies to everybody I thought would be interested, including the newspaper, and then I resigned. I also made maps showing lands that were and were not suitable for development, which angered the state and real estate industry.

I learned, where politics is concerned, if you play by the rules, some people are going to have an advantage over other people, and I didn't think it was right. After all, I was working for the public.

[After time spent working abroad, in the private sector, and as a professor at LSU, Paul was asked to serve as secretary of the Department of Environmental Quality.]

In 1988 I took over DEQ and set about trying to turn the DEQ into a functioning agency. When I went to the DEQ there were 350 people. When I left there were 850 people. We went from a budget of $15 million to $60 million per year, and most of this was self-generated through industry fees and fines. Roemer put another $10 million in the annual budget. Enforcement at the DEQ went up five times higher than in previous years. And we created a policy that everyone had to have a degree.

In 1989 we passed our own air toxics law, a year before the federal law went in. We began putting new regulations in place, and industry began spending more money on pollution control. Pollution levels came down and jobs went up, in contrast to what economists usually predict. We created about twenty-five thousand jobs in the manufacturing sector, a large number for Louisiana.

One special program we put in place was the environmental scorecard, where we conditioned a company's tax exemption. It was a huge controversy. If you got an A, you got 90 percent of the exemptions. Through that mechanism alone we lowered the pollution level by another 8 percent, which was a lot since Louisiana ranked high in toxic releases.

The way the scorecard worked was that the company automatically got 50 percent, and the other 50 percent they had to earn. They could earn it by the emissions-to-job ratio, which I started, where we'd take the toxic releases that they reported to the federal government every year and divide it by the number of jobs in the facility. The more toxic releases per job you had, the fewer points you got. So pollution became important. We also looked at the penalties they had and assigned them points. We also had bonus points for waste reduction. It got to be a contest with industry. But it also provided the public a way to evaluate the companies.

I was serving on Governor Roemer's transition team the first time I met Maureen O'Neill. She was working for the Sewer and Water Board in New Orleans when she came before us at a hearing, and she was very impressive. I asked Maureen if she was interested in the DEQ water position. I didn't know her very well when I asked her to serve in that position, but she said yes. I was also trying to get some women into government. I also appointed a woman to the legal division that I created, and I had a number of women involved in high levels in the DEQ. It was apparent that the cooperative skills of women were going to be more important than the competitive skills of men.

One of the things we did was open the agency. We called it the glass walls. The whole agency had to have glass walls. We opened up all meetings to the press. My lawyers hated it and fought me over it because, to them, law and penalties and a number of things have to be done behind closed doors. And some things do when you deal with personnel matters, and also if you've got a legal matter that can't be in the public eye because the law protects the rights of the people you are trying to assess the penalties against. So we closed some meetings, but not many. We made it very open and industry hated that. You shine the spotlight of publicity on many of these deals and the deals go away because people don't want to do them and have other people know what the deals were all about. The press could walk into my office at any time, and did. My door was open to the public and to the employees in the agency, which had never happened before.

Those interested in having an open agency liked it very much, but industry didn't like it because they had competition in the halls now. The environmentalists were there, and in some of those meetings in the past where deals had been made, now there were environmentalists sitting at the table.

When the Toxic Release Inventory data came out every year and TRI numbers and Louisiana was number one or number two almost every year, I would call in the top twelve dischargers to air, land, and water with the cameras and the press and everybody there and I would publicly ask these industries to reduce their emissions. When we did that once, the League of Women Voters picked up the top twelve industries and sent copies to headquarters of those industries. It turns out headquarters doesn't even know what the local plants are doing. They assume everything is OK until they hear differently. Industry has money to spend and it comes out of headquarters, but the money goes where the pressure is the greatest. Louisiana had never put pressure on these industries, so we weren't getting that money. So when you have lax enforcement, you don't have pollution control money to spend. Pollution levels dropped by 75 percent over six years. That's what industry learned. They looked bad. I am not anti-industry. We've got them and they are going to stay here, but I think they could be good citizens. We live in an industrial age, and we're going to have some pollution that we have to deal with, but I don't think we have to be number one.

One of the other things we did was to have committees appointed that were dealing with various matters in the agency. I had an overall advisory committee that was run by Wilma [Subra]. We had industry on the committee, but we also had environmental groups and the public in general. When we appointed committees to deal with new sets of regulations that were being developed, these committees actually wrote the regulations. We had staff there to help them, but environmentalists and industry would argue these things out and then write the regulations. We pushed through eighty-one sets of regulations in the four years I was there. It's important to have regulations because if you have a law on the books and you haven't written the regulations, you can't enforce the law.

The new policy that we came up with was that before any new expansion could occur, these chemical industries had to clean up the messes they had. They thought that was horrible, but to me it was just good housekeeping. You've got a mess, you clean it up, and then you get a permit to do something else. They began 125 ground water cleanups at the various plants. These plants were all contaminating the groundwater. Nobody had ever dealt with it until we put this policy in place. They began working at it.

Over all of those years there was never even a lawsuit against anybody I had appointed and nothing personally against me. We weren't doing anything wrong, but we were causing industry to spend about a billion dollars a year more on pollution control than they had spent prior to our term. And that's big money. I got a couple of threatening phone calls. One of them was from [then senator and future governor] Mike Foster. He said he was going to spend the rest of his life trying to get me—whatever that meant. I figured he was too busy trying to run the state government to worry about me.

[Women activists played a big role in Templet's administration of the DEQ. By focusing attention on critical issues and participating on advisory committees, they helped shape the direction of the agency.]

The environment today would be much worse without the women's involvement, and we wouldn't have had the many reforms we've seen. We probably wouldn't have known enough about Marine Shale to close them down without the mothers from Morgan City, and those women paid a high price. A grandchild died and there have been three or four children that died. We would be in a much, much worse situation than we are in now because it's the women who try to put the compassionate face on government and try to make government function. And I think it's because women have this sense of connection with continuity with family and with children. I don't think men have that much of a connection because they are all out there trying to make a buck. It's much better, for instance, for Marylee Orr to go on TV and say the air pollution is worse and to phrase it the way she phrases it than for me to go on TV and say there are too many parts per million in the air, the way scientists tend to approach these issues. I think the women are much better and more effective in dealing with the public. They've reshaped the whole landscape of the environment in Louisiana, and it's got a different face, which is good. It's a better face.

It's a departure from tradition because women in the past were taught to stay in the background and be the power behind the throne. That's changed. And I think it's more difficult for men to deal with women than it is for men to deal with another man. Industry has a way of dealing with me, but they can't use the same techniques with [women] necessarily. With me, they try intimidation. After I left the DEQ they had a whispering campaign where they would just talk to people—the leaders, the movers and shakers in society—and say, "Templet was bad. He was biased. He was radical." And, of course, a bunch of industry guys met with the president of the university and tried to get me fired. Because I'm tenured, they couldn't get me fired, but they did get my salary cut by $10,000. And the provost who was in the meetings told me all of this. So that's the route industry would take with me. Industry doesn't know how to deal with women. It's a bunch of old white males. They don't know how to deal with women that have a cause and really believe in what they are doing. They only know how to react to the old-style women, and this is a new style of woman.

### Afterword

You have to take a long view. You are working for posterity, for sustainability, for eternity. You are going to lose a lot. You are going to be discouraged a lot, but you have just got to regroup and come back again and again. You don't ever stop, but not many people can do that. When I look back over the thirty years I've been involved, I do see the successes. But you don't get to those thirty years except by having some kind of faith that what you are doing is the right thing, and, by God, I'm going to keep doing it.

What I liked about the environmental movement was that it didn't know any boundaries. The environment was important in almost every discipline that I looked at, and it affected people whether they were black, white, male, or female. So the only way we were going to address these issues was to have everybody involved, which means you have to transcend race, gender, age—and I think we have. Race was tougher. I think gender came easier. Age didn't ever seem to be a problem. Some of the old people, like me and Lorena in Alexandria, are really young at heart. They like fun and they have fun with what they do. It isn't all work.

# WILL COLLETTE

The desire to transcend boundaries as an environmental activist brought Will Collette to Louisiana during the 1980s, before national environmental organizations began focusing on the South. He spent eighteen years in the environmental justice movement. He served as the national organizing director for the Citizens' Clearinghouse for Hazardous Wastes (CCHW) from 1981 to 1990 and as the executive director of the Citizen's Coal Council from 1991 to 1999. Will is currently a strategic research analyst for the New England Region of the Laborers' Union.

### Narrative from Will Collette (b. Central Falls, Rhode Island, 1949)

I am the only college graduate in my family.[12] I worked and went to state college, paying for it myself. When I completed my BA at Rhode Island College, I majored in social work.

Will Collette

I became totally immersed in progressive social issues starting around 1968 and have been that way ever since. In 1969 and 1970 through 1972, I was a leader in Ecology Action for Rhode Island when it was lively and radical. I stopped being active in 1972 when environmentalism started being more middle-of-the-road and [was inactive] until Love Canal came along and environmentalism showed the potential to have a more working-class, social justice orientation.

In 1981 I got into the grassroots environmental justice movement when Lois Gibbs decided after her victory at Love Canal that she wanted to start a national environmental movement—a movement led by women and people of color. [She believed] that those two groups brought very unique characteristics to the table that were undervalued and needed to be valued.

My responsibility as her organizing director (of CCHW) was to think geographically about those parts of the country that were unorganized. And when I looked at the country as a whole, I saw the South as being a place that represented tremendous opportunity for new organizing. Nobody else really cared about the South. It was a write-off as far as everybody else was concerned. So for several years we were the only ones who were willing to work in the South. That was in 1981, and as I was looking at the map, it was pretty clear to me that Louisiana was probably going to be the lead state in the South because there was a higher concentration of grassroots organizations already in place, more than in any of the other southern states. My analysis was that Louisiana was going to be the place that would provide the spark that was going to spread across the South. So it made a lot of sense to invest resources and attention in Louisiana so that we could make it work. As CCHW started to mature, we started raising more money, and at one point 60 percent of our budget was allocated to doing work in the South, with Louisiana being the flagship.

I was also attracted by the romantic appeal of linking grassroots environmentalism with the historic civil rights movement. Even without the hard statistical data that came later, it seemed pretty obvious that there was a link between toxic problems and race.

I quickly started to buy into what became a deeply held conviction that women were going to be the heart and soul of the grassroots toxic movement. Women were stepping up to leadership roles in the grassroots environmental movement all over the country. Some were inspired by Lois Gibbs's example at Love Canal and nationally through CCHW. Most responded to need. They saw bad things happening in their communities that threatened their families, and they rose up to protect their children. My job was to help them fight to win.

Though we built relationships with local groups all across the region, Louisiana became an important part of the national grassroots movement largely because of its leadership cadre, which by no accident [was] nearly all women. As years went by, [Louisiana activists] got the recognition and respect and drew the interest of virtually all of the environmental organizations in the country. For several years, Louisiana was like everybody's favorite place, and everybody was dropping money, resources, and staff people and wanting to get a little piece of Louisiana's vibrant grassroots organizing movement for their own interests. One of the effects of that was that Louisiana activists started getting these national and international gigs to sort of spread what it was that they had. The organizations that they were invited by frequently had an agenda that may not have been the same as theirs, but the practical effect was that the activists got to spread the word all across the country.

One of the earliest principles that we incorporated into CCHW's organizing program was harnessing experienced grassroots leaders to help the new ones get started. We called it the mutual aid principle—helping other grassroots leaders. Women understand that . . . being a human being is being a part of a network of relationships. And I think that women also understood that pairs are a very efficient way of getting through the day, having your partner who gives you the strength and the backup you need. It was almost always in pairs. Pairings almost seem to be a natural way of women figuring out how to do the work. More often than not those pairings were "ying and yang." They were a pairing of opposites or a pairing of very different types of people whose different personality types balanced each other. An example is Ann Williams and Rose Jackson, an unlikely pair—an elderly white schoolteacher and a working-class, sweet, dear, African American woman. They personified what I saw as being the remarkable social change that the toxic movement was bringing to Louisiana and had the potential for doing around the country. When women came together to save their community from something bad or to make a situation better, that's an experience that makes deep and long-term changes in social relationships.

When Ann was hit with that SLAP suit, she was in a situation that was very dangerous because having a big multi-million-dollar lawsuit hanging over your head is not a pleasant place to be. Everyone loved Ann for her courage, and she earned everybody's respect and support during the very difficult period. She was on national TV when ABC's *20/20* show wanted to do a segment on these harassment lawsuits, and my advice to Ann was the only way to fight a harassment lawsuit is to harass them right back.

I wanted, as CCHW organizing director, to make sure that the women who were the heart and soul of the grassroots toxic movement didn't lose that emotional motivation that was at the heart of their passionate commitment to fighting to win. They were basically saying, "I don't care what the science says. I'm fighting to protect my children, my grandchildren, my family, and my community." There was a passion and emotion in that that we were scared might get . . . squeezed out of women if they gave into that symbol, if they got defensive about being called "hysterical housewives." Any hysteria that people were feeling I feel was driven by a very rational anger.

Many of the grassroots leaders, the women that I've worked with, particularly here in Louisiana, were indeed innocent. The best example was an evening in Lafayette where a group of drunken men screamed threats at us during a public hearing. The local group leader was Lorena Pospisil. She thought that because I didn't run in terror (which was what was running through my head) that everything was perfectly normal. It didn't even occur to her that we were in a dangerous situation. It was that tense and that dangerous, at least in my perception. But to her it was like, "You did really good. I liked the way you handled them." Meanwhile, I'm thinking that I'm going to call the sheriff so I can get out of town alive.

One of the things that we set out to do at the movement's peak was help states with a large enough base of local organizations to bring those organizations into a statewide program. LEAN certainly was in the first five of those organizations to be founded. LEAN has been the most successful of all of those larger organizations that were started. Almost all of them in the rest of the country are gone.

This is the South, and there wasn't a whole lot of experience, prior to LEAN coming along, of having a genuinely mixed-race organization where people actually were OK about that. I think LEAN actually shows an example of how you can build a social justice organization in the Deep South that's multiracial and for real, where there actually is shared leadership and the color matters a whole lot less than it does in most of the rest of southern society.

All social movements in this country, since the American Revolution, have a life cycle. There is a spark, a sort of launch and sharp trajectory. . . . [T]here is a period where you reach the top of the curve, and then there's a period of decline—sort of like a life span. When Lois and I were sitting on her back porch in 1981 and trying to figure out what CCHW was going to look like and how we were going to do things, I made a prediction that this grassroots toxic thing had maybe a five-year life span, maybe ten at the most. I was proposing that we adopt a plan for organizing this movement that assumed a five- to ten-year life span. Obviously, I was wrong by quite a number of years.

### *Afterword*

One of the things that Louisiana taught me, and I had this lesson hit me almost every time I've come to visit, is nothing is impossible. Absolutely nothing is impossible. The miracles that have been achieved in this state are a lesson for future generations and for people in the rest of the country that if you accept the possibility that you can win, you can win. And it's a tribute to the spirit of the women in the state that Louisiana has been the longest lived and, I would suggest from an objective standpoint, probably the most successful state for winning environmental justice.

# WILLIAM "WILLIE" A. FONTENOT

Before retiring in April 2005, William "Willie" A. Fontenot served as the community liaison officer for the Louisiana attorney general's office for twenty-seven years. In that position, created in response to the demands of environmental activists, he focused on assisting poor and minority communities, disenfranchised workers, others who were impacted by environmental pollution, bad government, or industrial decisions, and many others who felt they had nowhere else to turn.

Willie traveled thousands of miles across the state of Louisiana, as well as into other states, to educate and organize citizens and community leaders. He taught ordinary citizens, especially women, how to organize and navigate successfully through institutional and political systems. Willie mentored many of the women featured in this book. Today he remains a consultant to many groups and serves on the board of the Clean Water Fund.

### Narrative from William A. "Willie" Fontenot (b. Opelousas, Louisiana, 1942)

My family has lived in the Opelousas area for as long as I can remember.[13] My parents, my maternal and paternal grandparents, all grew up within a twenty-five-mile radius of Opelousas. My father, Austin Fontenot Jr., affectionately called "Little Austin," practiced law with his father in Opelousas. My maternal grandfather was also an attorney and the fire chief of Opelousas. Both sets of grandparents lived within walking distance of the Opelousas courthouse.

When my parents first married they lived in Washington, Louisiana, just eight miles north of Opelousas. When I was an infant we moved to Opelousas. It was during World War II, and most of my father's law practice was in Opelousas, and he didn't have enough rationing stamps for gasoline to travel back and forth from Washington to Opelousas.

My four sisters and three brothers were born and raised in Opelousas, and we all attended grammar and high school at the Academy of the Immaculate Conception. The first home in Opelousas that we lived in was called the Grover Mouton House. Grover was the governor of Louisiana during the Civil War, and for a short time Opelousas was the state capitol. We later moved to Ring Rose (built around 1775), located just north of Opelousas. Here we had our own garden, which was about five acres. We grew a lot of vegetables and strawberries. One of my chores was weeding the garden, which required a lot of weeding, especially the strawberry patch. We had to collect pine needles and put them under sometimes thousands of strawberry plants to keep them off the ground, so they wouldn't rot. We also had horses, cows, pigs, sheep, geese, and a lot of ducks.

Growing up, I don't recall solid waste as being a problem. We didn't have landfills because we didn't generate a lot of waste. The pigs ate the food that was left over, and paper waste was burned and the ashes dumped into a compost, and then trash and leaves were put on top of the ashes. Milk and soda pop came in returnable glass bottles, so basically everything was naturally recycled.

[Although Willie had a privileged background, as a child he learned the difference between the "haves" and the "have-nots."]

My life was probably a little different than my siblings because I had a set of two houses that I grew up in. When I was eight or nine months old, there was an outbreak of mumps with the kids, and my parents sent me over to my grandparents. I stayed there until the scare was over, but by then my grandparents were attached to me and asked if I could stay a few more days. I ended up staying between my home and my grandparent's home until I was sixteen.

My grandfather Fontenot was the most influential person in my life. We did a lot of outdoor activities together, where I learned to appreciate nature and its abundance. He took me pole fishing, and hunting, mostly for rabbits, squirrels, and birds. We shot all sorts of birds that I probably would not shoot today. We also went crawfishing. We'd put a number two washtub in the trunk of the car and go out to roadside ditches and ponds and get a half tub of crawfish and take them home and cook them up.

William "Willie" A. Fontenot

One of my fondest memories as a child were the trips I took with my grandfather when he took his laundry to an African American sharecropper family who lived in the area. Every week he would take the laundry and then a few days later pick it up. I enjoyed those trips because we often stayed awhile and visited.

We also knew other sharecroppers in the area, and my grandfather and I visited many of them in their homes. The head of one household was an African American World War I veteran, and on one of our visits he proudly showed me his Bronze Star, which he received in the army. I was very young but couldn't understand how somebody who had been a soldier in the war, received a medal, and was such a poor sharecropper. It was a learning experience for me that I have never forgotten.

[Willie learned early on about health issues related to the environment and Louisiana's lingering humidity—thought to be detrimental to residents—when a tuberculosis (TB) scare swept the country in the mid 1930s.]

My father had TB as a young man, so his parents sent him to law school in Arizona because the climate was drier. After the TB scare, every year they used to check us kids to make sure we didn't have the disease, so we'd get X-rays and patch tests. There was a lot of concern if somebody in the family had ever had TB that it could reoccur. So we grew up with the awareness of health problems. I guess if you weren't exposed to that, you wouldn't think much about it.

Growing up, I also had health issues. As a child my eyes crossed, and when I was about five years old, my mother took me to New Orleans to see a specialist. For the next ten years, I went to New Orleans once or twice a year to see the doctor. We'd either ride the Trailways bus from Opelousas to New Orleans or take the train.

On these frequent trips, we visited my mother's aunt, who lived in the Garden District of New Orleans. She [Anne McKinne Robertson] was the first city planner in New Orleans—the first official planner. Her interests were in the preservation of historical architecture and open areas such as parkways and the wetlands around New Orleans. I have to credit my great-aunt for instilling in me the importance of the historical restoration of Louisiana's magnificence architecture, the vast wetlands in the state, and how vital they all are to our culture, economy, and survival.

To get to my aunt's home, we had to ride the streetcar downtown. One event that has remained with me for a very long time was the seating arrangement on the streetcar. I remember the seats would have a couple of holes in the top of them, and they would move the signs, which read "White Only" or "Colored Only," back and forth on the car because when the train gets to the end of the track, they just reversed the car so that the front of the car now becomes the back of the car.

On one of these trips, I remember seeing some teenagers, white teenagers, who moved the "Colored Only" sign as far back in the streetcar as they could, forcing the black people back behind the signs. I had never seen anything like that and I was pretty stunned. I think I was about nine years old, but the memory has stuck with me. And I think it was probably the first racism that I had ever really seen or was aware of.

[Willie went to college for a year and then joined the U.S Navy for four years. He returned to the University of Southwestern Louisiana (USL) and graduated with a degree in political science. After graduation he married and had two children.]

In college we talked about environmental issues, but my activism didn't start until the early 1970s when I became involved with the New Orleans Sierra Club. Their issue was fighting the I-410 loop around New Orleans, also known as the Dixie Freeway, and the Lake Pontchartrain and Vicinity Hurricane Protection Project. The two projects would have levied off and opened up for development two hundred to three hundred thousand acres of coastal wetlands. Instead, today what you have in those areas include Bayou Sauvage, the national wildlife refuge, which consists of twenty-five thousand acres in New Orleans East. The original plan by the developers was to set aside fifteen acres for two wilderness parks called Little Oak and Big Oak. And all of the rest of the twenty-five hundred acres would have been developed. This wetland acreage is all inside the city limits of New Orleans. In addition, south of New Orleans is the fifteen-thousand-acre Jean Lafitte National Park, which would have also been developed. Those were the two major areas that ended up being protected that would have been totally developed if the Lake Pontchartrain and I-410 had occurred.

Although environmental issues were important to me, and I was involved with not only the Sierra Club but also the Audubon Society and the Louisiana Wildlife Federation, I also had a job working as an auditor for an insurance company.

[That would change in 1978, when Attorney General William J. Guste Jr. hired Willie, "creating a special position that gave Fontenot virtually free rein as an advocate of environmental causes."[14]]

When I started working in the attorney general's office in April of 1978, I was living in Baton Rouge, and every week I would drive down to New Orleans and spend most of a day with Dick Troy. He was the person in the attorney general's office who convinced Mr. Guste to hire me.

One of the fist women I worked with in my position as community liaison officer was Gay Hanks, from Kaplan, Louisiana [whose narrative appears in this book]. In 1978 she and other local residents were concerned about a dozen dumpsites where waste from the drilling and production of oil and natural gas was being dumped in waterways, canals, and along roadways. They were keeping diaries and taking pictures of the waste being dumped, waste flowing into local waters, pictures of dead livestock, dead fish and crawfish, copies of letters to officials, and newspaper articles.

We held a meeting with state agencies, and after this meeting officials in the Office of Conservation, the Environmental Affairs Committee, and the Department of Health and Hospitals started actually doing real enforcement of environmental laws.

In June 1980 I helped Hanks update and rewrite regulations governing the oil and natural gas industry. Before that, in January 1980, I also worked with Theresa Robert [whose narrative appears in this book] and Ruby Cointment, who were concerned about a proposed commercial hazardous waste disposal facility located in their community. I met with the two women on a regular basis and probably talked to them on the telephone weekly for five or six years.

This battle by the two women gave us a Louisiana Supreme Court IT decision in May of 1984, which provided the first interpretation of the Louisiana Constitutional Article 9, Section 1, which had been adopted in 1974. The IT decision was the first interpretation of the new Louisiana Constitution, and this decision has been used in more than a hundred more cases across Louisiana.

In 1980 I started meeting with Mary McCastle [whose narrative appears in this book] in Alsen, Louisiana, a small African American settlement just north of Baton Rouge. This was the first time that African American residents got seriously and successfully involved in dealing with environmental problems anywhere in the United States.

I also worked with Catherine Ewell, who lived next to the Rollins facility just west of Alsen. She also kept a diary on how the fumes were hurting them and noted how waste poured on their land from both Petro Processors and Rollins, and in 1969–70 they lost more than 150 head of cattle when waste from one of the facilities poured over Devil's Swamp and their cattle happened to be in the swamp.

The Environmental Control Commission (ECC) offered a resolution that the Office of Environmental Affairs should investigate Rollins and find out what was making people around this facility sick. At a meeting in 1980 the ECC staff reported that there were several places on the Rollins property which were generating extremely toxic and hazardous waste fumes. They also reported that there were more than a dozen places where the chemical liquids were flowing off of Rollins onto the Ewell land and into local drainage, which emptied into Devil's Swamp Lake, which was just west of Rollins.

In May 1980 at the ECC hearing, the Health Department staff reported that they had interviewed about 150 Alsen residents who all complained about health problems. This was the first time that residents near an industrial facility in Louisiana were able to successfully get officials from several state agencies to investigate and support their claim about environmental health problems.

I worked with many other women in the state of Louisiana after the stories about Rollins and Petro Processors helped to bring attention to waste pollution stories from industrial facilities and waste sites along the Mississippi River and other industrial corridors across the state like Lake Charles, Monroe, Shreveport, New Orleans, Lafayette, and Abbeville. What followed was, statewide, the public became outraged that our state was in such a terrible mess.

The women accomplished great things and most were involved because of personal reasons. Gay Hanks got involved after her teenage daughter died of leukemia. Theresa Robert was concerned about her children's health if IT was built in her neighborhood. Mary McCastle and Catherine Ewell were concerned about the health problems which all the residents began suffering after Rollins started dumping and burning hazardous waste.

Women played a very strong part in the push for more comprehensive and better-written statutes and regulations dealing with pollution. A mother talking about her concerns for her little children was always a very strong image. A mother holding a small child or baby and talking about health concerns was always an extremely powerful image. Mothers and fathers together with their children were also very powerful images.

Women tend to accomplish quite a lot because men tend to play by the rules because that is what they learn at school, in the military, and at whatever business they work for. Women very often have to struggle with raising a family, and if they are able to become very creative, which some do, they learn more about how to work with fewer resources, how to improvise, how to ask questions, and often how to challenge authority to meet the needs of their family. Not all women are automatic leaders, but they have a greater chance of doing that because raising a family can be a real struggle, which is an incredible training field. And I always tell them not to forget to pay attention to their families because these struggles may end in a few months or take years.

One of the things I taught the women was—I would hand out the pocket cards produced by the Public Affairs Research Council about public records and the laws dealing with open meetings. These cards gave people a sense of what their rights were to attend public meetings, to speak at these meetings, and to ask questions. They also learned that almost all records kept by government agencies are public records and that the public has a very strong legal right to look at these records.

Other things which I tried to teach people was to talk to their neighbors, to meet their local elected officials, and to work with the news media. Many people, especially in cities, have no idea whom their neighbors are. When people can come together and learn about common issues like pollution, they will be more likely to succeed. When we take the time to meet our neighbors and public officials, the results can become very dramatic.

## *Afterword*

Historically speaking, before the grassroots environmental movement swept the nation, major industries located in low-income and minority communities because the land was cheap and the people were basically invisible, without any real connections with their public officials, the news media, and other organizations, which might have been able to help them. And prior to 1970, there were no African American elected officials anywhere in Louisiana. There were also very few women serving as elected officials, and Native American elected officials also did not exist.

The women of the grassroots environmental movement brought these issues to the forefront. Today, the public is more educated about environmental issues and clearly there is a lot more awareness and concern than there was thirty years ago. There are still some real numbing problems out there, but because of these women's efforts they changed the way corporate America does business in Louisiana.

I would end then with my favorite quote. It is from Margaret Mead, though no one has ever figured out when she said it: "Never doubt that a small group of thoughtful committed citizens can change the world; indeed, it's the only thing that ever has."[15]

Chapter Eight

# "THERE WAS NEVER A QUESTION OF DATA"
## Perspectives from Ten Years Out

In 1962's *Silent Spring*, the book many people credit with giving birth to the modern environmental movement, Rachel Carson writes: "We stand now where two roads diverge. But unlike the roads in Robert Frost's poem, they are not equally fair. The road we have been traveling is deceptively easy, a smooth superhighway on which we progress at great speed. The fork of the road—'the one less traveled by'—offers our last, our only chance to reach a destination that assures the preservation of our earth." By 1970, Louisiana's elected officials and business leaders had made their choice and were rushing down the "deceptively easy superhighway" to which Carson refers. Far too many people favored short-term profit over long-term stewardship of natural resources. Soon, toxic wastes began to permeate Louisiana's air, waterways, and land.

The thirty-six activists whose stories appear in this book had the foresight to look for an alternative route. Their accounts often shock and anger us. From them we learn about elected officials who put money ahead of the well-being of those people they were elected to serve. We learn about minority and low-income families who paid with even their lives, so others could acquire wealth. And we learn about children who never reached adulthood because some companies failed to take appropriate measures to protect their neighbors.

But these stories and those of the other ten featured here also give us hope. In the words of the well-known grassroots environmental activist Lois Gibbs, "Ordinary citizens, using the tools of dignity, self-respect, common sense, and perseverance, can influence solutions to important problems in our society.... In solving a difficult problem, you have to be prepared to fight long and hard, sometimes at great cost; but it can be done. It must be done if we are to survive as a democratic society, indeed, if we are to survive at all."

The label "ordinary citizens" may sound like a misnomer given all that these women achieved in a relatively short period of time. But according to many of the women themselves, they were simply leading traditional lives before they became activists. They were ordinary individuals caught up in the routine of their daily lives but extraordinary when they realized they needed to take action. None of them answered the call in hopes of gaining personal recognition or reward. In fact, most of them would have preferred to avoid the burdens and stresses implicit in their public roles. But embrace these new roles they did. Although they were, after all, already living full lives taking care of their families, leading Girl Scout troops, teaching Sunday school, going to work, and tending gardens, their lives were never the same. And none of the women regretted their choices, even though the personal costs were high.

Much has changed since the women first began their work in the 1970s, 1980s, and 1990s, starting with the strategies used by their opponents. Louisiana's first environmental activists faced adversaries who blatantly exploited poor communities and harassed those who objected. Today, a subtler approach is employed. Petrochemical corporations doing business in Louisiana recognize the public relations' value of proclaiming themselves stewards of the environment, and they wish to avoid the lengthy legal battles that many of the women in this book waged so successfully. So whenever possible, the companies pursue their agendas in ways that attract little public interest. Lobbying for rule changes in legislation and cuts in the enforcement budgets of regulatory authorities, for example, can have huge impacts on the environment, without the raucous public hearings and bad press involved in more overt activities.

The nature of the challenge has changed as well. In the 1970s and '80s, Louisiana's environmental problems were clear-cut and egregious: chemical stews pouring from ditches into rice fields, truckloads of hazardous materials buried in illegal dumps, noxious fumes circulating through large neighborhoods. Thirty-five years later, we have come a long way, thanks in large part to what these women achieved. Yes, rogue landfills still exist, and industrial sites require constant monitoring by those outside the fence line. But regulations have been established, and many of the most dramatic abuses have been corrected.

Increasingly, today's environmental problems are created by multiple sources. For example, in the case of a large watershed that is polluted by runoff from several towns, or an urban area with high lead counts in the soil, responsibility cannot be assigned to one perpetrator. Instead, these issues must be resolved by multiple parties who need to work together over the long haul for the common good.

Hurricanes Katrina and Rita intensified the need for productive coalitions and created even more environmental problems. Besides the deaths, displacement, and destruction caused by the storms, over two hundred square miles of Louisiana's coastal wetlands were literally wiped off the map. The future of many surviving coastal communities is in doubt, as Congress and the state debate the pros and cons of various restoration plans. The interviews in this book were conducted prior to Hurricanes Katrina and Rita, but several of the women predicted the catastrophe that befell Louisiana's coastline and wetlands in August and September of 2005. Their prescient warnings against building too many human-made structures such as dikes, levees, and canals went largely unheeded and left the coastal areas vulnerable to widespread flooding and destruction.

To rebuild the state while continuing to improve the environment, Louisiana needs those who can bring diverse people together and keep them working passionately for a worthy cause. And yet, in some quarters, the national environmental movement that Louisiana helped found has fallen prey to infighting and division along race and class lines. The women in this book offer promising alternatives. Several of the women extended their leadership to areas hit hard by the storms.

In late 2005, after Hurricanes Katrina and Rita, environmental groups throughout the state went into action, working to facilitate recovery and rebuilding efforts. The leaders of twenty environmental organizations issued a joint statement calling for an "open, inclusive, transparent long-term recovery plan ... and an honest and effective hurricane and flood protection program for coastal communities" that "integrates an effective levee system with marsh restoration and protection of forests ... and (the prioritizing of) public health over speed of rebuilding." Wilma Subra is among the women featured in this book who have been involved in the recovery process. Early after Hurricane Katrina, she began testing the soil in flood-stricken areas to determine risk levels for contaminants. Marylee Orr, another activist who shares her story here, has also been a vocal advocate for safe, well-considered hurricane recovery operations. Countless volunteers have joined both of these women, a trend that bodes well for Louisiana's recovery.

Given the unique situation Louisiana's environmental activists now face, the models provided by these women demonstrate how much can be accomplished with tenacity, solid research, and creative bridge-building. The groundbreaking lessons these pioneers learned and shared in their stories here can help present-day activists make the most of their efforts. The road of environmental activism may have changed in the last thirty-five years, but the destination remains the same: to create healthy, life-giving communities for citizens today and future generations. We all have much to learn from the first Louisiana women who took up this challenge and began to pave the way.

In this spirit, we add final words from Wilma Subra. Her biography appears earlier in this book. Significant in this chapter is her more recent work.

# WILMA SUBRA

### Looking Back, Looking Forward: Narrative from Wilma Subra

Since 2000 there have been three big disasters that tested Louisiana.[1] My response to each one of them, like the responses of others, brought me in contact with national groups, but the local groups also had a very real role. I think that is the challenge for the future, for the readers of this book: to know how the local and the national can now work together.

When Hurricane Katrina hit, within forty-eight hours I was out in the field. It took us the first forty-eight hours to cut our way out and make sure everyone that we knew was attended to. And then I was out in the field when the dead bodies were still floating in the water in New Orleans. I did damage assessment, needs assessment, and then sampling the sediment sludge that came ashore with the tidal surge—all the way along the coast in Louisiana, Mississippi, Alabama because the farthest point to the east was Mobile Bay. I was able to go in there because I had worked with all of those communities along those areas. I knew the lay of the land. I knew where they lived. I knew their community situations. Each night, I'd call or I'd e-mail back to where they had been relocated and tell them what was going on with the issues and situations in their own community. Marylee Orr of Louisiana Environmental Action Network started sending in supplies; so, too, I would call her at night, give her the shopping list. The next day, she'd get the supplies and get them taken, a lot of times by horse trailer because FEMA had hired all the trucks. So you couldn't even rent a truck. Again, this was the local response, working to make sure the communities had what they needed.

Similarly, I was also providing information to various communities, so they could make decisions whether to come back and, even if it was for the day, what they could expect and what they needed to be prepared for. I also advised on the long run, what the health impacts were, short term and long term, of the sediment sludge. EPA actually came behind us and took additional samples. In Mississippi, for instance, EPA came in, did sampling around an industrial facility, and found in Bay Saint Louis that the whole crab population was contaminated with dioxin.

This is not to say that industry wasn't still pushing back. That is one change I have not seen. Still, this time, since we were using EPA-certified labs, there was never a question of the data. The process moved really, really quickly.

Something similar happened with the BP spill. I was once again immediately in the field, providing information. When the rig exploded, the first thing we were dealing with concerned the basic need to tell who had died, who had lived. There were a number of workers from this area. Family members had to wait until the supply boat that rescued the workers made it to shore in Fourchon before they knew what the status was. They had satellite phones onboard the supply vessel but wouldn't allow the workers to call home. That was the first twenty-four hours: I was involved then in an attempt to help the families understand the tragedy.

It took nine days for the oil to make it into shore in Louisiana. But as soon as it was a slick, it turned into an aerosol with tiny droplets formed as a result of high winds and high seas, and these started blowing onshore. From New Iberia, Louisiana, all across Louisiana, Mississippi, Alabama, and the panhandle of Florida, these droplets made people on shore very, very sick. Yet no connection was made with the oil spill.

I started then doing workshops along the coastal areas. I put together two lists, a list of the health impacts from the crude and a list of the health impacts from the dispersants. So they could take that information to their doctors.

Louisiana has proved a continual test, then, but, yes, things have changed. The biggest change is that now some of the national organizations have a presence in Louisiana. But it is important to remember that they are not a continual presence. When they get funding for a specific thing, they come in and they make a lot of activity occur. But once the project is ended, they're gone.

As a result of Katrina, and then Rita, everyone in the environmental community wanted to capture some of that money that they envisioned was available. They were here, and they didn't quite understand how to work with the grassroots groups. They tried to direct them and manipulate them, as opposed to assist them. There was a lot of bad fallout as a result of that.

That was the sequence generally felt after the Katrina and Rita money evaporated. Then the BP spill occurred in 2010, and a lot of them came back. So the communities had learned to be really, really careful.

We must not forget that these coastal communities had been impacted by environmental issues like landfills and incinerators and oil field waste issues for many, many decades. They were always resilient. But the last six years have been something harder to overcome: Hurricane Katrina, followed less than a month later by Hurricane Rita. These destroyed a lot of the wetlands. These destroyed a lot of their infrastructure. But again, resilience—and with assistance, the people could see there was a future ahead. And they started rebuilding. And if you talk to them, they talk about, well, once a hurricane moves through, we see the damage and we start fixing it and making it right, even though it's a huge task.

But then the BP spill occurred, leaking from April through the middle of July, and these people couldn't see the end. It wasn't an event that occurred, and then you moved forward. It was an event that kept occurring. And it's still occurring. We're fourteen months out; oil is still washing on shore, still continuing to contaminate the marshes, the wetlands, and the beaches, and continues to wash on shore. So those communities became very, very depressed. Their health was impacted by the crude. Their health was impacted by the dispersants. Their livelihood was taken away. A lot of them went to work for BP and became very, very ill. And they are getting more and more depressed every day. So it's not like the resilience could kick in.

Then we had the spring of 2011, with all the floodwaters. So the Mississippi River was extremely high from the rainfall in the Midwest. And then the Morganza Spillway was opened to divert a lot of the water down the Atchafalaya. So suddenly you had people in the Atchafalaya Basin and the backwater areas being put up and put out to save New Orleans and Baton Rouge. One more time, these communities damaged and destroyed, and it's just like how many times can they have a disaster and still come back?

And yet, you can walk into those communities. They walk and talk the issues. They know what's needed. It's just how do they get their message out to the national organizations and the national government?

The Native American communities below Houma, the Pointe-aux-Chien, the Houmas nation, are an example of this precarious state. In the midst of all of the BP issues, the Grand Bois waste facility was questioned; there was a DEQ hearing on an air permit. Now, the Grand Bois facility is an oil field waste landfarm facility. Before this hearing, it was found that Grand Bois had never even had to have an air permit. So the community turned out in force. The company had replaced one of the diesel-driven pumps that injected the waste down into the injection well with an electric pump. Questions were being asked about this pump, but they were going to allow their pits to have the same emissions they had always had. They were just requiring them to replace that one pump, as well as add a second pump.

The hearing officer talked to me before the hearing. "Tell me what this is." I said, "This is Grand Bois." After I told him about the pump and the emissions, he said, "I had no idea it was here." He said, "It's listed as US Liquids." I said, "US Liquids is in the community of Grand Bois." I said, "Did you go by the facility before you came to the hearing?" [He said,] "Well, no." I said, "It's right down the road." So they were holding a hearing that even the hearing officer wasn't aware it was Grand Bois, wasn't aware of what the situation was at the facility. As a result, the community members stood up and said, "Let us tell you what it's like to live with these air emissions." As a result, the DEQ sent out their mobile monitor. Yet, and this is significant, they put it in the wrong locations to catch the worst air. It is these kind of things that keep going on over and over and over.

For such reasons, the grassroots communities have become very savvy over the years dealing with environmental issues, but there is a difference in this climate of huge disaster after huge disaster. Always before, sometimes they'd win, or they'd win a little. But now they're feeling like they're not able to win or make positive progress. To compound the issues the national groups often think of the communities only as victims. They want victims to be able to bring to D.C. and show off to Congress. Without the victims, there's not a demonstrated need.

Overall, the history of the women in this book shows that you need both a demonstrated need in the form of people influenced by certain acts and facts about this need, the hazards. Initially, every community that was involved in an issue, after you'd go in and help them understand what the issues were, then they'd go meet with, say, their legislator, their police juror, or their parish [county] commissioner. Always the answer to these women would be, "Well, it's not against the law." The episodes are continual: dealing with solid waste, dealing with oil field waste, dealing with hazardous waste. "It's not against the law. There is no law on the books that prohibits it."

Today, not only do we have hazardous waste coming into Louisiana from out of state, we also have shale gas. The problems cross borders, state borders, as the waste does, but we need to look at this together as a society. In Louisiana, we have shale gas in North Louisiana, around Shreveport. We have the Barnett Shale in the Dallas–Fort Worth area. We have the Marcellus Shale on the northeast coast. And the waste, Louisiana's waste from the Haynesville Shale is disposed in Texas. Arkansas's waste was being disposed of in Oklahoma. The Pennsylvania waste is being disposed of in Ohio and West Virginia. And I've been working on a lot of those issues with a lot of those communities. And once again, it's that same story: "It's not against the law to transport your waste to another state. You don't need anybody's permission."

For those issues you need a national conversation *and* a local one; and you need legislation, as well as education, that address this issue. In some ways, then, the women of Louisiana created the blueprint for this: they saw problems, they educated themselves, they educated others in the community, [and] they educated policy makers. They went to hearings; they learned to speak in the jargon required.

Still, what we need to remember is all this takes time and takes a toll. One of the biggest strengths of the grassroots movement is that in their communities these people have become leaders. The grassroots leaders can serve as a reminder that economic progress might carry dangers.

Whenever you have an environmental issue, the industry and the regulatory agencies and the state government will say, "But we need jobs." And the issue is how many jobs are we going to trade for the health of the community? So every time you get in an environmental situation, they always bring up, well, this is how many jobs it's going to bring into your community. And as a result, the people doing the environmental situations have that many more problems dealing with the situation. Is it worth those jobs to have the community to become very, very sick? So when you read the paper in Baton Rouge or when you go down to the legislature, you always hear, "Jobs first. Jobs first." They're always looking into bringing in new industrial facilities. I mean, you can read it every day in the paper. And then you'll see, every now and then, a community go, "Well, if that facility's going to expand, remember, we're already suffering from that." But then those people get really quiet, because one of their relatives works for one of the facilities. And they're told, "Be quiet, or your relative is going to lose a job." So that's what happens. That's how they fight back to the environmental community; they start threatening the people who are speaking out with loss of jobs to their relatives. So it's a very, very difficult situation. Everyone wants new jobs. Everyone wants jobs for the communities. But they have to be safe jobs for the workers, as well as safe jobs for the community. And I think the BP spill demonstrated that. All the fishers had the fishing grounds shut down. And they wanted to go to work for BP because one, they knew those marshes and estuaries the best. That was their grounds. They thought they could protect them and they could do the best job of cleaning them up. And from the very beginning, BP didn't provide them with the proper training or the proper protective gear. So all of those workers got very, very sick. We had a work environment in 2010 where workers were being made sick. And there have been rules and regulations at the national level protecting workers' health and safety for a very, very long time. And there were hundreds of thousands of workers made sick. And these people, when they were made sick, if they complained, they were laid off. So a lot of them would come home at night, get back up in the morning, go back out and get sick again, day after day after day. And it demonstrated that if you don't have safe jobs, you not only impact the workers, you impact the rest of the community. We're going to be dealing with that health impact on those workers for generations. So safe jobs are important. Worker safety is very important. Community health is very important. And it's not to be given away in the name of just jobs.

Once the BP spill occurred and shale gas development started in some of these states, then all of a sudden, now, all the national groups want to be the leaders and want to be involved. So I think the weakness at the national level is they're policy-driven by D.C., inside the Beltway, not driven by the real issues out in the states. Yet, unlike the grassroots people, they have a lot of resources. They have technical people; they have attorneys that can file petitions and lawsuits on behalf of the communities. So in that aspect, they've really, really helped. As a matter of fact, the Earth Justice group actually filed lawsuits dealing with the vinyl chloride industry.

And as you know, in the Lake Charles area, East Baton Rouge, West Baton Rouge, and in the Plaquemine's area, there are a large number of vinyl chloride facilities. We just got a really great ruling that EPA had to develop regulations not just for the vinyl chloride, but the other chemicals that they release, and we had a hearing two months ago in Baton Rouge on the new proposed rules that are coming out of that. Without that kind of national support, especially from attorneys, we couldn't get across-the-board improvements.

A go-between or a bridge between the national and local groups has been Tulane Environmental Law Clinic. I always tell the story that in a number of communities where I worked, together we developed the issues and concerns, presented it at public hearings. Then Tulane, if the permit still was granted, Tulane actually appealed the permit, based on the data that we had developed and presented, and won many, many. So at the state level, Tulane's been really, really great. At the national level, we've needed the attorneys and the national groups to represent the communities and the pollution issues.

The environmental justice movement also has had very positive and very negative impacts. Before that name "environmental justice" was coined, we worked with all these groups doing just that, providing legal assistance, providing technical assistance. And then the environmental justice tag arose, and it divided. Instead of consolidating, it divided the communities. EPA started giving out environmental justice grants. So where you had a mixed group—mixed in any way, by race or income level or even at times by town or geographic area—suddenly that group divided since the environmental justice people had to form their own group to be able to get the money. And as a result of that, you lost some of that community-building impact. And it still drives it that way. Is this an environmental justice community or not? Is it mostly African Americans? Is it mostly Vietnamese? Is it mostly Native Americans? And people put that tag on it, and people treat those communities different. Instead of the issues getting dealt with, it's dividing. They have to be selective in which communities they deal with because of the environmental justice tag that's associated with them.

On the other hand, out of the environmental justice movement have come some really strong leaders. What I have always thought and what these leaders, many in this book, have thought is that you win some battles, and when you win some, it's great. But even if you keep on losing, you've educated and empowered the community, and they are a stronger, empowered community as a result of it. And so you never really lose everything.

Many of the policies and regulations we have put in place have stayed there, as well. After [Buddy] Roemer went out and [Edwin] Edwards came back in, he immediately got rid of some of the ones that dealt with the industrial facilities and Cancer Alley. But for the most part, they've stayed. Like we have one of the few ambient air standards in the United States, in the state of Louisiana. So they're on the books, and we can watch and see whether they're being enforced or not and then complain when they're not being enforced. So without the rules, we wouldn't have that ability to require enforcement. At the national level, I've been the voice of "You can have the best rules and regulations on the book, but if you don't enforce them, they don't exist." And that's the message I bring to the national level. But that's also the message I bring to the community: look to the rules and then look where they're not being enforced. We need to start documenting and going to the agencies and saying, "You really need to enforce the policies in place."

We also need to be lobbying the legislature about issues, and this was not done as often in the past as now. Louisiana Environmental Action Network actually has two and a half people that lobby, and they're registered lobbyists. And they're down at the legislature every single day during the session. And they're often requested to testify on bills. So they are very, very effective. Sierra Club has one, but they're a very part-time one. And then the industry lobbyists, the business lobbyists, they are always there. And then, the agencies themselves. If you go into a hearing, you would think that the agency is the lobbyist when they sit at the table and testify because they present it as the need for these or the lack of need for these, regulations based on the industry perspective. They are often the voice of industry.

The positive thing is that lobbyists are now required to have to report how much money they spend, and they are limited too on how much this can be. They are limited in how much they can spend on a meal with a legislator, for example. From the '70s to the '90s, when you'd go to a hearing and a committee, the first to speak would be the industry and the environmental agencies testifying. Then when the community had their chance to testify, the food provided by the industry arrived in the back room to feed the legislators. Well, now they can't do that, now that they have to have more transparency and reporting. So they're sitting there at their desks, listening to you—not in the back eating while you're testifying. So that's a positive change that has occurred. And the LEAN lobbyists actually interact with the grassroots communities on all the bills that will have an impact on what's going on in their community. LEAN lobbyists get the input of the communities, and they encourage the people to come to Baton Rouge for specific bills.

Not many other states have organizations like LEAN, so we are blessed in that respect with this umbrella organization of grassroots organizations. The other states have specific organizations in specific areas, but not an umbrella group of all the grassroots groups.

Louisiana has always had, too, some differences because of the prominent presence of the Catholic Church in the south of the state. A lot of the priests in the local Catholic Churches lent support to the grassroots movements. They put notices in the bulletin or they announced meetings during the mass. They offered the church halls for meetings. In some cases, the priest actually hired buses to take the community to Baton Rouge to the legislature. The priests participated with the people.

On the other hand, a lot of the environmental justice communities in recent times will be able to get their church hall for an initial meeting. But after you have one meeting there and you deal with the issue that you're discussing, then the pastor realizes that other members of his congregation work at a facility, that industrial facility gives their church money, so then those churches start backing away. Their hall is not available for the meetings because they don't want the wrong message being sent from their church to the rest of the community and from their church to the industrial supporters. A lot of the Catholic priests were called in by the bishop because industrial leaders had given money to the churches and these leaders would go to the bishop and complain: "If you don't get that priest to back off, I'm going to reduce my contributions." So the bishop would call them in. More often than not, though, the bishop supported the priest. It was amazing, and we should not forget we have this type of support.

On the other hand, there are other situations locally to understand. The agencies, both the Department of Environmental Quality and the Office of Conservation, are constantly changing and yet constantly staying the same. Under Governor Roemer, Paul Templet was secretary of the Department of Environmental Quality. And those were the best years as far as interacting with the communities and having the communities have access to what was going on in the agencies. Since then, it's been off and on. Some days, you're invited in. Other days, you're treated like "What are you doing here?" And then, with the security now, you used to be able to just walk in and go to whatever floor and whatever division you wanted to speak to someone and talk to the secretary. Now you have to actually sign in and have an appointment with someone. And they have to come down and get you. So you don't have that openness and transparency, or the chance to go in and deal with the agency on a one-to-one basis. Today, the appointments are difficult to set up and they're very limited.

The positive thing in the Department of Environmental Quality is they put all their files in an electronic database. So if you have a computer, you can access it from your home or your office. If not, you can go in the file room and sit at one of their computers, and they will help you. And so you can look up any of the documents that you want, all the way back to the beginning of the agency's existence—all the paper documents have been put on there. So that's been very, very helpful to the community.

But now, the Office of Conservation has a big role too, and they haven't received enough resources to put all of their data on an electronic database. Every time I meet with them, I keep bringing that up: that it would be really helpful if you didn't have to come to Baton Rouge and you didn't have to go to these different spots.

And, "Oh, so-and-so has that file. It's not available." So it's still that old style. But for the most part, they're the same people in the Office of Conservation that have been there since the '80s. A few new people have been hired on and have worked their way up the chain of command. But yet it's still the same people there. And there's still that reluctance; like when you show up to look at a file, they're still looking over your shoulder at what file you're looking at. And if you ask a question, they sort of like, "Well, let me check on that answer." You know, so it's not an open process at all.

The Office of Conservation is still granting most permits. So, therefore, we need Tulane to represent the communities and appeal. And in one case, we won the appeal on an injection well. The judge vacated the permit. So the Office of Conservation appealed it. And while they were appealing that decision, they allowed the applicant to reapply for the injection well. The Office [of Conservation] granted the permit, even before the decision by the appeals court. And then they petitioned the appeals court and said, "It's null and void because we've already granted them the permit." So the community was excluded from participating in that appeal process. So we still have a long way to go. We've made great progress, but we have a long way to go.

One of the big issues now is air emissions. It's been an issue around the industrial facilities for a long time, but people envisioned it was just a problem on Cancer Alley and in the Lake Charles area and that the rest of the state didn't have any air emission issues. There are many old sites that didn't have the right type of permits or didn't control the waste that has contaminated huge amounts of ground water and surface water. People don't know to ask about this; they go out to an area and see some property for sale and don't think to ask, "Well, is there a ground water plume? Is there a water source, or am I going to have to drill a well? And is that property going to be good if it's got a ground water plume?"

One of the interesting things with the oil spill is, if you notice, it was all the federal agencies involved. The command center of BP was really running it, but it was representatives of the federal agencies. The state filed a suit alleging that BP had violated the Clean Water Act and all that, but you didn't see a lot of state activity from the regulatory agencies. What you did see was the regulatory agencies getting involved, opposing the moratorium that was brought forth from the national level. So I think it didn't make that much difference in the state of Louisiana because it didn't really impact the rules and regulations as they were being implemented in the state of Louisiana. At the same time, the Haynesville Shale development was going like crazy. So the Office of Conservation was spending lots of time issuing permits for wells up there. So they were doing state business while the BP disaster was occurring; that is, the state regulatory agencies weren't that engaged with the BP disaster.

Another problem is that sustainability is not an issue that's discussed very much in Louisiana. And it's because oil and gas are driving our economy. It would be very critical to put together something like we had done under Roemer, where we were looking at what are the issues in the future, what do we need in place, and how can we have all the state agencies, including the economic development agencies, look at what kinds of things we need to promote for sustainability. Right now, with the budget cuts, the issue of sustainability is not high on anyone's list. It could be done. It could be done by engaging all these agencies, as well as the communities. And start moving forward with it. And that would be really, really important.

The dependence on oil, including a lot of foreign oil, is really critical to the whole United States. Knowing this dependency necessitates more than impulsive turns. What I was scared would happen after the BP spill is that the state government was going to say all of their fleet had to go natural gas. And that it was really going to push the development of natural gas in the Haynesville Shale in north Louisiana. And that area is very, very poor. And the people there are being abused by the industry going in and signing leases and then not paying them, or pulling back the leases and yet drilling and producing and really damaging and destroying the environment.

I think we need to push for alternative energies. We have an individual here, Herman Schellstede, in New Iberia, who's an inventor. And he came up with a method of putting wind turbines on old offshore oil and gas rig sites that were no longer used. And he beat his head against the wall with the state agencies. They would not work with him. So he went to Texas and is working with the Texas agencies. In Louisiana, we're so focused on oil and gas that we can't see beyond. We cannot come up with alternative technologies.

These alternatives will require new leaders, but what these leaders can learn from the stories of the early activists is how they kept moving forward in the face of adversity. They should also know how many issues they were dealing with, not only the environmental issues, but also the personal issues and the community issues. Sure, they got diverted at times, pulled in all these different directions. Yet you can make progress if you just keep moving forward. And I think that their stories serve as role model stories and help community leaders realize it's not going to be easy.

If you come to stand on the shoulders of these leaders, you will be involved in this for the rest of your life. It's not a short-term commitment. It dominates your life. The women in this project show how they have always been the ones who made do, who made time and made space. I think the new leaders can see this in their stories.

Historically, grassroots movements have short lives. The Louisiana movement has lasted more than thirty years. The women and men in this book set the process in motion that has led to the huge environmental awareness that is now present in

Louisiana. Their care-giving extended from a personal to a public space. There is every reason to be proud of them and to build on what they began.

# SUPPLEMENTAL LIST OF WOMEN ENVIRONMENTAL ACTIVISTS

This book does not include interviews with all of the courageous and visionary women who worked to protect Louisiana's environment in the 1970s, 1980s, and 1990s. Some of the women died before the project began, and some we were unable to speak with because of time and resource shortages. Although they are not featured in the book, they nevertheless made extremely important contributions and we are indebted to all of them.

Please forgive me if your name is not on the following list. I did not intentionally omit anyone. Listed are the names of some of the women I met during my activism; other names were given to me by friends. Dr. Velma Campbell of Colorado was a catalyst for bringing medical treatment issues related to the environment to the forefront. Ruby Cointment (Gonzales, Louisiana) worked with Theresa Robert to stop the IT Corporation from building a hazardous waste facility in her community. Helga Cernicek (deceased), formerly of New Orleans, participated in Louisiana wetland research that provided important data to LSU staff members and students alike. Brenda Davis (Westlake, Louisiana) organized her community to plant nearly fifteen thousand cypress seedlings on the Calcasieu River over a five-year period. Barbara Dodd (Covington, Louisiana), one of only two volunteer lobbyists for the environmental community, brought a seasoned and progressive voice to many discussions with government employees and legislators. Ruth Duhon (deceased), formerly of Sulphur, Louisiana, was a founding member of the High Hope Road Committee. Catherine Ewell, formerly of Zachary, Louisiana, lived on the Ewell farm adjacent to Devil's Swamp and was the first to keep meticulous records about air and water pollution in the area. Doris Falkenheiner (Baton Rouge, Louisiana) participated in restoring the Atchalalaya Basin's wetlands; she also served on the legal advisory board of the Tulane Environmental Law Clinic. Mary Fontenot, of Baton Rouge, Louisiana, helped collect thousands of signatures to stop the burning of PCBs at the Rollins facility in Alsen, Louisiana. Charlotte Fremaux (New Orleans, Louisiana) helped Frank Ehret Jr. establish the Jean Lafitte National Historical Park and Preserve. Evelyn Fulgenz (deceased), formerly of Lake Charles,

Louisiana, successfully lobbied members of Congress to defeat ocean incineration in the Gulf of Mexico. Maxine Hargar (Sulphur, Louisiana) spent thousands of hours researching complicated environmental documents and putting them into laymen's terms for environmentalists to use at public hearings. Patricia Norton Hudnal (San Francisco, California) was the first female appointed as secretary of the Department of Environmental Quality, Baton Rouge, Louisiana; in her position, she not only represented industry, but also became an advocate for citizen involvement, especially for African Americans living in communities like Alsen and Willow Springs; opening the door for citizen input caused the demise of her state job. Emma Johnson (deceased), formerly of Alsen, Louisiana, kept meticulous records about the pollution problems in the area. Mabel Rigmaiden Jones and her mother, Beaulah Rigmaiden, of Westlake, Louisiana, passed a petition in her neighborhood to close the BFI landfill; they were also founding members of the High Hope Road Committee. Pam Kaster (Baton Rouge, Louisiana) worked with Citizens for a Clean Environment in stopping the burning of PCBs at the Rollins incinerator. Dr. Carolyn Morillo (New Orleans, Louisiana) was a principal supporter of the Ecology Center. Joan Phillips (deceased), formerly of New Orleans, was a leader in raising awareness about the need to address coastal wetland loss; according to Dr. Oliver Houck, founder of the Tulane Environmental Law Clinic, she saved Lake Pontchartrain. Anne Plettinger, of Baton Rouge, Louisiana, was involved in the highly secretive Manhattan Project as a nuclear physicist. Nancy Roberts (Baton Rouge, Louisiana) was a member of Friends of the Environment, which focused on air pollution. Bunny Snow (Lafayette, Louisiana) worked on issues pertaining to multiple chemical sensitivity and sanitation; she also opposed a statewide landfill and garbage incinerator that would have been relocated in the recharge zone of the Chicot Aquifer. Ramona Stevens (deceased), formerly of Prairieville, Louisiana, became an activist when her husband took part in the BASF (a large, German-based chemical company) lockout from 1985 to 1991; she helped local citizens organize, took samples to identify pollution, and challenged local and state government and industry. Kathy Wascom (Baton Rouge, Louisiana) is one of only two volunteer lobbyists for the environmental community in Louisiana; as president of the Louisiana Wildlife Federation, she received an award for spearheading the LWF's used motor oil recycling project. Marsha Whatley (Pineville, Louisiana) became an activist after her younger sister died of leukemia; she successfully pushed for a statewide tumor registry; she was also the first person in Louisiana to testify on behalf of the rare and endangered red wolf, not yet extinct at the time. Eloise Wall (Baton Rouge, Louisiana) was a founding member of

Citizens for a Clean Environment and spent many hours successfully raising the Louisiana legislature's awareness of environmental issues. Karen Wimpleberg, of New Orleans, Louisiana, was one of four founders of the Alliance for Affordable Energy, dedicated to promoting fair, affordable, and environmentally responsible policies in Louisiana and the nation.

# NOTES

## Introduction

1. Jim Beam, "Why Is This Earth Day Different," *Lake Charles American Press*, April 22, 1990.

2. "BFI, ICG Pass Dumping Buck," *Lake Charles American Press*, October 23, 1982. BFI Chemical Services, Inc., a subsidiary of BFI, operated the facility until mid-1983, when operational control of the facility was transferred to CECOS International, Inc., another BFI subsidiary.

3. "BFI, ICG Pass Dumping Buck."

4. *Lake Charles American Press*, October 24, 1982.

5. "BFI, ICG Pass Dumping Buck."

6. Ibid.

7. She died several months after the health study was conducted.

8. David Snyder, "The Poisoned Land," *New Orleans Times Picayune, Special Report*, September 8–13, 1985.

9. The affected areas included fifteen parishes or eleven thousand square miles, extending west to the Sabine River, east to the Atchafalaya River, south to the Gulf of Mexico, and north to Vernon and Rapides Parish.

10. BFI constructed both a landfill and an injection well at the facility. We were successful in the closure of the landfill and partially successful with the injection well. They can no longer take waste from other companies. They are allowed only to inject waste from their own waste stream.

11. For more on open range cattle and this testimony, see Jim Schwab, *Deeper Shades of Green* (San Francisco: Sierra Club Books, 1999), 224.

12. Ibid.

13. Schwab, *Deeper Shades of Green*, 208. In 1986, Louisiana led the nation annually in the discharge of toxic pollution with more than 715 million pounds being emitted into the air, land, and water.

14. "Report on Solid Waste Landfills," 1989, Louisiana Department of Environmental Quality (DEQ), State Agency Files, Baton Rouge, LA; "Report on Hazardous Waste Dumps," 1990, DEQ, State Agency Files, Baton Rouge, LA; "Report on Hazardous Waste Landfills," 1995, DEQ, State Agency Files, Baton Rouge, LA; "Report on Injection Wells,"

1996, Louisiana Office of Conservation Report, State Agency Files, Baton Rouge, LA. Copies available from Wilma Subra.

15. "Report on Hazardous Waste Dumps." An underground waste plume is similar to a plume of smoke. Like smoke, the groundwater flows out from an underground source of contamination and forms a larger area of contamination.

16. The Superfund Program was set up by Congress in 1980 to pay for the cleanup of numerous abandoned hazardous waste sites around the country.

17. Personal interview with Lois Gibbs, director of the Citizens' Clearinghouse for Hazardous Wastes (CCHW), January 29, 2000.

18. In 2011, Edwards was released from federal prison after serving eight years for a corruption conviction related to the gaming industry.

19. Huey Long was governor of Louisiana, 1928 to 1932. He also served in the US Senate from 1932 until his death in 1935. Like Edwards, but with a record of building, Long was a populist, sponsoring many reforms that endeared him to the rural poor.

20. Barbara Allen, *Uneasy Alchemy* (Boston: Massachusetts Institute of Technology, 2003), 10–13, 164 n 18.

21. Save Ourselves v. Louisiana Environmental Control Commission, No. 83-C-1480 (452 So. 2d 1152, 20 ERC 2214) (La. May 14, 1984). See also Theresa Robert in chapter 2 of this book.

## Chapter 1

1. Division of Administration, "About Louisiana: History and Culture," http://doa.louisiana.gov/about_industry.htm (accessed March 10, 2012).

2. For more on the cases against Marine Shale, see U.S. v. Marine Shale Processors, Inc. (W.D. LA), United States Department of Justice website, http://www.justice.gov/enrd/3639.htm (accessed March 10, 2012); U.S. of America, et al., Plaintiffs, United States of America, Plaintiff-Appellee, Cross-Appellant, v. Marine Shale Processors, Defendant-Appellee, Southern Wood Piedmont Company, Intervenor-Appellant, Cross-Appellee, No. 94-30419, April 18, 1996, http://caselaw.findlaw.com/us-5th-circuit/1340583.html (accessed March 10, 2012).

3. Peggy Frankland interviewed Sally Herman in June 2000.

4. Peggy Frankland interviewed Fernell Cryar in June 2000.

5. At the time of these interviews, neuroblastoma was considered rare by doctors. In 2010, the incidence of neuroblastoma was "10.2 cases per million children under 15 years of age." See John M. Maris, "Recent Advances in Neuroblastoma," *New England Journal of Medicine* 362 (June 2010): 2202–11. Also available online at http://www.cncfhope.org/Neuroblastoma_Research (accessed August 17, 2012).

6. Jennifer Abraham interviewed Barbara LeLeux in June 2000.

7. Jennifer Abraham interviewed Catherine Holcomb in June 2000.

8. Peggy Frankland interviewed Monica Mancuso in June 2000.

9. Peggy Frankland interviewed Helen Solar in June 2000.

10. Peggy Abraham interviewed Miriam Price in June 2000.

## Chapter 2

1. "Report on Solid Waste Landfills"; "Report on Hazardous Waste Dumps"; "Report on Hazardous Waste Landfills"; and "Report on Injection Wells."
2. "Report on Hazardous Waste Dumps."
3. Allen, *Uneasy Alchemy*, 3–4, 15–162.
4. John Wilds, Charles L. Dufour, and Walter G. Cowan, *Louisiana, Yesterday and Today: A Historical Guide to the State* (Baton Rouge, LSU Press, 1996), 75–76; Eddystone C. Nebel III, *Factors Affecting the Location of the Petrochemical Industry in the Gulf South* (Baton Rouge: LSU Press, 1971), 51–58.
5. Jennifer Abraham interviewed Ann Williams in November 1999.
6. A Petition for Damages and Injunction was filed in the 24th Judicial District Court for the Parish of Jefferson on August 19, 1988: Delta Environmental Services, Inc. and J. Stuart Ellis, Jr. vs. Ann Williams and Plaquemines Newspaper Publishing, Inc.
7. Jennifer Abraham interviewed Rose Jackson in June 2001.
8. Marvin Legator (1926–2005) was an internationally recognized toxicologist and recipient of the prestigious Hollander Award for his contributions to the field of toxicology.
9. We were unable to corroborate this statement with Louisiana Department of Health and Hospitals (LADHH).
10. Jennifer Abraham and Peggy Frankland interviewed Marietta Herr in several meetings over 2001 and 2003.
11. Peggy Frankland interviewed Ruth Shepherd in March 2000.
12. Save Ourselves v. Louisiana Environmental Control Commission, 452 So. 2d 1152 (La. 1984).
13. Peggy Frankland interviewed Theresa Robert in June 2000.
14. Save Ourselves v. Louisiana Environmental Control Commission.
15. For more on the Ecology Center, active from 1970 to 1983, see Ecology Center of Louisiana, Inc., Special Collections, Monroe Library, Loyola University, New Orleans, LA.
16. Peggy Frankland interviewed Kay Gaudet in March 2001.
17. Plaquemine is near Baton Rouge and is not located in Plaquemines Parish

## Chapter 3

1. "Girl Scout Promise," Girls Scouts, http://www.girlscouts.org/program/basics/promise_law/ (accessed March 15, 2012).
2. Peggy Frankland interviewed Lorena Pospisil in April 2000.
3. Peggy Frankland interviewed Shirley Goldsmith in June 2000.
4. Peggy Frankland interviewed Gerry Ardoin in January 2000.
5. Peggy Frankland interviewed Janice Crador in January 2000.
6. Randy Roach later became mayor of Lake Charles.
7. Sasol acquired the facility in 2001. For information on EDC in groundwater, see Sunny Brown, "Wait for settlement payoff has Mossville plaintifs growing angry," *Lake Charles American Press*, December 10, 1999.

8. Conoco owned the VCM plant before selling to Condea Vista, so it was also sued. Mossville residents reached a $16 million settlement with Conoco and its parent company, DuPont, in 1997.

9. Peggy Frankland interviewed Debra Ramirez in November 2000.

## Chapter 4

1. The Toxic Release Inventory was first issued in 1988 but was established in 1986. The inventory is part of the 1986 Emergency Planning and Community Right-to-Know Act of 1986 (EPCRA), which was commonly known as SARA Title III. Section 313 of EPCRA established the Toxics Release Inventory (TRI) Program. The goal of the TRI national database is to empower citizens, through information, to hold companies and local governments accountable in terms of how toxic chemicals are managed.

2. For example, the Gordon sisters were among the women in New Orleans who brought such reform. See Kate and Jean Gordon, *Louisiana Leaders: Notable Women in History*, http://www.lib.lsu.edu/soc/women/lawomen/gordons.html (accessed March 15, 2011).

3. Peggy Frankland interviewed Jessie Price in November 2000.

4. David Snyder, "The Poisoned Land," *Times Picayune*, Special Report, September 8–13, 1985; Wilma Subra, "On regulations, 29B, governing oil and gas exploration and development," e-mail to Peggy Frankland, March 14, 2012.

5. Peggy Frankland interviewed Gay Hanks in June 2000.

6. Saint Jude's Research Hospital is a state-of-the-art center for children with pediatric cancer and other catastrophic diseases.

7. Jennifer Abraham interviewed Mary Brasseaux in April 2000.

8. Jennifer Abraham interviewed Florence Robinson in October 2000.

9. Jennifer Abraham interviewed Mary Ellender in November 2000.

10. Olin is now closed.

11. Jennifer Abraham and Peggy Abraham interviewed Carol Savoy over two sessions in May and November 2001.

## Chapter 5

1. See, for examples, Mary Gehman, *Women and New Orleans: A History* (New Orleans, Margaret Media, 1996).

2. The New Orleans League papers tell many examples of environmental concerns from 1915 onward. League of Women Voters, Manuscript Collection 556, Louisiana Research Collection, Howard-Tilton Memorial Library, Tulane University. For one example from the press, see "Leaguers Plunge into Water Study," *New Orleans Times-Picayune*, January 20, 1957.

3. Susan Tucker and Beth Willinger, "Distinctions," in *Newcomb College, 1886–2006: Higher Education for Women in New Orleans*, edited by Tucker and Willinger (Baton Rouge: LSU Press, 2012), 127.

4. Jennifer Abraham interviewed Mildred Fossier in March 2000.

5. Jennifer Abraham interviewed Mary McCastle and Simms McCastle in January 2000 and Willie Fontenot in September 2003.
6. Peggy Frankland interviewed Florence Gossen in September 2000.
7. Peggy Frankland interviewed Clara Baudoin in September 2000.
8. Jennifer Abraham interviewed Liz Avants in November 2000.
9. Peggy Frankland interviewed Les Ann Kirkland in November 2001.
10. Peggy Frankland interviewed Mary Tutwiler in October 2000.
11. Save Ourselves v. Louisiana Environmental Control Commission, 452 So. 2d 1152 (La. 1984).

## Chapter 6

1. Peggy Frankland interviewed Sister Helen Vinton in October 2000.
2. Peggy Frankland interviewed Lorna Bourg in October 2000.
3. OMB Watch, a nonprofit research and advocacy organization, was formed in 1983 to lift the veil of secrecy shrouding the White House Office of Management and Budget (OMB).
4. Jennifer Abraham and Peggy Frankland interviewed Marylee Orr in January 2002.
5. Linda Price King, *Chemical Injuries in the Courts: A Litigation Guide for Clients and Their Attorneys* (Chesapeake, VA: Environmental Health Network, 1999); Brian Keating, Sanford Lewis, and Dick Russell, "Inconclusive by Design: Waste, Fraud, and Abuse in Federal Health Research," May 1992, http://archive.org/details/InconclusiveByDesignWasteFraudAndAbuseInFederalEnvironmentalHealth (accessed August 19, 2012).
6. Peggy Frankland interviewed Linda King in November 2001.
7. Jennifer Abraham interviewed Wilma Subra in June 2000.

## Chapter 7

1. Sharon Dyer interviewed Buddy Roemer in February 2004
2. Sharon Dyer interviewed Carroll Wascom in February 2004.
3. Peggy Frankland interviewed Maureen O'Neill in June 2000.
4. Sharon Dyer interviewed Kai David Midboe in November 2003.
5. Sharon Dyer interviewed Dan Borne in February 2004.
6. Borne could be referring to "Incidence of Early Loss of Pregnancy," *New England Journal of Medicine* 319, no. 4 (July 1988): 189–94. This article found a 31 percent rate of miscarriage, but 22 percent of these miscarriages were so early that no confirmation of pregnancy had occurred. The percentage of women who miscarried after they had been clinically diagnosed as pregnant, which were the types of pregnancies Kay Gaudet was tracking, was only 9 percent. Because miscarriages do occur often, scientists recommend studies of less frequent indicators, such as premature births, birth defects, and problem pregnancies.
7. Tulane University, School of Public Health and Tropical Medicine, "Final Report: St. Gabriel Miscarriage Investigation," New Orleans, 1989. Critics point out that the study

area included the entire eastern portion of Iberville Parish on either side of the Mississippi River. By aggregating data from such a large area, the study made it impossible to detect a miscarriage cluster in the much smaller zone around Saint Gabriel. An outside review of the study found the results "inconclusive at best" (James O'Bryne, "Study of St. Gabriel Miscarriages Flawed," *Times-Picayune*, May 16, 1990).

8. For a summary of these issues, see chapter 5 of Allen, *Uneasy Alchemy*.

9. Jennifer Abraham interviewed Bob Kuehn in July 2000.

10. Peggy Frankland interviewed Audrey Evans in January 2002.

11. Jennifer Abraham interviewed Paul Templet in 2001.

12. This text was compiled from an interview Peggy Frankland had with Will Collette on November 17, 2001, as well as from e-mails and an essay.

13. Jennifer Abraham interviewed Willie Fontenot in January 2012.

14. Jim Schwab, *Deeper Shades of Green* (San Francisco: Sierra Club Books, 1994), 215.

15. Fontenot's career ended abruptly in 2005 after he took a group of graduate students from an Antioch New England Environmental Studies class on a tour of a neighborhood where homeowners had to relocate after a 500,000-gallon storage tank erupted at an Exxon/Mobil plant in 1989. Exxon guards demanded that the students show their IDs even though they were not on company property. Two weeks later, Willie was notified by then Attorney General Charles Foti to submit his resignation and clear out his office.

## Chapter 8

1. Jennifer Abraham interviewed Wilma Subra in July 2011.

# INDEX

Page numbers in *italics* refer to illustrations.

Abbeville, Louisiana, 153
Aerial spraying, pesticides, 146–48, 154–56
African American, xxi, xxiv, 34, 37, 46, 80, 94, 97, 118, 158, 198, 205, 223, 225
Agency for Toxic Substances and Disease Registry (ATSDR), 165–66
Agrico, 49
Air Control Commission, 123
air quality/emissions, xiv, xx, 11, 20, 46, 47, 59, 68, 81–83, 97, 100, 108, 119–25, 133, 157–58, 170–71, 239
Alliance against Waste and Action to Restore the Environment (AWARE), 132, 134, 136, 137
Alsen, Louisiana (Rollins Environmental Services), 97, 100–101, 118, 119–23, 158
Anderson, Bob, 122, 158
Ardoin, Gerry, 70–74, *71*; activism of, 70–74; background of, 70; faith and, 70; ICE and, 70, 72
Aristech Chemical, 209
At Sea Incineration (ASI), 68, 69
Atchafalaya Basin, 191, 193, 196, 233
Audubon Society, 42, 116, 225
Avants, Liz, 132–35, *133*, 160; activism of, 134–35; AWARE and, 132, 134, 137; Kirkland and, 136

Babich, Adam, 175
Barthelemy, Sidney, 42, 43, 115, 117
BASF Corporation, 189
*Baton Rouge Advocate*, 122, 158
Baudoin, Clara, 125, 126, 127–32, *128*, 184; activism of, 129–32; background of, 127–29; health issues and, 129; lawsuit and, 130–31; politics and, 131–32
Bayou Sauvage National Wildlife Refuge, 40, 43, 115–16, 224
Bayou Sorrell, 48, 134
Bhopal, India, 160, 169
Big Diamond Trucking Services, Inc., 74, 78, 105, 107, 183
Big Oak Island, 43
Bizalion, Anne, 147
Boese, Bob, 143
Boggs, Lindy, 115, 188
Boggs, Tommy, 188
Borne, Dan, 197–203; background of, 197–98; on cancer, 201–2; chemical industry and, 198–200; on regulation, 199, 203; on women in the movement, 200–201
Bourg, Lorna, 151–56, *152*; activism of, 153–56; arrest of, 155; attempts to intimidate, 156; background of, 152–53; Head Start Program and, 153–54; recognition received by, 151; SMHU and, 146, 151, 155
BP oil spill, 232, 233, 239
Brasseaux, Mary, 94–96, *95*; activism of, 96–97; background of, 94–96; cancer and, 95; HOPE and, 94, 96
Breaux, John, 8, 54, 68, 155
Brown and Ferris Industries, Inc. (BFI), xiv, xv, xvi, xvii, xviii, 44, 47, 67
Bryant, Pat, 205

Calcasieu Estuary, xiii, 177
Calcasieu League for Environmental Action Now (CLEAN), 44, 48, 65, 67

251

252  INDEX

Calcasieu Parish, xiii, xiv xv, xvii, 5, 70–73, 101, 103, 104
Calcasieu Ship Channel, 101
Campbell, Velma, 242
Cancer, xix, 22, 26, 39, 47, 56–57, 67–68, 75, 79, 92–93
Cancer Alley (Cancer Corridor), 201, 239
Carson, Rachel, *Silent Spring*, 46, 191, 228
Cenla, Louisiana, 62
Cernicek, Helga, 242
"chemical valley," 163
Chemical Waste Management (CWMI), 103, 104–5
Chernobyl, 160
Chicot Aquifer, xvii, 92, 104, 126, 141–42
Chief Seattle, 48
Ciba-Geigy, 55
citizen involvement, 195, 196, 199–200, 205–7
Citizens' Clearinghouse for Hazardous Wastes (CCHW), 7, 164, 217, 218–19, 220–21
Citizens for a Clean Environment, 122, 159–60
Civil Rights Act of 1964, 205
Clean Air Act, 54, 202
Clean Air Action Committee, 54
Clean Water Act, 188, 202
CNN, 155
Coalition for Community Action, 118, 121
Coastal Zone Management, 192–93, 213
Cointment, Ruby, 51, 110, 225, 242
Collette, Will, 30, 174, 217–21, *218*; background of, 217–18; CCHW and, 218–19, 220–21; environmental justice and, 218–19; King and, 164; LEAN and, 159, 160, 174
Community Alert Network, 133
Concerned Citizens Committee of Cenla (CCC), 60, 63, 77, 105, 107
Condea Vista, 80, 82, 83
Conoco, 80, 82, 83, 248ch3n8
Crador, Janice, 74–80, *76*; activism of, 75–79, 106, 107; background of, 74–75; CCC and, 105; faith and, 79–80

Crowley, Louisiana, and proposed medical waste incinerator, 94
*Crowley Post Signal*, 97
Cryar, Fernell, 3, 4, 9–12; activism of, 9–11; background of, 9; on economic status and environmental quality, 12; recognition received by, 3; on women activists, 11
Culture (Louisiana), Creole and Cajun, xiii, xx, 5, 15, 112–13

Dakrill Community Action Group, 35
Davis, Brenda, 242
Department of Agriculture Environmental Pesticide Committee, 146, 150
Department of Environmental Quality (DEQ), xiii, xxii, xxiii, 56; and Alsen, Louisiana, 100, 122; changes in, 238; creation of, 49, 176–77, 193; Edwards and, 7; environmental scorecard and, 174, 214; Grand Bois waste facility and, 23–34; IT case and, 193; Little River and, 90; Marine Shale Processors and, 17; Oakville and, 38; Office of Water Resources, 189–90; and Paulina, Louisiana, 204; political influence and, 206–7; under Roemer, 176–78; transparency and, 214–15, 238; Waste Management and, 142–43; Western Waste Industries and, 73
Department of Health and Hospitals, 20, 125, 225
Department of Natural Resources, 78, 193
Department of Transportation and Development (DOTD), xiv, 213
Depression era, 12, 31, 62, 65, 88, 91, 101, 113, 146, 162, 197, 211
Devil's Swamp, 99, 119, 226
Dodd, Barbara, 242
Doland, Jack, 72
Dow Chemical, 132, 133, 134, 138, 193, 194, 212
Doye, Estelle, 101
DuBois, René, *The God Within*, 60
Duhé-Datsun Law Firm, 122
Duhon, Ruth, 47, 242
Duke, David, 43, 193

Earth Day, 124, 213
Ecology Center of New Orleans, 51, 243
Edwards, Edwin, 117; advisory committee and, 42; Baudoin and, 131; DEQ and, 43, 193–94; Ellender and, 198; environmental issues and, 47–48, 64, 68, 79, 134–44, 145, 172, 174; Freeport-McMoran and, 188; Goldsmith and, 69; hazardous waste and, 52; Industrial Tank Corp. and, 50; Marine Shale Processors and, 7, 9, 10, 28; Midboe and, 191–92; politics and, 202; Roemer and, 176; Vermillion Parish and, 166–69
Edwards, Marion, 188
Ellender, Allen J., 189
Ellender, Mary, xvi, 101–5, *102*; activism of, 103–5; background of, 101–5
Environmental Affairs Committee, 225
Environmental Control Commission. *See* Louisiana Environmental Control Commission
Environmental Health Network, 162, 165
environmental issues: churches and, 108; environmental scorecard, 214; grassroots vs. national organizations and, 235–36; health and, 138–39, 157, 158, 164–65, 201–2, 249ch7n6; jobs and, 160, 171, 234–35; national perspective on, 234; poverty and, 164; race and, 121; regulation and, 199, 202, 206–7, 236–37
environmental justice, 194, 204–5, 218–19, 227, 236
environmental movement: Catholic Church and, 237–38; lobbying and, 237; in Louisiana, 229, 230; political influence and, 63–65; religion and, 59–60; transcending social barriers and, 30–31; women activists in, 11, 86, 110–12, 160, 191, 195–96, 200–201, 216–17, 219–20, 226–27, 228–29, 230–31
Environmental Protection Agency (EPA): environmental justice and, 205; Hurricane Katrina and, 231; Little River and, 89; Love Canal and, 11; Marine Shale Processors and, 17, 171; recognition received by, 3; USEPA study and, xvii
Esso Standard Oil Refinery, 132
Evans, Audrey, 38, 207–11, *209*; attempts to intimidate, 210; background of, 207–8; Oakville and, 39; Office of Management and Budget Watch and, 208; Tulane Environmental Law Clinic and, 207, 208–11
Ewell, Catherine, 225–26, 242
Ewell, Dave, 119, 120

Falkenheiner, Doris, 120, 242
*Family Circle*, 157
Firestone Rubber Co., 103
fish kills, 88, 148–49, 150
Folse, Kim, 7
Fontenot, Mary, 242
Fontenot, William "Willie" A., 134, 221–27, *223*; activism of, 224–27; and Alsen, Louisiana, 119–23; background of, 221–24; Crador and, 77, 79; end of career of, 250ch7n15; Kirkland and, 139; memories of racism and, 224; and Oakville, Louisiana, 38; Pospisil and, 63; Robert and, 51; Savoy and, 107; Sierra Club and, 224; and Willow Springs, Louisiana, 104
Formosa Plastic, 209
Fossier, Mildred, 112–18, *113*; activism of, 43, 115–17; background of, 112–14; Bayou Sauvage and, 40, 43; education and, 111; Freeport-McMoran and, 188; Herr and, 42–43; O'Neill and, 185; racial issues and, 114–15; on women and success, 117–18
Foster, Mike, 8, 64, 206
Frankland, Peggy, 48, 104
Freedom of Information Act, 135
Freeport-McMoRan, 116, 117, 188
Fremaux, Charlotte, 242
Friends of the Environment, 200
Fulgenz, Evelyn, 242

Gaudet, Kay, 53–58, *54*; activism of, 55–58; background of, 54–55; Kirkland and, 138; personal costs to, 57
Gibbs, Lois: activism and, 206; Love Canal and, xx, 56; national movement and, 218, 219; Orr and, 159, 160
Givens, Dale, 89, 126, 135, 174
Goldsmith, Shirley, 48, 59, 65–69, *66*; activism of, 67–69; attempts to intimidate, 77–78; background of, 65–67; CCC and, 77; CLEAN and, 65, 67; Contraband Bayou and, 67–68; faith and, 67
Gossen, Florence, 123–27, *124*; activism of, 125–27, 132; attempts to intimidate, 127; Baudoin and, 129–30; illness in family of, 125; Save Our Homes and Land, 125
Grand Bois waste facility, 233–34
Grand Lake, Louisiana (Big Diamond Facility) 75–77, 78
Greenpeace, 19–20, 26
Groundwater contamination, xvii, 8, 83, 106, 119
Gulf Coast Tenant's Organization, 205
Gulf South Research Institute, 167–68
Guste, William J., Jr., 79, 225

Hamilton, Alice, 111
Hamilton, Rachel, 42
Hanks, Angela, 92
Hanks, Gay, 90–93, *91*; activism of, 92–93; background of, 91–92; Fontenot and, 225, 226; illness in family of, 92; VAPE and, 90, 92; Wascom and, 184
Hargar, Maxine, 243
hazardous waste: health effects of, 56–57; illness and, 67
Hazardous Waste Council, 7
Head Start Program, 153–54
Help Our Polluted Environment, Inc. (HOPE), 94, 95
Herman, Sally, 3, 4, 5–8; activism of, 6–8; background of, 6; effects on personal life of, 8; faith and, 8; Marine Shale Processors and, 5, 6–8, 170, 172; recognition received by, 3, 7

Herr, Marietta, 40–44, *41*; activism of, 42–44; background of, 40–42; Bayou Sauvage and, 40, 43; Fossier and, 42–43, 117
High Hope Road Committee, xviii, 44, 47
Hodge Paper Mill, 88
Holcomb, Catherine, 4, 15–17; activism of, 16–17; background of, 15–16; on balance between the environment and economic necessity, 17; on lobbying, 16; Marine Shale Processors and, 20; recognition received by, 3
Home Box Office (HBO), *America Undercover—The Toxic Time Bomb*, 104
Houck, Oliver, 175, 243
Houmas nation, 233
Hurricane Audrey, 102
Hurricane Katrina, 229–30, 231, 232
Hurricane Rita, 230, 232

Iberville AWARE, 56
Iberville Parish, 30
Illinois Central Gulf (ICG), xiv, xv
Industrial Pipe, 35
Industrial Tank Corp. (IT), xxii, 51, 52, 226
Injection wells: BFI and, xiv, xv, xvii, xviii, xx, 30, 47; Big Diamond and, 74–76, 79, 106–8; Wascom, 180–83
Iowans for a Clean Environment (ICE), 70, 72
Irving, Steve, 51
IT decision. *See Save Ourselves v. Louisiana Environmental Control Commission*

Jackson, Rose, 32, 35–40, *36*; activism of, 38–40; background of, 36–38; Dakrill Community Action Group and, 35; Industrial Pipe and, 35, 38–39; LEAN and, 35; transcending social barriers and, 219–20
Jean LaFitte National Historical Park and Preserve, 40, 224
Joe Brown Park, 116
Johnson, Emma, 120, 243
Johnston, Bennett, 198
Jones, Mabel, 47, 243

Kaplan, Ben, 153
Kaster, Pam, 243
Kent, Jack, 7, 16, 28, 171, 172
King, Linda, 162–66, *164*; activism of, 163–66; ATSDR and, 164–66; background of, 162–63; *Chemical Injuries in the Courts: A Litigation Guide for Clients and Their Attorneys*, 162; EHN and, 162, 165; Herr and, 6–7; "Inconclusive by Design: Waste, Fraud, and Abuse in Federal Health Research," 162; Kirkland and, 136; and Oakville, Louisiana, 39; in West Virginia, 162–63
Kirkland, Les Ann, 136–39, *137*; activism of, 136–39; AWARE and, 136, 137; Avants and, 132, 136; background of, 136; faith and, 136; LEAN and, 136; Orr and, 160; Spanish Lake landfill and, 56
Kjerulff, James "Pete," 77
Knapp, Leonard, xviii, 68
Ku Klux Klan, 32, 43
Kuehn, Robert, 175, 203–7; background of, 203–4; Tulane Environmental Law Clinic and, 203, 204

*Lake Charles American Press*, 70
Lake Pontchartrain, 178
Land farm, 77, 107
Landfills, hazardous waste: BFI and, xiv, xv, xvi, xvii, xx, 26, 30, 34, 46–48, 63, 65, 67, 92; CWMI and, 100–103
Landfills, solid waste, 30, 55, 56; Lafayette Municipal landfill, 123–24, 126, 129–30, 132; Rapides Parish, 60, 62, 63; Spanish Lake, 138; Western Waste, 70–74
Landowners Association, 193
Landrieu, Moon, 114, 115, 116
League of Women Voters, 42, 111, 215
Legator, Marvin, 39
LeLeux, Barbara, 3, *4*, 12–15; activism of, 13–15; attempts to intimidate, 14; background of, 12–13; lessons learned by, 15; Marine Shale Processors and, 12, 13, 20; recognition received by, 3
Lindsey, Joel, 192

Little River, Willow Springs and, xvii, 86, 87, 88–89, 90
Livingston Louisiana (BFI landfill), xiv, xv, 67
Long, Huey, xxi, 86
Long, Russell, 198
Louisiana: coastal erosion and, 33; environmental issues and, 85, 145; hazardous waste and, 30; map of, 2; Marine Shale Processors and, 5; oil and natural gas in, 4, 31, 85; political culture of, 85–86; poverty in, 153–54; shrimping in, 4; timber in, 4; women activists in, 86
Louisiana Chemical Alliance, 198
Louisiana Chemical Association (LCA), xxiii, 178, 197, 198
Louisiana Department of Environmental Quality. *See* Department of Environmental Quality
Louisiana Department of Health and Hospitals. *See* Department of Health and Hospitals
Louisiana Environmental Action Network (LEAN): Collette and, 220; Fontenot and, 116; Jackson and, 35; Kirkland and, 136–37; lobbying and, 237; Orr and, 157, 159, 200; Pospisil and, 61; Robinson and, 97
Louisiana Environmental Control Commission, xv–xvi, xxii, 49, 51, 103–4, 120, 125, 193, 226
Louisiana Ethics Commission, 52
Louisiana Foundation of Excellence and Science Technology and Education, 198–99
Louisiana Health Department, 11
Louisiana Interchurch Conference, 60, 62
Louisiana Manufacturer's Political Action Committee, 199
Louisiana Nature and Science Center, 116
Louisiana Resource Recovery Development Board, 127
Louisiana Supreme Court, 49, 51, 193, 206, 225
Love Canal, xx, 11, 56

Lowenthal, Margaret, 68
Lower Mississippi River Warning System, 185

Madden, Martha, 19, 174
Malek-Wiley, Darryl, 139
Mancuso, Monica Laughlin, 3, 4, 18–21; activism of, 18–21; attempts to intimidate, 14; background of, 18; Holcomb and, 16; LeLeux and, 13
Mar Services, 183, 184
Marine Shale Processors: closure of, 8, 183; hazardous waste and, 5, 6–8, 16, 24, 26, 170–72; jobs and, 8, 9, 10, 24; political influence and, 7–8, 9, 10, 17, 27–28; regulation of, 24; settlement with, 3
Martin Chemical, 169
McCastle, Mary, 34–35, 118–23; activism of, 119–23; background of, 118; CCHW and, 34; Coalition for Community Action and, 118; Fontenot and, 225; Rollins and, 226
McCastle, Simms, 118–19
McKeithen, John, 42
Mead, Margaret, 227
Midboe, Kai David, 191–97; background of, 191–92; Coastal Zone Management and, 192; environmental justice and, 194; politics and, 193–94; Robinson and, 97, 100; Sea Grant program, 191, 192
Miller, Mary Ann, 72
Miller, Richard, 138, 208
Minville, Lynn, 155
Mississippi River, xiii, 31, 32, 35, 36, 43, 188–89, 199, 233
Morgan City, Louisiana (Marine Shale Processors incinerator), 3, 4–5, 15, 26, 170–72
Morial, Dutch, 42, 115
Moses, Marian, 155
Mossville, Louisiana, 80, 82
Mossville Steering Committee, 83
Mothers against Air Pollution, 122, 157, 158–59
Mud Movers, Inc., 47

NAACP, 47, 176
National Superfund Committee, 93
Native Americans, xxiv, 147
Neuroblastoma, 16, 19, 22, 42, 111, 113, 170
New Orleans, Louisiana, 22, 26, 31, 40–43, 46, 48, 93, 111–16, 123, 157, 172, 186–89
*New Orleans: The Glamour Period*, 114
*New York Times*, 57
Newcomb College, 42, *111*, *113*, *170*
North Dugas landfill, 123
Norton, Pat, 43, 119, 174
Norwood, Cathy, 104
Nunez, Pete, 77–78
Nuns, 12, 111, 148, 152, 153

Oakville, Louisiana, 4, 34, 35, 38, 39, 40
Odom, Bob, 146, 148
Office of Conservation, xviii; BP spill and, 239; changes in, 238; Crador and, 77; Fontenot and, 225; public hearings by, 181–82, 183–84; regulation and, 239; transparency and, 238–39; Underground Injection Control program and, 180–84
Office of Environmental Affairs, 226
Office of Management and Budget Watch, 208
Oil Chemical and Atomic Worker's International Union (OCAW), 138, 208
Oilfield waste: industry, 30, 31, 85, 90, 105, 107; radioactive, 188, 190
Olin (chemical plant), 102
O'Neill, Maureen, 178, 185–91, *187*; background of, 185–87; DEQ and, 204, 214; environmental issues and, 187–91; Fossier and, 117; gypsum dumping and, 43; Lower Mississippi River Warning System and, 185; at New Orleans Sewerage and Water Board, 187–88; Office of Water Resources and, 189–90; at Planning Commission, 187; regulation and, 200, 202
O'Neill, Melanie, 7
*Oprah Winfrey Show*, 57

Orr, Marylee, 11, 122, 157–61, *159*; activism of, 158–61; background of, 157–58; faith and, 161; Hurricane Katrina and, 231; hurricane recovery and, 230; LEAN and, 157, 200; Mothers against Air Pollution and, 122, 157, 158–59; Oakville and, 38; recognition received by, 157

Pauline, Louisiana, 204
PCBs (polychlorinated biphenyls), xvii, xx, 38, 68, 101, 104, 122, 158–59
Perez, Leander, 31
Petro Processors, 226
Petrovich, Luke, 33, 38
Phillips, Joan, 243
Plaquemines Parish, 31, 37, 39
Plettinger, Ann 243
Pointe-aux-Chien, Louisiana, 233
Pospisil, Lorena, 60–65, *61*; activism of, 62–65; background of, 61–62; CCC and, 60, 63; LEAN and, 61; recycling and, 63
PPG, 83, 156
Price, Jesse, 86–90, *87*; activism of, 88–90; attempts to intimidate, 89, 90; background of, 90
Price, Miriam, 4, 25–29, *27*; activism of, 26–28; background of, 25–26; Cryar and, 11; frustration of, 27–28; Holcomb and, 16; illness in family of, 26; Marine Shale Processors and, 19; Subra and, 171
Price, Nicole, 22, 23, 28, 29
Protecting the Environment and Ecological Resources (PEER), 31
Public Affairs Research Council, 227

Ramirez, Debra, 59, 80–84, *81*; activism of, 82–84; background of, 80–82; faith and, 82; Mossville Steering Committee and, 83
Rapides Parish, Louisiana, 60, 63, 92
Ratard, Raoult, 122
Research Associates, 51
Restoration of Little River, 89
Rigmaiden, Beulah, 243
Rigmaiden, Herbert, xviii, xix

Roach, Randy, 79
Robert, Theresa, 49–53, *50*; activism of, 51–53; background of, 49–50; Fontenot, 225, 226; Industrial Tank Corp. and, 49; LEAN and, 49; SOS and, 49, 51
Roberts, Nancy, 243
Robertson, Anne McKinne, 224
Robinson, Florence, 97–101, *98*; activism of, 100–101; background of, 97–99; recognition received by, 97
Roemer, Charles Elson "Buddy," 175–79; background of, 175–76; Chemical Association and, 178; in Congress, 176; DEQ and, 176–78, 204–5, 206–7; environmental issues and, 10, 43, 52, 56, 57, 64, 68, 143, 176, 179, 190, 202; environmental scorecard and, 174; governorship, 176; Marine Shale Processors and, 17, 23–24, 28, 172; Office of Water Resources and, 185, 189; politics and, 202
Rollins Environmental Services, 99, 116, 119–20, 122, 123, 225–26
Rollins-Purle, 123
Rural Advancement Foundation International USA, 146
Ruston, Louisiana, 86, 89–90

Safe Drinking Water Act for the United States, 188
Saint Gabriel, Louisiana, 56, 138, 201
Save Our Homes and Land, 125, 127
Save Ourselves (SOS), 49, 51
*Save Ourselves v. Environmental Louisiana Control Commission*, xxii, 49, 51, 143, 193, 225
Savoy, Carol, 105–9, *106*; activism of, 78, 106–9; attempts to intimidate, 109; background of, 105–6; CCC and, 105, 107
Savoy, Mike, 78
Schellstede, Herman, 240
Screen, Pat, 121
Sea Grant Program, 191, 192
shale gas, 234, 240
Shea, Leo, 152

Shepherd, Ruth, 44–48, *45*; activism of, 46–48; attempts to intimidate, 46; background of, 44–46; CLEAN and, 44; High Hope Road Committee and, 44, 47
Shrimp and Petroleum Festival, 3–4
Sierra Club, 42, 57, 138, 174, 224, 237
Sigur, Alexander, 153
Simoneaux, Frank, xv
*Sixty Minutes*, 147
Snow, Bunny, 243
Solar, Helen, *4*, 21–25; activism of, 22–25; background of, 21–22; Cryar and, 11; faith and, 23; frustration of, 24–25; illness in family of, 22, 26; Marine Shale Processors and, 19; Subra and, 171
South Louisiana Against Pollution (SLAP), 7, 160, 220
Southern Advance Paper, 88
Southern Mutual Help Association (SMHA), 146, 147–48, 149, 151, 154, 155
Southern Wood Piedmont Association, 5
Spanish Lake Bluff swamp, 138
Spanish Lake landfill, 56
Stevens, Ramona, 38, 160
Stine, Tim, 72
Subra, Wilma, 166–73, *168*, 231–41; activism of, 169–73; background of, 167; BP spill and, 232; Brasseaux and, 96; Crador, 77; Cryar and, 10, 11; DEQ and, 215; at Gulf South Research Institute, 167; Hurricane Katrina and, 230, 231; LeLeux and, 13–14; Midboe and, 196; public hearings and, 183; recognition received by, 166; Savoy and, 107; Tutwiler and, 142, 143; VAPE and, 168–69; Wascom and, 181, 182
Sudduth, James E., 74
Sullivan, William, 80
Superfund Sites, xx, 92–93, 134, 170
Sustainable Agriculture Working Group, 149

Tauzin, Billy, 8, 17
Taylor, Cecil, 213
Templet, Paul, 211–17; attempts to intimidate, 216–17; background of, 211–13; DEQ and, 64, 142, 177–78, 204–5, 212, 214–17; Midboe and, 192; O'Neill and, 189; politics and, 213
Tensas Wildlife Area, 193
Thompson, Herbert, 78
timber industry, 85, 88
Toxic March, 205, 208
Toxic Release Inventory (TRI), 85, 134–35, 169–70, 194–95, 215, 248ch4n1
Treen, David, xvi, xxiv, 176, 191; DEQ and, 193; environmental issues and, 52; hazardous waste and, 68; Midboe and, 192
Tritico, Mike, xvii, 47, 67, 68
Troy, Dick, 225
Tulane Environmental Law Clinic, xxiii, 208–11, 236; Foster and, 206; Kuehn and, 203, 207; LEAN and, 200; Oakville and, 34, 38, 175; recognition received by, 206; regulation and, 239
Tutwiler, Mary, 140–44, *141*; activism of, 141–44; background of, 140–41; education and, 111; lawsuit and, 143; War on Waste and, 140, 141

United Church of Christ Commission for Racial Justice, *Toxic Wastes and Race in the United States*, 60
Urban League, 204
US Liquids, 233

Verdine, Hazel, 82
Vermillion Association to Protect the Environment (VAPE), 90, 92–93, 168–69
Vermillion Parish, 90, 153–54
Vernon Parish, 92
Vinson, Odell, 108, 183
Vinton, Helen, 146–50, *147*; activism of, 148–50; arrest of, 155; background of, 146–47

Wall, Eloise, 200, 243

Wascom, Carroll: background of, 179–80; citizen distrust of government and regulators, 182–84; public hearings and citizen input, 181–83; Underground Injection Control (UIC) Program's duties, 180–81; on women and their role in the movement, 182–84

Wascom, Kathy, 243

Waste Management, 43, 116–17, 141–43, 189

Water pollution, gypsum dumped in Mississippi, 43, 141, 143

Watson, Jack, 48

Weeks Island, 169

Welch, James H., 78, 181, 182

Western Waste Industries, 70–74

Whatley, Marsha, 243

Williams, Ann, 31–35; activism of, 33–35; background of, 32–33; Jackson and, 38; lawsuit against, 34, 160; lessons learned by, 35; PEER and, 31; recognition received by, 31; transcending social barriers and, 219–20

Williams, Martha, 33

Willow Springs, Louisiana (BFI landfill), xiv, xv, xvi, xviii, 33, 44, 46, 47, 65, 75

Wimpleberg, Karen, 244

Winfrey, Oprah, 138, 201–2

www.ingramcontent.com/pod-product-compliance
Lightning Source LLC
Chambersburg PA
CBHW030338240426
43661CB00052B/1669